MAD FRANK'S BRITAIN

Frankie Fraser
with James Morton

Virgin
BOOKS

For all my grandchildren and great grandchildren carrying on the family tradition

First published in Great Britain in 2002 by
Virgin Books Ltd
Thames Wharf Studios
Rainville Road
London W6 9HA

A catalogue record for this book is available from the British Library.

ISBN 1 85227 973 7

Typeset by TW Typesetting, Plymouth, Devon
Printed and bound by CPD Wales

CONTENTS

INTRODUCTION

When I get an offer of work nowadays it's usually television or radio, but if a friend or friend of a friend wants some real help I'm always happy to try and give a hand.

I had a call a bit ago from a man I've known for years. His son was on his toes. Could I help? Of course I said yes, I could. Get the boy to ring me. I'd only seen him once to my knowledge. It's like if you're in a coffee shop and someone comes in and the man you're sitting with knows him. You get introduced and that's it. Next I hear the boy's in London and he's lost. That's the thing with mobile phones. The thing is it's a Saturday and this kid is red hot. It's a case of the most dangerous man in Britain, until the next one comes along that is. I give him directions how to get to South London and a bit later he's on the blower saying he's lost again. He's been asking people directions but you know how it is. Everyone you ask's a stranger himself and if he isn't he's got a cleft palate. The kid says he's in a motor outside the Post Office in King's Cross just opposite the station and I tell him to stay where he is – get the motor round a corner, of course, and I'll come and get him. What else could I say? I didn't want to frighten him saying he was even hotter there with the police cleaning out the druggies and brasses and their pimps.

I hop a lift and we was there inside ten minutes. There's a little turning just up the Euston Road and we double-parked there. I go round to the Post Office and there's the kid. We walk back to the car I'm in and suddenly I see two coppers. It was just one of them things but all they did is walk on by. I rushed him back to his car and got in it with him, but he said it would be better if he followed on behind and we got home safe.

In a way things turned out well. When Marilyn had gone she'd taken the kitchen cupboards and things with her and though I'd been down to IKEA and got some new stuff, I hadn't put it up. Funny thing is, now she's living in the same block where the Twins was nicked. So, the good thing was I wasn't having people round because I didn't want them to see the state of the place.

There was no danger of my family or friends coming round. I'd been fobbing them off for months. The other good thing was the kid was good with his hands and he had stuff on the walls in no time.

We parked his car – it was a ringer, of course – in a side street and every morning we'd be up at half seven, quarter to eight to move it into the car park. Fiver a day it is. We'd load up with silver and shove it in the machine. If you'd left it in the side street you'd have been ticketed for sure. 'Greedy bastard,' the wardens would think. 'Too mean to pay for the park round the corner', and they'd have blistered it straight away. The car was safe enough during the day in the park but if you'd left it there at night it would have been stripped. Nice car it was. Not too flashy and not too beaten up. No one would raise an eyebrow at it. Like that advertisement all those years ago, 'Not too little, not too much.' So once it was dark we moved it back to the side street where kids wouldn't be so likely to break in. Moving the car was the dangerous part. There's a great big modern police station in Manor Place near where the Baths used to be, took over from the old nick Carter Street in Walworth. There's squad cars going up and down Browning Street the whole time; that and coppers on the beat. I said to the kid he should walk on ahead and I'd follow a few yards behind. I'm often seen on my own in the road but there's never anyone with me regular, so if they had see another person they might have wondered. With me behind, if they had come looking I could have gone steaming in like a terrier and tried to cause enough trouble for him to get away. I'd never have succeeded and I'd have been nicked for certain, but it might have given him that bit of time if there hadn't been too many of them. I'd have had to try.

You couldn't invent what happened next. All my life and all the people I've known and they've known and the kid and his friends have known it's never happened to them. One morning we go to drive the motor round to the park and the boy said, 'Oh, Christ'. I thought what had happened was someone had banged into it or scratched it but what's happened is someone's nicked the front plate. Why not both? Well, I suppose whoever done it had the first one off and then there's a twitch on the curtain and they don't fancy hanging around for the second. I reckon someone must have wanted the plates for a short time job.

Along the Walworth Road you can buy anything. Anything that is except plates. We walked up and down it until we come across one shop which said they could make some up but not until the next day. Then the fellow tells us there's another shop in a little cul-de-sac where they might be able to help, so round we go. Blow me, on the pavement there's a man talking to two coppers. I was all for walking on by but the kid says, 'No they've seen we look like we're going in the shop, if we spin off they might get suspicious.' First thing the woman wants to know is have we got the insurance certificate? I pat me pockets. 'Blind me, I've left it behind.' 'Have you reported it?' Then she says she can't do it 'til the next day anyway. And so out we come. We got a cab back to the shop that sent us to her and there's another man there. He'll fix us up by four in the afternoon.

So I get a lift to go back that afternoon but now there's the worry the woman may have done her duty and given the station a bell. 'Officer, these two men . . .' Maybe there's some law that shops who make up plates have to report things. I thought the best thing was to go back on my own and if there's trouble then the driver can at least get back to the flat and get the kid out. But no, it goes sweet as anything. 'Do you want me to wrap it?' the man says. 'Yes, it's better with it on the bus.' I don't let on I've someone waiting across the street. As soon as I got back the kid went straight down and put it on. The driver was terrific, she'll know who I mean.

You might think with my connections it would be easy to ring up someone, even one of my boys, for plates but I didn't want to know. It wasn't the money, though someone would have charged three or four hundred. Speed was of the essence. One of my boys could have rung someone up but he might not be there and then he would have to ring someone else and before you get it right there's half a dozen people know I want some plates. There was always the worry that the law might have nicked the plate and it was a get up.

I liked having the kid around. I don't smoke and he didn't and I don't drink in the house and nor did he. A couple of times he went away to do a job here and there but I didn't ask, though he told me one had been a right touch. Then he says he'd better be getting on. I didn't ask him where he was going. It's better you don't know then it can't slip out somehow. The last night we sent out to the local Italian, *La Luna*, and had a decent meal brought round with a good bottle of wine; a sort of celebration, and we had a good laugh about the plates. And he was gone the next morning. He wanted to pay me but I never took a penny. Putting the cupboards up was good enough. I had a nice card saying thanks and I had a Christmas card as well.

LONDON

For those who haven't read my other books I come from a family in Waterloo. I was born in 1923 the youngest of five of us. The first three was never in trouble and neither was my parents although my father, who was half Red Indian, may have done a bit of bird in Canada for manslaughter. I don't really know. My parents was dead straight but they was also dead poor and I reckon that's why Eva, my sister, and me started stealing in the first place, bringing back money for the stuff we'd nicked and sold. As a kid I was a bucket boy for the Sabinis, the racecourse gang, and then I started work proper on my own, working for Billy Hill who was big in the 1940s and 1950s a lot of the time. I was given a five stretch for the affray in Mr Smith's Club in 1965 when Dickie Hart was killed, and then ten in the Torture Trial and a further five for the Parkhurst Riot, all consecutive, and I lost every day's remission. When I was let out finally in 1989 I was 66 and I'd done just about getting on for forty years inside. And, of course, since I didn't go away until my teens it meant I'd only been out about six or eight years of my adult life in total. In prison I was always in trouble. I've had three kids who've also done heavy bird by Kathleen and a fourth, who's never been in trouble, by my wife Doreen. The Carters I mention is a local family who I had trouble with over the years after Eva, my sister, married Jimmy Brindle. I think that's about all you need as background.

When I first read about the Dome robbery I had the utmost admiration even though it didn't work. I thought what a brilliant coup. I didn't know any of the men except Terry Millman, the one who died. They was my sons' and even grandsons' ages. I think Terry was related to the Carters by marriage, a good man. But, no disrespect, the more the story come out and the more I studied it, the more I thought they needed their brains testing. One of them had a brother-in-law for a copper. That's bad enough for a start. Then it looks like they'd already done a run across the Thames in a speedboat as an escape in another blagging. Even if it wasn't them the coppers don't need too much in the way of brains to think that once someone's done it a second team may have a try and they're going to be on the lookout at things beside the Thames which may be targets. Then again did they really think them jewels was real? I wonder if the public can get their entrance money back. They'll never be able to say I saw the Millennium Diamond or whatever. Do you think they can get at the Dome people for false pretences? I mean no one in their right mind's going to go and look at them if they're imitations.

That's the trouble with big jobs. There's too many on them. Billy Hill used to say that you're your own best partner and he's right. There's wives and there's girlfriends and people they've spoken to. It can be accident or it can be a bit of malice if one of the women have found their fellow's having it off round the corner. Then there's people who listen out so they can get a reward. In something like the Dome there had to be twenty or more knew something really big was going off, and that's a good fifteen too many.

It was like in the Train when Renee Wisbey was knitting balaclavas for them all and Marilyn and her sister found them. They was all staunch, of course, but it only shows how easy it is for things to leak out. That's another thing with the Dome. You don't do jewels or paintings if you can avoid it. You do money. If you do jewels you've got to bring someone else in to sell to and, very likely, if it's a big job they've got to bring in someone as well, and before you know the whole of Hatton Garden's in on it. Think of the rabbit that must be going round. You don't even know who the police is watching which is what seems to have happened. Quite by chance they was watching a man and he went to the Dome. The next day or a bit after they see someone else at the place and from there on it's all on top.

I've often wondered why the Train Robbers needed the farm. Buying it or pretending to they was involving people who weren't full members, probably only half hooky so to speak. If a man's been sent to buy property just near where a big job has gone off he don't need to be the Brains of Britain to know what it was all about. There's always the worry he won't stand up if the police get hold of him. The Train men could have all gone up to the railway in separate vehicles that night and been back in London before anyone knew what had happened.

I still think that the great mistake the Train men made was not to have involved Billy Hill and I think that one or two agree even though their pride won't let them admit it. That, and Billy would have been greedy. He'd have wanted the pickings. But, there again, there was plenty of pickings to go round. No one ever quite knew how much was on the train. It was a robbery where you could let someone be a bit greedy. What I'm sure about is that if Billy had been around there wouldn't have been thirty years all round.

Personally I think it was the same with the London Airport robbery at the end of July 1948 when so many good men was betrayed and picked up a lot of bird. Billy would have done it different. That was one of Spotty's things. He'd picked the job out and it all seemed so sweet then it all come crashing down. Billy Hill and me was in Wandsworth when it went down. There was meant to be over £600 grand in diamonds and money in a bonded warehouse with the prospects of more on the way. The idea was they should dope the coffee of the warehouse staff and it would be a doddle, but instead when they got there they found the man they'd been dealing with on the inside had gone hooky on them and talked to the police. Instead of doped staff there was wide-awake coppers.

Some men got away but Jimmy Woods picked up nine and his brother George an eight. Teddy Machin, who Billy calls Terrible Ted in his book, got away and so did Franny Daniels but Alfie Roome really went off his head whilst he was doing his ten. He was known as Donk and when he come out he attacks his wife who was working on a newspaper stall at the gates of the Ford factory at Dagenham. When people chased him he swallows poison and dies there on the pavement. What a waste of a good man. Billy always reckoned if he'd been running it there wouldn't have been a disaster. He knew so many top coppers, one of them would have got the word to him and he'd have pulled the team out. That was one of Jack's troubles. He didn't have any high-ranking coppers behind him. It took the starch out of Jimmy and Georgie Woods as well. They'd been doing so well out of their blaggings they thought it was too easy. They're both dead now I'm sorry to say. In fact I'm not sure that there's anyone left who was on the job.

Much better was that robbery at London Airport in February this year.[1] Cash, and only two of them involved by all accounts. It had to be an inside job. What was even better is they seem to have gone back and done it again in March. There's a story that the money is for terrorism but I'm not so sure. People have been saying if you've had a £2 million touch why repeat it, but then if you've made £3 million out of a drugs run why do it again?

Every time I go down Waterloo way I see the IMAX there. If my father was still alive he'd never believe it. The Royal Children's Hospital is about the only thing standing from my day let alone his. I got taken into it when I ran my bike into the kerb and fell over. Blood all over the place there was. I've still got the scars. My grandmother stayed on in Cornwall Road, where I was born, until she died. I think the actor Charlie Drake's father had a place at the end of the street. I've bumped into Charlie in my travels once or twice and I've meant to ask him but I've never got round to it.

As you know I live off the Walworth Road and the gentrification that's going on there is amazing. You've got what I call Beehives all over the place. They're young people, not working class, you see in the Beehive pub round the back of the Elephant. There's Sutherland Square and now it's out of this world. The houses used to be in flats but they're mostly single dwelling units, as the estate agents say. Maybe there's one or two that's not been done up but they're the exception. There's no noise, no traffic. There's a little square in the middle and that's got a locked gate now to keep out the druggies. It's enlightening, it really is.

When I was young, if you had a car you was looked at askance and it was a good way of attracting the coppers. That was the way to get nicked or have to hand over a few quid. The Campbells, who also lived in Howley Place, had a little baby Austin 7. It stood out like a sore thumb in the Cut but they had two pie shops, Harris near the Windmill Pub down by the Blackfriars Road and

---

[1] 2002.

Woods was the other, so they could account for how they'd got it. People stood with their mouths open watching them drive around on a Sunday. Tom Thumb Brindle could have had a car and be left alone because he was a street bookmaker and was paying up anyway. But little Frank having a car – not a good idea.

When there was talk of legalising bookmakers the police was some of the biggest opponents. Their pensions was going to come to an end. There must have been five street bookmakers between Waterloo and Blackfriars they could tap. I'd run errands for the bookies or be a lookout. The bets were tiny, 3d or 6d, and for the day's running about I'd get 2d or 3d.

When I look back I don't think there was much in the way of what you call domestic burglaries when I was young. For a start there wasn't much to burgle. If you'd done our place there was only my father's blue serge suit and you'd have to do the drum at the weekend because it was the only time it was out of hock. There wasn't any cash even though my parents never had a bank account, either one of them. And we wasn't any different from most of the families round us. Of course those with shops was more vulnerable because they'd have cash. Even people like them didn't trust banks. I think they was afraid they'd be shopped to the tax people. I know now there's a theory that burglaries happen within a mile of the screwer's home but it wasn't like that when I was young. There was more a spirit between people. If my father had thought I was doing someone's home he'd have beaten me blue and then died of shame. But it wouldn't have occurred to me.

There was one good man who did a lot of work just before I was born. Charles White was known as the Clapham Climber because that's where he did a lot of his work. Don't forget that would be half country in those days. He'd started his life as a blue-flyer stealing lead. He picked up a ten from Darling in 1923. Darling said he wished he could have had him flogged but Charlie was in poor shape.

Country houses and rich people's drums in Mayfair was a different thing and there was some fine burglars. For a start there was my friend Ruby Sparks. That's how he got his nickname. He did some Maharajah's drum and come away with a whole lot of rubies. He didn't know what they was and he more-or-less give them away to the fence who conned him they was worthless.

As far as the country houses was concerned George Smithson, known as Gentleman George, was about the finest when I was growing up. He looked a bit like a vicar, which was a help, and he'd often have a sort of college scarf round his neck which give him this air of respectability. He was another who had a double life. He'd been well educated and he lived with his wife and kids in Kensington and until the first time he goes down they didn't know what he was up to. What was good was he was fearless and he didn't cause damage for the sake of it. In them days everyone had dogs and he was good with them. There's a story when he did a job in Upton Magna there's a big black Labrador or Retriever in the chair by the desk. Smithson's so good the dog doesn't really wake up except to be patted when he's leaving.

Mostly Smithson worked alone, which is really the best way to do things, but for a time he worked with George Ingram who wasn't his class of thief. Ingram's real name was Alfred Tragheim. What you want to be if you're a creeper is to be soft on your feet. A good creeper like that Welshman Raymond Jones could stay in someone's room half an hour and they'd never wake up. I think they liked the challenge and the danger. That sort of thing was never for me. George Ingram was clumsy, and like me he never settled to his bird. On and off he did a two-and-a-half-year hunger strike in Dartmoor. Smithson copped three long sentences even so, despite how good he was, including a six in Scotland in 1923 and a week later he got another two added at the Bailey. After that he give it all up and wrote a book. Ingram drew a six at the same time and he wrote a book and all.

When they come a cropper in Scotland the bogeys up there thought it was the biggest capture they'd made in years and, in a way, I suppose it was. It come about because they hadn't got their escape laid on. They was relying on trains and in them days the porters as well as the railway police watched the passengers. They'd screwed a big house in North Berwick and was trying to get themselves back to Edinburgh and they was seen waiting for a train. In fact they had a pull from a copper and he'd let them go, so it looked like they'd got away with it. It seems like it was the first time George used the name Ingram. But a couple of phone calls was all it needed. They thought they'd get off before the train arrived in Edinburgh and they jumped off in Portobello and picked up a tram, but the bogeys had found out they wasn't on the original train and they was watching for them to get to the station. In a briefcase they had all the stuff and a burglar's kit as well as a couple of horseshoes for luck.

I never carried horseshoes or wore green or things like that but I never liked the 13th. I was born on that day and the times I've been nicked over the years outside or in prison on the 13th is remarkable. When Dodger Davies and me was nicked when the car wouldn't start in Oxford Street that was a 13th. I've always planned to keep quiet that day but the times I've come out the punishment block, think I'll take it easy, get the day over with and I've been swagged straight down again is almost countless. I still don't like it.

Another good thief, much nearer my time, was Ernie Watts. He was top class and I think he only did a couple of years in the nick early in his career. He'd had a good education but there wasn't enough money to send him to Christ's Hospital, even though he'd got a scholarship, and it was after that he took up thieving in a big way. There was plenty of stories about him, like how he once had a challenge over how many smash and grabs he could do in a night and he got up to twelve. Then there was another how he had the police, who was following him, neck-deep in a pond before he could get away. He was a funny devil though. He was a diabetic and he topped himself – I don't know if it was an accident or not because he'd tried twice already – when he come back from a job just out of London. He give himself an overdose of insulin. By then he'd already met up with Bruce Reynolds who was top notch himself and really took over Ernie's organisation. I had a drink with Bruce not too long ago. He come down my nephew Jimmy's Tin Pan Club in Denmark Street.

But even smash and grab, which was one my games, wasn't that easy. You had to do it right otherwise if you threw the brick it more or less bounced back off the glass, and if you didn't hold it right when you smashed against the glass then you ended up getting a shower of glass on you and a load of splinters. That happened to Ruby at first. He had to use those Bulldog clips to keep the cuts together until someone could sew him up.

INTERNMENT AND THE SABINIS

Before the War I saw Oswald Mosley but I never really went and watched his marches. It was nothing to do with me and there wasn't any money in it. There wasn't any anti-Jewish feeling around the Elephant like there was in the East End. I don't recall ever seeing any Jewish boys my age at all. There certainly wasn't any at St Patrick's, which of course was a Catholic School, and I don't think there'd be many at St John's which was C of E, nor St Andrew's in Joanna Street in Lower Marsh. In fact the only Jewish people I knew was Max Cohen, the tailor, when I went down the East End to get my suits, and Hymie Harris who was the South London tailor we used. There was a man, Levy, at the Elephant and there'd be one or two who'd buy crooked gear but generally they kept themselves to themselves. I think I was thirteen when one of the Chaps took me over to Max Cohen's. A suit probably cost 30/- and you had to put down £1 as a deposit. That was about two years after I saw the first black person in my life. He was in the Boy's Brigade. He was a terrific guy.

I suppose the Jews controlled the pawnbrokers but there was never one behind the counter. Harvey and Thompson were the biggest round us. In went Dad's blue serge suit, with a waistcoat of course, on a Monday and out it came on a Friday. I'm sure he never knew. His pride wouldn't have stood for it. It was the same with the tallymen. The men who owned the firms may have been Jewish but the people who come round knocking for the weekly money wasn't. You hardly knew their names. If you paid up regular then they was just John or Jim. It's funny to write it now but in South London when I was growing up you didn't know what Jewish people looked like. There was no illustrated magazines like today. I think *Picture Post* was the first and that only come out just before the war. There was things like the *Illustrated London News* but that wasn't for the likes of us. We weren't going to be interested in what Lady Muck had said when she opened the flower show.

It all ended in tears for the Mosleys and a lot of others when the War came. Lady Mosley was in Holloway with my sister when Eva was doing a shoplifting sentence. She'd been locked up at the beginning of the War so she couldn't be a go-between between her husband, who was in Brixton, and the British Union. She was let out around the same time as Eva who always spoke highly of her. Of course there was privileges for the Mosleys. They let him come and visit her in Holloway and there was a ruckus. At that time Eva's eldest daughter, Beverley, was a bit under a year old and when our mother got a visiting order they wouldn't let us take the kid in to see Eva. Me and Dido Frett was on the run at the time but I took my chance and went in and Dido had to stay outside at the gate holding Beverley. There were visiting boxes, about a foot by two foot, with thick glass with wire netting. You only got twenty minutes visiting in those days anyway. How could they be so cruel and not even think they was being cruel?

Once Italy joined in the War with the Nazis then there was arrests of Italians and half Italians all round. In all something like 600 people was detained. There was the Quaglino brothers who had the famous restaurant in Bury Street, and there was the head chef at the Cafe Royal and a couple of clowns from Bertram Mills' Circus. They'd been with the circus for fifteen years but they was thought to be dangerous people who'd attack cabinet ministers and people like that. Of course it was a load of nonsense and they was released after a few months. Naturally the Sabinis was among them and they and Bert Marsh got sent down to internment at Ascot racecourse, which I suppose was at least appropriate. They didn't even speak Italian. It was a way of breaking up the gang. A sort of reprisal for the gold Bert Marsh got out of Croydon airport before the War.

Some of the Italian boys I was at school with was detained under those section 18B regulations. Mario Florentini was one and he ended up in Walton. He was only about seventeen when he was locked up. I don't know what danger they thought he could be. He would go to Italy every summer to a camp and I suppose they thought he was bringing back messages. He was a very talented musician and he was on BBC radio for years after the War. The last time I saw him was in an Italian restaurant in Frith Street. Bobby Warren and Italian Albert were with me. Mario was playing the violin and came over to see us.

The Italians still had cell tasks just like the rest of us. Protocol went out the window. If they complained it was, 'Yes, but there's a War on. Rules don't apply.' The Jewish mobs took over then but it wasn't personal, it was business, as they say. They just took advantage of anti-Italian feeling. Albert Dimes went in the air force but he soon walked out. Tony Mancini was one of the few big Italians left outside to rally the flag and he soon got topped for the murder of Hubby Distleman in the Palm Beach.

I remember talking to an Italian kid, Tony Nappi; he was with me and Jimmy Brindle when we went to see Albert Dimes after the Spot fight. He'd been in Chelmsford in 1941 and he was saying how he thought it looked like him and the others was going to be badly done up. Not just by the Jewish prisoners but everyone was in on the war effort. Thankfully, nothing come of it.

When I think of the trouble there's been in Glasgow between the Protestants and the Catholics it's surprising there was never anything like it in London. I think we was the only Catholics in Howley Place but no one ever said a word out of turn to us. There was no bigotry at all. St John's was the big Protestant school and they had a very good boxing team. St Patrick's was always having bouts against them and playing them at football but there was no religious quarrels. Our teachers were Irish or Italian and they encouraged us to support Celtic, which is what our school's football colours were, but that was about all. Of course we had fights on the streets but there was nothing religious in it. Eva and I used to go to the Protestant Youth Club and no one said we shouldn't. I suppose it was because London was more sophisticated, being a bigger city than Glasgow.

MRS VIOLET VAN DER ELST

Mrs Violet Van der Elst was the woman who did so much to try and stop topping. She was the first person to try and really kick up a fuss. I'm not sure she was all she said she was but she did wonders. She'd made some money out of her second husband and she was a good businesswoman in her own right, selling cosmetics. She reckoned she could stop hanging inside six months. That was in 1935 and it took nearer thirty years. The first one she tried to do something about was a bloke in the navy, a fellow called Brigstock who'd done a Chief Petty Officer on their ship. She got a petition with 80,000 signatures, and when that didn't work she got another 100,000. It didn't do any good. The authorities said they wasn't on the right bit of paper and only her signature counted.

Then she tried to stop Reggie Woolmington being hanged. He was a funny man. In fact when it come to it he didn't need her because the House of Lords said he wasn't guilty of murder. He'd written a note to his boss something like, 'I'm not coming to work today. I've shot my wife.'

She was quite willing to put herself in the firing line. When Brigstock got topped she had aeroplanes flying black banners over Wandsworth with STOP THE DEATH PENALTY on them and sandwich board men parading. That's when the coppers did her for obstruction.

Next thing she's down in Brighton in April protesting over Percy Anderson who'd done his girlfriend on the local golf course. She'd said he'd been going out with other girls and he'd lost his rag and strangled her with a shoelace. It's amazing how many people do others with shoelaces. I suppose sometimes it's the only thing that comes to hand easy enough. Anyway, once he's strangled the kid he goes off paddling for half an hour. Usually in that sort of case the bloke's tried to rape the girl, but there wasn't anything like it in Percy's case and as a result there was a big petition for him to be reprieved. Violet had 'Abide With Me' played over the loudspeakers in vans she'd hired. People must have thought it was the Cup Final. That was when she got done for assaulting a copper.

In all she got arrested seven times and summonsed seventeen. Most of them were dismissed and when they wasn't the magistrates give her things like conditional discharges. The biggest pros against her was at the start of the War when she got done under the Official Secrets Act. What happened was when Wandsworth got a hit in the bombing one of the cons managed to get hold of the medical records of the fellows who'd been topped there with things like how long they'd actually lived after the drop and what drugs they'd been given to keep them quiet before it went off. Anyway she realises it's dynamite. She'd got a sort of butler-companion and she got him to give the bloke a tenner or something like that, which was all she had in the house. Tells him to come back at the end of the week when there'll be more. Next, she takes the pages to a photographer – no copier you can use yourself in them days – and tells him to guard them with his life whilst he's photoing them. What does he do? Goes to his boss and what does his boss do? Goes to the coppers. Next thing she's at Bow Street. She was fined a tenner and ten quid costs and she undertook not to publish what had been in the documents.

She may have been an exhibitionist but the cons worshipped her. Funny thing, she was just as keen to pros people as she was to save them from topping. One of the people she prossed was Lord Edward Montagu who worked for her for a bit. She'd won a few quid from her bookmaker and she said he'd been and taken a cheque of hers and cashed it for himself. He said she'd endorsed it to him but he went down. He doesn't seem to have held it against her though because they seem to have become quite friendly later on.

Lord Edward Montagu was involved in a funny way in a murder case himself. It was one of those unsolved ones. A good one too – just like an Agatha Christie play. It was a few years before he became involved with Mrs Elst. What he was in them days was a film extra and he'd put up $200 along with a lot of people to go and film a travel documentary in the South Seas. The whole thing was being run by a man who calls himself Captain Walter Wanderwell and he was scamming them all. He'd been an enemy alien in the First World War when he'd had another name altogether. I can't think right now what it was. Anyway in early December 1932 his Lordship and the Captain and the others are all on the boat which is moored at Los Angeles when a man puts his head through a porthole and asks where Wanderwell is. He's told he's in the saloon and the next thing there's a shot and that's the last of his wanderings.

Who did it? At this stage you can never say for certain but the chances are it was a fellow who'd been taken for his money by Wanderwell and dumped in Panama. He was identified as being the man who asked where the Captain was and he'd got a gun of the type that shot him but that was about it. He got a not guilty but when it come to it he was deported to Australia and was killed in the Second World War.

Another member of the family, Lord Montagu of Beaulieu, was involved in a case which started off a campaign to stop homosexuality being a crime. It was in 1953 it was. He and a couple of friends were charged with indecency. It had all come about when Montagu reported the loss of his camera and it somehow got turned around and he was in the dock. Then a couple of RAF servicemen said they'd been involved as well. The servicemen had been well at it with each other but the pros said Lord Montagu and his friends had lavished hospitality to seduce them. When it come to it the lavish hospitality seemed to be some cider and a meal cooked on a gas stove, which don't seem that lavish to me. Anyway the jury convicted but when Lord Montagu and the others were being driven away to the nick the public gathered round the car and cheered them and booed the pros's witnesses.

DOUBLE JEOPARDY

There was another fellow I remember. This was a fellow, Leonard Thomas, who'd been convicted of trying to kill his wife in 1949 and he got a seven. He'd stabbed her at their home in Chelsea. In them days you couldn't be done for murder if the person you'd tried to do lived for more than a year and a day. That's how Harry Roberts, who did the policemen in Shepherd's Bush, was lucky. Previously he'd done a man who lasted the year and then died so Harry couldn't swing for it. This fellow Thomas's wife died inside the year and so he got put up for the murder. He said they couldn't try him because he'd already been convicted of the same offence. Same circumstances but a different offence, said the judge, who was Devlin who tried that doctor Bodkin Adams and wrote a book about it. Made himself very unpopular over it he did – the book that is, not Thomas. Thomas was sentenced to death but he got reprieved and funnily he only served about five years. Not bad.

When it comes to it not a lot of Chaps were topped over work. Babe Mancini was one, and Harryboy Jenkins and Flossie Forsyth were a couple more. It was much more usual for straight people to swing but there was one back in 1928 when Frederick Stewart, who was a burglar, was hung. His game was sounding the drum, knocking on people's doors of an afternoon and if there was a reply putting up a moody saying he was looking for so-and-so. It was going all right until a fellow in Pembridge Square come back and surprised him and Stewart shot the man with a gun he'd bought for an oxford. The man was looking through the glass panel of the front door and Stewart fired from the other side. He come a tumble because a copper remembered that he come from Warwick Mews and that afternoon when a woman had answered the door at another drum he'd said he was looking for Warwick Garage. The copper put two and two together and thought it was worth a spin and it was. Stewart said it was an accident but he drew that judge Avory and he might just as well have put his hands up, saved time.

Sometimes I sit in a coffee shop in Kingsway waiting for James Morton so we can discuss the book. I like to get there early and I get a corner seat so I can watch what's going on. It's got big plate glass windows and you can just about see all human life there is passing. One or two people recognise me and they wave or give a thumbs up and sometimes they'll come in and ask me to sign my autograph on a paper napkin. There's two things I think when I'm watching. One is how many people smoke despite being told its bad for their health. I can just about see Holborn Tube station from the coffee shop and the second people are off the forecourt they're lighting up. The second is I rarely see a slim woman. You hardly ever saw a fat woman when I was young. Not unless they was getting on and they were boozers. There was no McDonald's or Kentucky Chicken and all the others. There was Lyon's Corner House and the fish and chip shop and the pie and mash and you couldn't afford to go there very often even though it was cheap. Now it seems like Kingsway's just wall-to-wall restaurants and cafés and takeaways. No wonder people's fat. The young ones and all. And you see people eating in the street. When I was young if my mother had seen me eating in the street she'd have taken the food away and smacked me. It's like these young women, and men for that matter, who comb their hair on the tube. If Eva had done that my mother would have thought it a terrible disgrace. Back in my time I remember an old lady turning to one woman and saying, 'Don't do that my dear. You may know what's in your hair but we don't.' She wouldn't have dared now. She'd have had her eye poked out with the comb. I know there aren't so many nits about today but that's not the point.

Back then to get a girl into trouble, as it was called, was a major offence and a shame. For her and you and the family. That's why there were abortionists. They were almost always women, sturdy, a bit school-mistressy. You'd never sus them out, a bit severe. An ordinary woman would be too squeamish. Remember if it went wrong they was risking a murder charge and a certain five years for manslaughter. No home leaves then, no nothing.

It's funny thinking back on how things and manners have changed. We wouldn't have thought we was dressed unless we had a trilby on. And if you met some woman you took it off and kept it off until she sort of nodded to say you could put it back on again. I'm amazed sometimes when I watch the racing on the television and some man's won a big trophy. He goes up to collect it and he never even takes his hat off to the woman who's presenting it to him. It was even worse when they had the minute's silence for the Queen Mother, some of the men, not just in the crowd, but those who should have known better didn't take their hats off.

The coppers, detectives that is, was made to wear a hat in them days. You certainly wasn't allowed in the CID without one even after the War. And good publicity it was too. There was a famous photograph of a copper, Beveridge it was, raising his hat before he made an arrest. It was a funny case, that was. Beveridge was the one who put a temporary stop to the war between Bill and Jack Spot and the Whites.

Anyway, the woman he raised his hat to was Florence Ransom and he did it in High Holborn. It was back in July 1940. She'd been the mistress of a man, Lawrence Fisher. He'd got a wife and a nineteen-year-old daughter and they lived in a village called Matfield near Tonbridge, whilst she and Lawrence lived on a farm in Oxfordshire. She kept things in the family because although Lawrence didn't know it, her mother was the housekeeper and her brother Fred was the cowman.

One day she goes visiting the Fisher women and she takes a shotgun wrapped in brown paper with her. Since none of them came out alive except her and she wasn't saying, it never come out how she got them into the orchard where she blew them away. The maid ran out hearing the shots and she got it as well. What Mrs R. didn't realise was she'd dropped one of her white leather gloves and, since these things are usually family, it was only a matter of time before Beveridge took his hat off. She was found guilty, of course, but she got a reprieve and she ended up in Broadmoor.

I didn't drive then. I'd had my brief taken away from me when I was sixteen out working with Patsy Lyons down King's Cross way. I wasn't even driving but I lost it for ten years and after that I never bothered. There used to be a juvenile court in the Euston Road at the old Friends' Meeting House. We'd all go for our cases and wait in the hall discussing what we'd been up to. I remember there was one kid was going to get probation and he was asked if he was willing to do it. 'Yes,' he pipes, 'but I don't want to have Mr Smith supervise me.' 'Why ever not, Tommy?' says the beak. 'Because he makes me take me clothes off and dance on the table with only me boots on,' says the kid. In those days people would think he was just a little liar but they'd take more notice now. Back then he probably lost his chance of probation and got detention.

I've never ever had a licence since, incredible though it may seem, and now I'll never have one. It wasn't until after I come out from the Spot slashing that I got a car, an automatic it was. Until then Jimmy, Eva's husband, used to drive me. Once I'd got the car I drove all over the country with the gaming machines, and I must have been a good driver because I never got a pull and I never had even the smallest accident. I was never a wheelman though.

I think you've really got to be born a wheelman. People like Roy James, who was on the Train and one or two other top class jobs, or Danny Allpress were just naturals. Probably wheelmen's fathers were often van drivers and they'd want a car of their own to go out with the family. That's where the kids would learn. They'd probably nick Dad's car and give it a spin round the block a few times. Don't forget the streets was empty compared with today.

A top wheelman would work for up to five teams during his career. He'd have a reputation and firms would approach him.

There weren't a lot about. Even though the driver usually got a bit less than the others who actually did the job a lot of people was frightened of getting a five or a ten back then, prison was so hard. So a wheelman could pick and choose.

Down Kingsway towards the Aldwych there used to be the Stoll, big theatre it was. It got pulled down but there's now the Peacock just round the corner. That's been through a few names in its time. People could queue for the gallery and you could rent little stools for about sixpence so you didn't have to stand whilst you waited. As far as I remember the big show at the Stoll was *Kismet*. Before the War though, Eva and me and another kid used to do a bit of a song and dance and get pennies and ha'pennies from the crowd. I remember one night, there waiting to go in was my eldest sister, Peggy, with her boyfriend who she married later. We saw her and give her a nod, saying she'd have to give us something otherwise we'd shame her by stopping and saying she belonged to us. Her husband joined the army and he stayed in after the War, did well and served his full twenty years. She's still alive.

There used to be trams which ran in a tunnel under Kingsway down to the Embankment. When Jimmy Brindle, who went on to marry Eva, and me went over to see our Italian pals in Clerkenwell we'd often take his car down the tunnel. It was all right if there weren't two trams in it. We'd have a few drinks in us and we'd be hooting and laughing but eventually we realised the authorities would be after us. We never drove through it after we'd been working. You might have to in an emergency but you was far too likely to get blocked because it was several hundred yards long. You can still see where it come up or went down, depending on which way you were going, just over the traffic lights at Holborn Station on the way to Southampton Row.

BRIGHTON AND THE SOUTH

I was never in Lewes Crown Court myself. Not in the dock, anyway. I've watched a few trials from the gallery and when I did a bit of work for Harry Rogers from Brighton all those years ago, like torching a rival bingo place in Eastbourne, I also had a look at a juror at the court. You only had to get hold of one in them days although you always tried for two as a sort of insurance.

The building itself is really pretty if you like that sort of thing. It's in the High Street and just about opposite the hotel, The White Hart, and people reckoned that after the Old Bailey it had had some of the best cases in the country. One of them was Tony Mancini. No relation of the Tony Mancini who got done for topping Hubby Distleman in the Palm Beach during the War. This one was a bit before the War, in the '30s. It all came on top because of someone leaving a body in a trunk at Brighton station. I've said before how I can't understand how people think they're going to get away with that sort of caper. It's a bit like those mafia killings where they leave the body in the boot of a car at Miami airport. Two days later and it's going to smell like anything. Of course you can't do it at stations now with security. They don't have lockers or a left luggage now for a start. But even when you could, and though it's not as hot in Brighton as it is in Miami, it was going to get the stationmaster in soon enough.

What happened was a bit of bad luck for Tony. At the beginning of June 1934 someone went and left a trunk made out of plywood in the cloakroom at Brighton and by the middle of the month it had started to stink. They opened it, of course, and there was a woman's body without a head and legs. Maybe that's why they called it a trunk murder, just joking. They had that pathologist, Bernard Spilsbury, down to have a look and he decided it was a girl about 25 years old. A bit later they found her legs at King's Cross station. There was about 700 women reported as missing at the time but they never managed to identify the girl. She'd been in the club so it could have been a boyfriend or a botched abortion, but why leave the body at the railway station?

Over the years there's been quite a few heads rolling around. After Billy Moseley was killed in what they called the Torso case, his head turned up in a lavatory in Islington, during the trial I think it was. Then, a bit after Jimmy Waddington was killed in Romford over some trouble or other, someone chucked his head at the local nick one night. In New York, when the Westies killed someone in the bit they called Hell's Kitchen, they took his head for a farewell tour of the bars giving it a drink and putting a cigarette in its mouth.

Anyway, as for Tony he'd kept the body of his brass, Violette Kaye, in a trunk at Kemp Street near the station. His story was that he'd come home and found her dead on the bed and since he'd got form he didn't think anyone would believe him and he'd panicked and hid the body. He was defended by that brilliant brief Norman Birkett who told the jury to 'Stand Firm'. When they give a not guilty, Birkett says to Tony 'Go home and be a good boy to your mother', which shows how soft some briefs can be even if they're brilliant.

Years later, I met Tony in a club, in Brighton. His real name was Cecil Louis England and he had almost more aliases than I had Christmasses at home – Antoni Pirelli, Luigi Mancini, Hyman Gold and Jack Notyre were some of them. He was born in Newcastle back in 1908. He'd been on the fringes so to speak for years. I half remember he was mixed up with Darby Sabini and his mob at one time. He worked as a counterman and bouncer in pubs all over the place. I'm not sure he wasn't a dancehall gigolo at some time either. A bit before he died he went and told some reporters he had actually killed the girl. He got a few quid for his story but I don't hold with doing that. Keep your trap shut in cases like that is my motto. Up in the North there was a fellow a few years back got acquitted of killing a brass but he gets put away for something else. He's another who can't keep his trap shut; he tells a screw all about how he did it. They can't do him for the murder again, but they did him for perverting the course of justice and he got a six.

The club where I met Tony was owned by Bud Flanagan of The Crazy Gang, on the front it was, near the derelict pier rather than the big one near the Aquarium. For the life of me I can't think of its name at the present. Lovely place it was; lovely baby grand piano. Bud opened it just before the War – 1938 or 1939. It ran for years.

Over time you get a few women who stuff their leavings in trunks. They've usually had a bit of help though. One was the brass in Paris called Gabrielle Bompard. At the end of the nineteenth century she and her boyfriend killed one of her clients. He got topped and when she was released she became a bit of a celebrity, being invited to people's boxes at the races and things, so idolising the likes of us is nothing new. Then a few years later there was a woman, Maria Goold, who did a woman in Monaco. This time her husband was helping her. They were about as incompetent as I was the time I did a smash and grab in Oxford Street just after the War and the car wouldn't start. They thought they'd take the body to Marseilles and ship it to London. When they got there the body wasn't just ripe, it was leaking blood. They both got a guilty but, when it come to it, she died of typhoid and he topped himself.

I suppose the most famous was that Winnie Judd who got known as The Tiger Woman in the 1930s. She did a couple of her girlfriends and went with their bodies from somewhere in Arizona to Phoenix. Made sure they arrived at their destination so to speak. Same as the Goolds in the South of France, someone noticed the trunks were leaking. She was going to be topped but they reckoned she was insane. I read she was released a few years ago.

I've written about Brighton before and how it was an open town with that Chief Constable Ridge who rode on a white horse up and down the promenade. He was a good drinker and he'd be in the clubs with the best of them. I remember there was a Chief Constables' meeting in Brighton one year and Ridge had a whole lot of them in a club where I was, all of us having a drink together. Didn't do me no harm.

But Brighton wasn't too good for a number of people I've known. Alf Gerard was one. He died down there when he was on the run. He'd been a good man in his time; a good crook and a good cook and if you was in a spot he was one to have at your back. Funnily, like so many of us he wasn't a tall man, just a big one. For a time he had a restaurant, The Blue Plaice, south of the river. There's so many stories about how he died – cirrhosis is one of them and that he choked on a lobster is another. I like the second one better.

Then there was Alan Brown. He didn't die down there but he just about signed his warrant. He didn't turn up from release and when he was found down in Brighton at Britannia Court it was with what they said was the biggest haul of amphetamines they'd found so far.

People who say the death penalty stopped killing is mostly wrong, I reckon. I suppose there's an argument, and as a rule we didn't go out with guns on a job, so I suppose to that extent they're right, but take the case of Victor Terry. The day his friends get topped he goes out and does a bank job and shoots the guard.

The people who were topped were also my friends – Flossie Forsyth and Norman Harris. They'd gone down for killing a bloke down Hounslow way; kicked him to death with those shoes they called winkle pickers. There was all sorts of petitions but it didn't do them no good. Flossie got topped at Wandsworth and Norman at Pentonville in November 1960. That was the way it was. Normally if you was one side of river you would be hung in Wandsworth and the other Pentonville, but by then the authorities didn't like topping two people in the same case in the same prison on the same day anymore. Not like in Canada where they literally used to tie them together and hang them back to back.

Anyway Vic hears about them on the radio and sets off for Worthing with a couple of mates, and when the bank guard tries to take the shotgun away from him it goes off and he's killed. Vic and his girlfriend then went on to Portsmouth where he bought himself another shotgun and from there it's off to Scotland. There's rewards out all over the place. I don't know what he was thinking because he gets in a taxi there and tells the driver to keep the change from a ten-bob note when the fare's only a tosheroon. With his cockney accent he must have stood out like a camel in a back garden.

After that it's only a matter of time before him and his girlfriend gets picked up in a hotel in Glasgow and he's brought back down to Sussex. Vic runs a diminished responsibility defence. Says he's possessed by the spirit of that New York gangster, Legs Diamond, and so he's not responsible. There's two doctors say he's genuine and the one for the pros who says he isn't, of course. What the judge does is, instead of reviewing the medical evidence out loud, he gives the jury a copy of the transcript of what the three doctors have said which he's marked in red ink where he thinks something's important. When Vic gets a guilty there's an appeal and he's unlucky. The Court of Appeal says the judge was wrong but what it was all about was whether Vic was pulling the wool over the trick cyclists. It depended not on them but on what the jury thought of Vic. That was the end. Poor old Vic was topped at Wandsworth just like his mate Flossie. Twenty-sixth of April 1961 it was. They did things much quicker then than they do now.

I'm too lazy to go on holiday really. I think the last time I went abroad was with Marilyn to Mexico and I can't say I did enjoy that. I go down to Brighton a lot. The neighbours were good to Doreen and my boy Francis when I went away for what turned out to be twenty years. There was no ostracising them even though there was a lot of publicity. But, there again, I'd been a good neighbour. There was never any trouble with any of them and I kept the house looking nice, of course. It was the first place I had which had a bath of its own. Doreen lived there all the twenty years and that's where I first come out to when I was released. It was sold when she died but Francis still lives in the area with his family. I go down quite often. There's a little jazz band plays of a Sunday at the back of Montefiore Road. Good they are too. I listen to it and put a few bob in the hat. One man come across when they was having a break and said, 'Do you remember me, Frank?' Blow me, it was the man who had the corner shop all those years ago.

I used to be a good swimmer, after all I saved Billy Murray when he got into trouble near what's now the Oxo building when we was kids, but I've given it up now. I swam a bit after I come out from the twenty but I've always been a bit worried about showing my back with the scars on it from the floggings. I don't want people upset or staring for that matter. One thing the school did was take us to the Lambeth Baths every couple of weeks or so. If you didn't have a costume they rented one for you from the attendant. I don't recall getting lessons from any master. It was more or less left up to the older boys to show the younger ones how. We used to walk past my Gran's in Cornwall Road, and when she knew I was coming she'd throw me a ha'penny or perhaps even a penny – mouldies they was called. On the way back I'd treat myself and friends to the bread pudding you got home made from the corner shop in Oakley Street – it's Bayliss Street now. It was gorgeous. Her house is gone now but it was there until ten years ago, when it was one of the ones which had to come down for the Jubilee Line extension.

For the life of me I still can't understand why Freddie Foreman went and admitted the killing of Frank Mitchell and tipping the body out into the Channel. There wasn't any need. I don't think he got much dough for it and it didn't help his reputation any for it. It didn't help when it looked as though him and the grass, Albert Donaghue, stood and looked at each other on the escalator. I know that can be done by filming them separately and then cutting the film but it didn't do no good.

Mitchell's body's never been found but the one that turned up near Newhaven was that of Scotch Jack Buggy. He'd been done in the Mount Street Bridge Club in Mayfair where he'd been causing a bit of grief trying to get the money back for my friend Roy James from the Train. Roy had left it to be looked after whilst he was away and the money seemed to go for a walk. Jack, who'd been in the nick with Roy, was just trying to help. For his pains he was shot, wrapped in a carpet to get him out of the club and then bound with baling wire and tipped overboard. He floated up just about Derby Day 1967. Years later a couple of people was charged but their case was chucked out at the Bailey.

Of course that's where Lord Lucan is said to have disappeared, over the side of the Newhaven–Dieppe ferry after he was meant to have killed the nanny, Sandra Rivett, by mistake for his wife. It seems amazing it's back in 1974 his Lordship went AWOL. Mind you, I'm not sure he's not still alive somewhere like South Africa. He could easily have been hidden away. There's still a lot of people who don't believe he's dead. There's also a lot of people who don't believe that JFK and Elvis are gone either, or that singer Jim Reeves, so maybe they're all together somewhere.

If you went the other way out of Brighton you'd get to Shoreham on the way to Worthing. That's where the body of a biker turned up in the harbour. Just down the road was Shoreham and in April 1973 a body come out of the harbour there with its legs tied to a block of concrete. Clive Olly, the fellow's name was, and he'd been reported missing at the beginning of March. It turned out he was a member of the Mad Dogs Chapter of the Hell's Angel's (Brighton). The Mad Dogs seem to have been a bit of a poor relation because they didn't have bikes of their own.

It seems Olly'd had it off with the girlfriend of Brian Moore, another Mad Dog. Moore had put Olly in a van and hit him with a truncheon and then thrown him in the harbour. Him and another fellow was convicted of the murder. They had a girl with them and she was convicted of manslaughter, but that got slung out on appeal.

One man got a re-trial over what went on in a hotel in Brighton. Not the usual sort of hanky-panky the town's been famous for, but when the jury got sent to a hotel overnight some of them put together a ouija board to get a bit of advice. The fellow was Stephen Young and he was meant to have shot Nichola and Harry Fuller at their cottage in Wadhurst in 1993. Harry used to boast about how much money he had on him and the pros said that was why Young went and shot him. He was in debt but the day after the topping he went and paid six grand into his bank account. They never found the gun but it seems the bullets were like some the coppers found at Young's place.

The jury goes off to the Albion Hotel for the night and around eleven o'clock four of them go to one of their rooms and since they don't have a ouija board they put together the letters on bits of paper. They get a wine glass and the glass moves to the letters spelling words out. It says it's Harry Fuller and so they ask it, 'Who killed you?' and it says, 'Stephen Young'. After that they ask it how and where the money is and things like that, and then it tells them to vote guilty. Anyway although they agree to say nothing about it one of them blows it all out at breakfast. They still find Young guilty but one of the other jurors gets in touch with a brief. Now one of the problems is that the Court of Appeal can't ask jurors what's gone on in the jury room once they've retired to consider the verdict but it's a bit crafty. The court says the jurors weren't in the jury room at the time and so it can hear what went on. They quashed the conviction and give Young a re-trial, but it doesn't do him any good. It's another guilty.

It's funny how you think if people are part of a firm then the only harm that's going to come to them is in the way of business. It's not right of course. Take Charlie Clarke who was with the Twins. He wasn't generally liked. He kept a room for Ronnie as a hideaway for him in Walthamstow. He'd been a grass for years but Ronnie Kray never found out, which was just as well for Charlie. He also set up Lennie McLean, 'The Guv'nor', to get a beating. They was going to strangle Lennie with chicken wire but he escaped and as a result Charlie had to pay good money in compensation.

He was another who moved to the seaside and later he had one of his legs off. In March 1989 he's stabbed to death at his home in Dover. Apparently he surprised a kid, Shane Keeler, when he was screwing the place. Funny, because Charlie had been a good cat burglar himself in his day. Keeler pleaded guilty to man-slaughter on the grounds of diminished responsibility but he still got lifed off. Charlie was 71 at the time.

I suppose one man who did more harm than any three judges put together was that pathologist Bernard Spilsbury. When I was young he was the great God in the courts. All he had to do was turn up and say some man had done it and the jury was knocking their heads on the box saying, 'Yes, Sir Bernard, of course Sir Bernard'. But now it seems that he wasn't necessarily all that great. One of the men he did for was Sidney Fox and there's been an argument about whether he was right in that case ever since.

Sidney and his mother were a pair of confidence tricksters but by October 1929 they was well down on their luck and they'd got rooms in the Metropole in Margate. I think things was so bad for them that she was wearing all the clothes she had on top of each other. She'd been ill and they put it about they'd been visiting the graves of his brothers in France. Her story was that she was the widow of William Fox, founder of Fox's Flour Mills. What she was really was the widow of a railway signalman. It's true her boys had been killed in the War, but they'd never been near the graves. Sidney liked to be called Captain Owen Smythe.

Just before midnight one day he runs down the stairs saying there's a fire in his mother's room and a fellow comes and pulls her out. It seems like the armchair and the carpet was on fire. Poor Sidney was so upset they had to give him a shot of something to quieten him down. What he was worried about was a pony that was in his mother's bag. They found the bag but there was no dough in it. His story was that he woke up, smelled burning and tried to get in his mother's room but got beaten back.

He was nearly home and clear because the doctors at the inquest reckoned she'd fallen asleep and part of a newspaper had caught fire and set the place alight. What did for Sidney was that he'd taken out insurance on her for £3,000, which was good dough then, and the policy was due to expire about twenty minutes after she snuffed it.

It all came on top for him when he tried to get the money from the insurers. They got in Spilsbury who reckoned there was no soot in her lungs and she must have died before the fire started. By this time Fox was inside for getting credit by fraud and he never come out. What Spilsbury reckoned was that he'd given his mother a few doses of port and then he'd strangled her. He'd then gone and shut the doors before he raised the alarm. He said he'd done it to stop the fire spreading, which isn't a bad answer. But the really funny thing was that if you strangle someone you can't help not breaking what's called the hyoid bone and this hadn't been broken. Spilsbury said he had seen bruising but the other pathologists, Sydney Smith and Keith Simpson, said it wasn't there when they saw the body and it could have just been putrefaction. They reckoned the jury convicted just because Spilsbury was Spilsbury.

Fox never appealed and he got topped in April 1930. I suppose it come out right because a bit before Mrs Fox died Sidney had been having it off with a widow and she'd woken up and found the gas tap on. He'd persuaded her to make a will in his favour and then insured her as well. She give him the chuck after that and he's walked off with her jewels. He got a year-and-a-half for that. Some people think he did his mother because the old girl had Parkinson's and he was practising euthanasia, or 'old dear topping' as we call it. But even years later Smith wouldn't have it as murder.

I think people in insurance companies have got smarter over frauds these days. You used to be able to have a fire and there was no questions asked. Provided you didn't do it too often everything was all right. Mind you when Joe Wilkins and me set fire to the place off Wardour Street we was lucky to have that hooky assessor help us out. Of course, some people don't go about it the right way. I saw one in the papers where the husband got a good payment from the insurance, going about like he was crippled for life, and then he goes and leaves his wife. She's so cross she shops him. There's a story, I don't know if it's true, of an assessor who hounds an Irish builder who's slipped off a ladder and can't work anymore. The man's convinced the builder's a fraud but he can never catch him going ten-pin bowling or anything. Anyway the fellow gets a big pay out in the High Court and he's being wheeled away when the insurance assessor runs up beside him and says he'll never stop chasing him and he'll get him one day. The man just smiles and says, 'It won't do any good. I'm booked to go to Lourdes next Monday.'

Being in a wheelchair doesn't stop you working though. In fact it can be a good cover. There's just been a woman in America, Ernestine Williams, 65 she was, run a gang of pickpockets from a wheelchair. She'd got high blood pressure, she was arthritic and she'd had kidney failure, but you have to admit she was game. The team worked from Miami up to Atlanta and they was clearing $1,000 a day each. She'd started off as a family business using three of her kids and one of her grandsons and she'd expanded. She taught her fifteen dips the tricks of the trade, like who you should nick from. She reckoned elderly whites in supermarkets was the easiest touch. She used to trade the credit cards her team nicked with crack cocaine for the kids she was using. By the time she was nicked herself it was reckoned she'd cleared hundreds of thousands of dollars.

Going back to Spilsbury, he started out his career as the pathologist in Crippen's case and he went on from there. Eventually he topped himself. He'd had a stroke as long back as 1940 but it still didn't stop him working. Then he had another couple, and then at the end of 1947 he went and gassed himself in his workroom. I reckon it's impossible to say just how much harm he did to people over the years.

In my time there wasn't that many policemen killed. I think until the early 1950s there'd only been four in the previous ten years. I know people will say one is more than enough but it shows how violence had grown in recent years. There was a copper, Evan Davies, shot whilst questioning a couple of youths in a Cardiff air raid shelter at the beginning of the War. They was never nicked. Then there was a William Avis only a couple of months later in February 1942, while he was searching a house in Bognor Regis. Then come Nathanial Edgar who killed Donald Thomas in Southgate in February 1948. There'd been a lot of burglaries about that time in the area, which had some big houses, and the copper was patrolling Wades Hill. Edgar was found in Clapham with a Luger under his pillow. It was funny how he went wrong. He'd been captain of his school's cricket team but once he'd been called up at the end of the War he become a deserter. He'd done six months in detention and he was on his toes again. He was lucky they was discussing abolishing hanging at the time because he'd have swung for sure otherwise.

But the one which created a big stir was a kid who'd escaped out of Feltham Borstal in June 1951. I think it was because he was so young. He'd been bullied there and he did it to show that he was as tough as anyone else. Derek Poole he was. He come from Chatham and he got himself back there and barricaded himself up. He killed a copper, Alan Baxter, before he shot himself. There was something like 200 coppers at the siege.

Portsmouth was the place we'd be taken to go over to the Island. We'd go down on the train and then let out at Portsmouth Harbour and have to walk in our handcuffs across to the boat with everyone watching. Sometimes there'd be a chain looping through the cuffs. Then it was in a big cabin to ourselves and at the other end a coach to take us to the nick.

Portsmouth was also where Alfie Hinds' father did a big raid in the 1930s. He got the cat for it and it ruined his health. It was also the place where the fellow Harold Loughans, who was missing a few fingers on one hand, was meant to have strangled a woman who ran a small hotel. Mrs Rose Robinson she was and she ran the John Barleycorn in Commercial Road. At the end of November 1944 she'd been found strangled and there was scratches across her throat. Whoever done it got away with a bit under £500. It was one of the few mistakes Spilsbury made that ever got showed up. He was appearing for the defence that time.

Loughans got nicked because he was heard saying he'd done the woman but although Keith Simpson give evidence that even without his fingers he could have strangled her, the jury at Winchester disagreed and when the case was reheard in London Spilsbury gave evidence. What he said was that it was impossible for Loughans to have killed the woman because when he had caught his hand in the machine that took off his fingers, in trying to pull away he'd also done in the muscles in his arm and he wouldn't have had the necessary strength. Loughans got a not guilty but within a couple of months he got a five for screwing. Then he got a fifteen years PD. When he come out in 1963 the *People* had done a series on the barrister J. D. Casswell who'd prossed him back in 1944 and in it they said Loughans had been lucky to get away with the murder.

It's as I've said so many times. The likes of us shouldn't go near the libel courts – Darby Sabini, Jack Spot and me are just some who've all come croppers. Anyway Loughans had a run at the paper though I don't know where he got the money; in those days you didn't get legal aid for libel and it was illegal for a brief to take it on and share the winnings.

Joseph Moloney was the brief for the paper and he was the one who later prossed us at Parkhurst. It was a jury trial and he was able to put Loughans' form to him and he called Simpson to repeat what he'd said nearly twenty years earlier. He'd kept his notes all those years. Anyway the jury said they reckoned Loughans had done it, and they was right. He'd got stomach cancer and a bit before he died he walked into the paper's offices and made a confession saying he hadn't long to live and he wanted to put things straight. They took a photo of him writing out that he'd killed Mrs Robinson.

There was another man who had a deformed hand who said he couldn't have done a murder. He was Ronald Lewis and he went down for killing a nurse in 1969. He pleaded guilty and now he says his brief persuaded him to and he was shielding someone else. The last I heard he was still inside. He'd had a bit of trouble with his home leaves. First he tried to top himself in a hotel in October 1989 and then he'd gone to Grendon and it turns out a woman who'd been seeing him when he was in Leyhill complained he'd been round to her home and made threats. He says he never did but it's been enough to have him kept inside. He may be out now and I hope he is but, if so, it's only recent.

It was down the road in Southampton that Lady Docker lost her jewels; back in 1958 when I was doing time for Spot it was. She'd left about 150 grands-worth of stuff in the boot of Sir Bernard's Roller. They'd left about £20,000 of stuff behind. The assessors put up the usual ten per cent. It was a well-planned job. The boot wasn't forced so someone had a key. Bernard said he thought there was only two keys in existence, one with him and the other with his manservant, but there must have been three. Billy Hill went to see Her Ladyship and said he'd do what he could to get the stuff back. This time he didn't manage it like he'd managed for Gordon Richards when that good climber Billy Benstead nicked his racing trophies.

Hilly had met her at a party at Gennaro's in Soho when his book come out. Albert Dimes had given her a slap when he went into the upstairs room and found Billy giving her one. Albert could be a bit straightlaced and he thought it showed disrespect since her husband was downstairs.

I suppose the biggest murder case there's been in Southampton come in the 1920s when a fellow, William Podmore, did a man who worked in the same company, Vivian Messiter. What had happened was Podmore, who was a sort of an all-rounder, had applied for a job as a salesman at the Wolf's Head Oil Company. Sensibly he didn't give his own name and he was calling himself

William Thomas. Once he'd got his feet well in, he starts writing up fictitious invoices and collecting the commission on them. When the company sends Messiter round to see what's going on Podmore kills him with a hammer and hides the body behind boxes in a garage.

There's no way you can just leave a body like that and, of course, someone sniffs it out. There wasn't a lot of evidence against Podmore – a few letters which tied him in – and he had a brief who was really big at that time, Edmund O'Connor, who appeared at the inquest. He wasn't a barrister, just a solicitor but people said he would have been as good as Marshall Hall if he'd gone to the Bar. He defended my friend, Freddy Ford, over some gambling clubs and drinkers he was running.

In those days – in fact up to the Lucan case – an inquest jury could name the killer and that worked as a sort of committal proceedings. O'Connor was brilliant; he managed to get a verdict of murder by persons unknown and Podmore walked. Like getting chucked at the magistrates' court it didn't count always as an outright acquittal and they could charge you if there was new evidence. Podmore didn't last long on the outside because he picked up a six months for an earlier fraud in Manchester and then on his release he collected another six months for robbery. Then he was nicked again for the murder, and this time they'd got those so-called cell confessions made to other prisoners.

From what I read of the committal proceedings O'Connor produced a trick really worthy of Marshall Hall at his best. Podmore was quite a small man, not much taller than me, and O'Connor challenged one of the doctors to try to move the 'body' of Messiter, a much bigger man. He'd got one of Podmore's friends to play the part. All the doctor succeeded in doing was to rip the buttons off the man's shirt. It must have been a bench of lay justices. A stipendiary wouldn't have allowed that sort of thing. O'Connor also did a lot with the jail evidence, but the beaks committed Podmore and when the trial come the pros had its house back on the bricks. There was an application for a reprieve but the Home Secretary said the there wasn't any doubt. By the time Podmore was topped, O'Connor was reported to be in Paris looking for a so-called mystery enemy of Messiter who might have done it. More likely he was off drinking and gambling because that was the downfall of him. He ended up penniless and doing a seven for fraud.

MIDDLESEX AND HERTFORDSHIRE

When I read how the police complain they can't get convictions and juries throw cases out I think they've only got themselves to blame. Over the years when I was young there wasn't really any point in challenging police evidence. Juries who come from the middle classes had no experience with policemen except that they saluted and told them the way to Piccadilly Circus when they was lost. Then over the years, little-by-little, it come to them that the coppers lie same as anyone else. What's worse the magistrates and judges are as much to blame. The defence briefs knew coppers were lying but when they got up on the bench themselves it was the same old story, 'Brave old PC Jones, why would he lie, members of the jury? Have twelve good policemen risked their pensions and prison conspiring against Fraser?' If they'd put a stop to it back in the 1950s and 1960s then things would have been a lot better.

Take that thing with notebooks. Coppers used to say notes had been made up independently with no help from their mates and yet they was word for word and full stop for full stop the same. How could they be independent? So they got over this by saying they'd refreshed each other's memory in the canteen some five or six hours after the interview. There's a story about that top brief who's got a junior brief behind him who's meant to be taking notes. The judge misses something and asks what a witness has just said. The man behind the leader didn't get it down and the senior brief gets up and says, 'I'm afraid he hasn't written down what the witness says but he and I will be compiling it in six hours time in the wine bar.'

I think the first person really to go on the attack in a murder case over verbals and statements was the man who became Attorney General, Peter Rawlinson, when he was defending Alfred Whiteway in what they called the Towpath Murders in Teddington back in 1953. Here was the man on trial for his life and people said that Rawlinson had gone in a bit strong against the copper Bert Hannam. He was cross examining him over Whiteway's confession and he didn't half lay into him, saying he'd more or less composed it himself. It didn't do Whiteway any good. He was on trial for the murder of a young girl and there was another one who'd been killed as well so he wasn't going to get any change out of the jury. But Rawlinson was one of few who dared give it a real go. It was a bit of a funny case altogether. The copper who found an axe which Whiteway was supposed to have used took it home for himself. When he was asked why he'd done it he said it was the rule that if a driver found anything in the car he could claim it.

Hannam may have got away with it that time but he come a cropper with the case over that doctor, Bodkin Adams, who was meant to have done his patients in at Eastbourne. Mind you, more or less the whole of the pros' witnesses come a cropper in that.

What's come out over the years is that it wasn't just verballing but they had a thing called scriptwriting. If there was a bank job or a hi-jack, something like that, then there'd be one officer who's job it was to write up a script giving all the coppers their parts to play. The result was when it come to court they couldn't make a rick by one of them saying he could see DS Smith the whole time when DS Smith was saying he was round the corner. Then when it was all worked out, the copper would give the script to each of the others and they'd write up their parts in their notebooks.

You don't associate Potters Bar, at the start of what used to be called the Great North Road, with murder but there's been a couple of what you could call good murders there and in Wheathampstead, which isn't that much further up the road. That wasn't solved and nor was one of the ones from Potters Bar.

The first was back in 1947 when a fellow Albert Welch, who was known as Snakey to his workmates, left a note for his wife Phyllis on the kitchen table saying he'd gone for a walk and wouldn't be back for tea. They lived on an estate which is near where the rubbish tip is nowadays on the way to the M25. He wouldn't be back at all. Next day she told her neighbour, who was a retired copper, and she reported him missing. He'd taken his ration book and identity card with him but he didn't turn up for six months until a kid was looking for golf balls in Potters Bar Golf

Club, where Tony Jacklin used to be the assistant or the pro, and turned up a hand with manicured nails. Bit by bit as they dredged the pond up come Albert, or what's left of him. Someone had cut off the head and burned it. They managed to get a fingerprint which identified the bits as Albert but Mrs Welch wouldn't have it that it was her husband. She never went to the funeral saying it wasn't him they was burying. She said he'd got rough workman's hands but his mates said he always wore gloves to protect them. I suppose it's possible the fingerprint was wrong but if it was no one can say where Albert finished up. No one ever found out a reason or who killed him.

Funnily there was another murder at Potters Bar Golf Club about eight years later, when a boy called Michael Queripel hit a woman, Elizabeth Currell, with a tee-marker. He was only seventeen and he got detained. You'd think that Queripel was such an unusual name you'd never hear of two of them in your life but in 1993 a little girl called Stacey Queripel was found in the woods near where she lived in Bracknell. At first they thought she'd caught her necklace on some branches and strangled herself but then they realised someone else had done it. At one time they arrested her mother but she was released. She told the coroner that she'd gone to check on Stacey and found her missing so she'd got her lodger to go searching for the little kid with her. No one was ever prossed over it.

The case in Wheathampstead was one of those real mysteries which ran for years. A girl called Ann Noblett was a seventeen-year-old who disappeared at the end of December 1957 on her way home from a dancing class. Some men with their dog found the body a month later in some woods about seven miles from where she'd last been seen. She'd been raped but what was really odd was that she'd been kept in a deep freeze. The family got a detective agency to look into things and three years later they lit on a man who was wanted on a fraud charge and had left the country. He said it was nothing to do with him. Him and another man had a refrigeration company. I think the family tried to bring a private prosecution but it never got off the ground.

Private prosecutions for murder are rare but not as rare as it used to be. What's more common now is that families, where they don't like a not guilty verdict, bring a civil action where they don't have to prove so much. O. J. Simpson's a classic example and there was one in Scotland not long ago, as well as the one brought by the family of that doctor in St John's Wood. But there was a proper private prosecution over the death of a girl in Sussex back in August 1948. There's always a danger with them. Either the Director of Public Prosecutions can step in and offer no evidence and there's nothing you can do even if you don't agree or, worse probably, if the fellow gets acquitted you can be liable for a lot of dough.

Anyway Joan Woodhouse's body was found by a fellow in the grounds of Arundel Park. There was a neat pile of clothes by the body. She'd been dead about a week. They thought she'd been raped and strangled. She'd been living in the YWCA in Blackheath but originally she come from Barnsley. She'd arranged to go and see her father over the Bank Holiday and that's where she told her roommate she was going but instead she goes down to Sussex. The copper Fred Narborough was in charge and he could never get enough together to make an arrest. Of course they fancies the man who found her. The family instructed a private detective and the Yard then got that Reginald Spooner to have another look. He says there's no evidence but the family isn't satisfied, and that's when they took out a private pros. The DPP steps in and this time he does go on with the case. Two hours later to great cheers the magistrates say the man hasn't got a case to answer and that was the end of things, although the family did try and get what's called a Voluntary Bill of Indictment, which means a case goes straight to a jury. That's what the pros did in the case of the prison officers they said had attacked the Birmingham Six. This time though the judge wouldn't grant one to the Woodhouse family. It seems that Spooner thought since a big relationship had broken up she'd committed suicide and that accounted for the neat pile of clothes, but Narborough never agreed with this. He always reckoned a man would speak up out of turn in a pub somewhere and then he would have him. But if there was such a man he never did.

It's not often you get two killings in exactly the same place. Well, I suppose you can if you're thinking about Chicago or some club or other, maybe a beach or some moor, but off hand I can't think of many like that here. One place was an exception and that was Rooks Farm at a place called Stocking Pelham out in Hertfordshire. That's first of all where Muriel McKay ended up, poor woman, and then a kid called John Scott gets done there as well.

The McKay case was famous. It was one of the first kidnappings for ransom there'd been in Britain and the coppers didn't have much experience in dealing with it. That and the fact the Hosseins didn't have lifts going up to the top floor, certainly not as far as crime went. For a start they kidnapped the wrong woman. Two brothers, Arthur and Nizamodeen, from Trinidad they were. Arthur was quite a good tailor down the East End. They'd been watching television and seen Rupert Murdoch who had bought the *News of the World* talking to David Frost about what a beautiful wife he had and what he was worth, and they decided they'd kidnap her and get a million quid for her. They went to Fleet Street and by chance saw Murdoch's right-hand man, Alick McKay, get in a blue Rolls and they mistook him for Murdoch. They follow the car out to Wimbledon and went back and kidnapped his wife.

They took her out to the farm and no one quite knows what happened to her. She needed medicine and she may just have died because she didn't get it. They sent off the demand for a million and there was drops of money arranged. I think they even had a million printed up in fake notes. Anyway it didn't do no good but the Hosseins was using their own car to go on the run for the money and a copper took the number. After that it was just a question of time and the next morning they picked them up. Both of them got life. I knew them in prison a bit. They kept themselves to themselves. They weren't that popular for having done that to a woman but I never heard of anyone giving them a seeing to. They're still in I think. No one ever found out what happened to Mrs McKay. The best bet is they fed her body to the pigs but they never would say.

After the brothers had been put away, a publican down the East End, Tony Wyatt, bought the place. Seventeen-and-a-half grand it cost him back in the early 1970s. Anyway, in September 1972 there's a wedding reception for his sister-in-law, Avril Hurst, and during the festivities John Scott gets himself done with a sickle. It was a bit of a funny case. The holes in the kid's body is plugged up and he's dressed in fresh clothes and taken to Ranelagh Road, out Leytonstone way, and left in a van. Schoolkids found him a day or so later which must have put them off their lunch.

Tony Wyatt was done for the murder. He said he'd only killed Scott because he was being offensive to the women at the party and Scott'd attacked him when he'd tried to get him to go. He pleaded guilty to manslaughter at the Bailey and was defended by that good brief, Michael Corkery. He got three years and was out just after one. He never even lost his licence. What made the whole thing so funny was that he couldn't have moved the body all on his own and yet no one was done with him, although that copper Bert Wickstead was involved and he used to pride himself on how he solved cases. At the time Wyatt was a big witness for the pros in the case Wickstead was running against the Tibbs family and there was a number of other witnesses at the wedding. The farm was sold again and this time it was worth around £46,000.

BROADMOOR

Back in 1953 I got taken from Durham straight down to Broadmoor in a taxi. It was a long drive in the days before the motorways and there was an overnight for the screws which meant overtime. That pleased them and paid for a part of their holiday. No one told me where I was going. I just found out when I got there. They didn't actually talk to me on the journey. I went straight into Block 6, the refractory block, and I stayed there the whole time. At one time you did every day of your sentence if you was in Broadmoor; there was no remission. The benefit was the regime was easy there. But as years went by prisoners tried to get in and out of Broadmoor and back to prison just before the end of your sentence. If you was doing say a seven then you did a couple, went to Broadmoor for a couple of years and back to the nick. You'd be out in four years and eight months if you'd lost no remission and it had been an easy run.

Generally you worked your way up through the blocks and apart from Block 1, which was a sort of assessment block at the time I was there, the lower the number the more the privileges. There was some wealthy people in Broadmoor over the years and in Block 2 some of the men had others being sort of batmen or valets for them, giving them a few bob a week. Even if I'd got out of refractory I'd never have done that.

I was in Broadmoor just after John Allen, the so-called Mad Parson, had escaped. He got the name because he'd been part of the Broadmoor concert party, a sort of end-of-pier show, and had dressed up as a vicar for one of his parts. He'd managed to hang on to the collar and the stock front and he climbed out one night, jumped into some telephone wires which broke his fall and he was off. November 1947 it was. There was a big hue and cry but he was clever. He wore slippers and carried his shoes and the bloodhounds followed the scent to a pond where he'd thrown them in and the dogs got confused. I don't think bloodhounds are that bright myself. Some got used in the hunt for Jack the Ripper and that lot got lost. Anyway, Allen gets a lift into London from a fellow. That happened then. If you saw someone walking by the road it was courtesy to offer them a lift. It can't happen now. Women are generally too frightened. Men ought to be as well. I read of a case the other day where some girl made a speciality of getting herself lifts and then telling the men that if they didn't give money she'd go to the police and say they'd tried to rape her. Back then vicars in particular were respected, and if you saw one then of course you'd stop. Allen was dropped off at South Kensington tube and he made his way to Paddington and got a train to Devon.

He was out two years before he got nicked up St John's Wood way. He'd been working in a baker's. Back in 1937 he'd been some sort of chef when he killed the little girl of one of the women he'd been working with. Nothing sexual or anything like that. He just got in a temper because the mother had been chosen to bake some cakes in preference to him. Up till then he'd been devoted to the kid. He got the death penalty and was reprieved and sent to Broadmoor. He'd been in the hatch twice already before he killed the girl.

There'd been a few murders in St John's Wood about the time he escaped. One was a brass and another was a woman beaten to death in her shop one lunchtime and, of course, Allen was in the frame. He was put on an ID but he was never picked out. He got sent back to Broadmoor but they only kept him another couple of years. By then he certainly wasn't mad. When he was back inside he applied for a rebate of tax he'd paid whilst he was working on the run.

I remember one of the times when Alfie Hinds escaped, the papers got hold of Allen for his comments about what he would be doing if he was in Alfie's position. He wrote a book and all. He'll be well in his eighties if he's still alive. Several people got out of Broadmoor and stayed out, but there was one who come back. He'd been sent there in the 1880s, James Kelly his name was. He always talked about escaping and that's just what he did. He joined the merchant navy and went to America. Then at the end of his life he came back and demanded to be let in, said it was his home. He'd been out 39 years. It dwarfs Ronnie Biggs really. And he was meant to be mad and all.

I suppose the really big man who was in Broadmoor just before me was Ronald True. He'd been the one who'd killed a brass down

Fulham way and got reprieved. People said it was because he was well connected, as when a poor kid called Jacoby, who's never had any sort of a life, kills an old girl in her hotel, he swings. I've written about both the cases before.[1]

True had been the sort of King of Broadmoor of his day. He'd been another leading light in the concert party. People were always speaking about him. He died in 1951. He'd been there 28 years, happy as a sandboy. There was talk that he knew some of the Royal Family, and that counted a lot even if it wasn't correct. People was very snobbish in them days. If you was Sir Charles Brown or Sir William Smith then people looked up to you no matter what you'd done. There wasn't any of these knighthoods for sport or acting you have now. I think Stanley Matthews must have been the first. You wouldn't have got one for rowing up and down a river in them days. Maybe it was Gordon Richards, the jockey. There used to be a joke on the music halls, 'If they made Gordon Richards a knight why can't they make Wigan a pier?'

Another toff who was in Broadmoor a bit before me was Thomas Ley. You don't get too many times when a former cabinet minister, even if it's an Australian one, gets done for murder. But that's what happened a bit after the end of the War. November 1946 it was when the body of a bloke named John Mudie was found in a chalk pit down in Surrey.

Really Ley's story was a good one. He'd gone from here with his parents to New South Wales when he was eight, back in the 1880s, and had been a paper boy. He'd left school at ten and become a junior clerk in a solicitor's and he'd managed to work his way up and qualify. He even had his own firm, and by the time he was 25 started to go into politics. He got into the State Parliament and then wanted to go for the big time. There was a whiff about him even then. His opponent claimed there was bribery involved and he disappeared when he was on the way to a meeting with Ley.

Then there was another bit of trouble. Ley was a director of a company and when that got investigated the man who was causing trouble disappeared over a cliff top. Then there was another man

---

[1] See *Mad Frank's London*.

died, with Ley a bit too close. I suppose he was really a serial killer, not for kicks but he just cleared people who was a nuisance out of his way. Anyway this time enough was enough and they kicked him off his Parliament seat and he came back to England. He'd got a middle-aged mistress by then; Maggie Brook was her name. He tried to get a sweepstake off the ground and did a good bit of profiteering in the War.

By the end of the War his girlfriend was getting on a bit. She was 66 and you'd have thought getting on for retirement from it all, not looking at other men. But Ley got the idea in his head she was having it away with his son-in-law and then later with a barman called Jack Mudie. I don't suppose for a minute she'd had it away with the son-in-law, and all poor old Mudie had done was just speak to her. But it was enough to do for him. Ley recruits a man, Lawrence Smith, and together they find out Mudie's address, lure him to Beaufort Gardens where Ley is living and strangle him. Then they take the body to a chalk pit near Woldingham.

It's not that long before the body's discovered. The trial was a big one. Lord Goddard, the man who it was said had two pairs of trousers with him when he give someone the death sentence, was the judge. The story used to be that he had to change because he'd come as he was saying the words. His family denied it but, like Mandy Rice Davies said, 'They would, wouldn't they'. My friend Alfie Hinds, who was up in front of him more than once, used to say you knew he'd lost interest in your case when he started picking his nose.

Ley ran a number of defences and that top pathologist Keith Simpson really got on Goddard's wick by saying that it was possible Mudie had topped himself. I don't know how he come to work that one out. Then there was another Aussie who come along to say he'd tried to do a screwing at Beaufort Gardens, had found a man tied up and he'd pulled on the ropes. God knows where they found him and how much he must have been paid to say that. It didn't do Ley and Smith no good whatsoever. They both was sentenced to death – I don't know if Goddard had three pairs of trousers that day. Ley was going completely round the bend by then and a bit later he was found insane and sent to Broadmoor. That was what saved Smith. They couldn't really top him if the man who'd started it all was reprieved and so he was lifed off. Ley didn't last long. He had a brain haemorrhage within a few months. That was the case where a neighbour of ours in Howley Place, the all-in wrestler Chopper Sims, give a bit of evidence. You could see him at the Ring, Blackfriars and the other shows before the War. It wasn't his real name of course.

Ronald True wasn't the longest inmate in Broadmoor by a long chalk. A lot of people lived a long time there, if they kept out of the refractory block that is. One of the reasons people did is that they didn't have any worries. Everything was done for them. The other reason was the air was so clean. The place is just on the edge of Windsor Forest. When Allen was in there was more than 50 inmates over the age of 75. There was a fellow, Peter Murphy, who'd been in Broadmoor 55 years when he died at the age of ninety. He played the drums in the band they had. That was in the 1930s. Then again just before me was Frank Smith who was there from 1893 to 1947.

Bill Giles was the oldest man in Broadmoor. I'd gone by the time he died in March 1962. He was 87 and he'd been there over 75 years. He'd been sent there in 1886. The place hadn't been open 24 years then. He'd set fire to a hayrick and that was the last he saw of the outside world. He was so small he was kept in the women's wing for the first five years until they decided he was big enough to stand up to the violent men in the main block. That's where he stayed. He was the best floor scrubber they ever had. People did come and see him for the first few years but gradually he outlived them all. I don't suppose he was dangerous for years but there again he wouldn't have been able to cope outside. Just think, he was in during the Boer War let alone two world wars. He was there before there was proper electricity and the motor car. He must have been taken there in a horse-drawn van. When he died, there was spokesmen saying how people used to play tricks on him, nailing his bucket to the floor, and how he enjoyed it saying he'd have them expelled. Just like he was a schoolmaster. They give him a new suit each year and a birthday present. There was stories about how he corrected new nurses if they got the routine wrong. Made him out to be a proper little character. But what a life for the poor devil. Now he'd have had probation.

Another big thing happened when I was there and that was the death of a kid, John Berridge, from cyanide poisoning. He'd been in a few years after shooting his parents in Pembroke Dock back in 1959. Now how did he get the poison? Or who give it him? There was all sorts of rumours flying around. Of course, we all fancied the screws, but when it come to it the coppers reckoned it was either one of the inmates or that he topped himself. A whole load of inmates give evidence and there was a lot of talk about how easy it was to get poisons at the time. There was also talk that he'd been blackmailed over tobacco debts. It seems like someone had shoved the cyanide into chocolates, just like in an Agatha Christie book, and John had picked them out.

There was another even more fantastic story. Young Berridge had been in the RAF and the reason he gave for topping his father is that whilst he'd been in Germany some fellow speaking perfect English had asked him to be a spy for the Russians. There was a bit of boodle in it and he'd agreed and told the man about some practice bomb or other. When he come home he told his father and the old man said he was going to report him to the authorities. That's why he blew him and his mother away. No wonder they put him in Broadmoor. Anyway one story which come out at the inquest was that he'd had a parcel which he said had come from the Russians and that it contained cyanide.

My friend Timmy Noonan, who was with us on the Parkhurst Riot, was one of the witnesses. The jury went and decided it was suicide. Seventeen of them there were. For once no one could say I'd had anything to do with it. I was on Block 6 like I've said and this took place on Block 4.

I've said before how I was advised there was two sorts of medicine they give out, one which put you to sleep and one which just about put you to sleep permanently, and most of the people in the refractory were on one of them. We'd be woken at seven and slopped out and then it was down to breakfast. There was a series of tables and benches cemented into the floor so the inmates couldn't use them as weapons, and you had the equivalent of plastic spoons to eat with; some of the men just used their hands, shovelling it in with both of them. The screws sat at one end of the room so they could watch us. You'd have three or four men on each table. The screws would supervise breakfast and once that was cleared away we sat at these tables until it was time for what they called airing court, which was our half-hour's exercise. When you went on exercise you walked in a sort of courtyard where the walls was smooth so you couldn't injure yourself by rubbing your face against them.

A lot of the men were just slumped over the table with their heads on their arms and they only moved when it was medicine time. They'd come to life and then they'd slump over again. Then there was lunch and the same thing happens until it's tea and then we went back to our cells at seven in the evening. And then it was the same the next day and the one after. If you wanted to go to the toilet you had to put your hand up and go under the supervision of the screws. If you weren't mental when you come in, there was a fair chance you soon would be.

In fairness the screws weren't bad. They never tried to provoke me. They knew there was nothing wrong with me and I behaved myself. There wasn't a minute's trouble from me. I was there for a rest from the prison screws and the prison screws was having a rest from me. So, I got some privileges. The screws would have the morning papers and they'd hand the linens out for those who wanted to read them. The trouble was if someone who was really daft got hold of it first then when it was your turn it might be in shreds already. So they was good. They'd let me have the paper first so's I could read the sports. The other good thing was they put the radio on. Now that was unheard of in prison at the time.

As for treatment I never got none but then, as I say, I wasn't ill. Some of them were getting electric shock treatment which was popular in them days. The men was in fear of the next dose. There had been talk earlier of me having it but fortunately, what with the fractured skull I'd had when I was a boy, that went away.

All in all though it was better than prison. The food wasn't bad by prison standards, not good but not that bad either. There was none of that cell work sewing mailbags we all hated so much. There couldn't be – you couldn't leave the inmates with needles. They couldn't give you bread and water, just a bit more of the liquid cosh. Visiting was better too, about every fortnight and it was at a table, not through glass. It wasn't far for Eva to come, and you could get more letters. She was terrific, she was always writing in, keeping up the pressure, making sure they remembered there was nothing wrong with me.

People today would be appalled, but that was how it was on that block fifty years ago. Jack Rosa was in there when I went in and he pulled a bit of trouble and got sent back to refractory so I had a bit of company. He was still there when I left.

Things got a lot better over the years and there was people who set up Broadmoor's League of Friends so that relatives and friends of the prisoners could get a lift to and from the station. They'd also go and see people who didn't have no visitors. It went belly up for one woman visitor, Rita Fry. She and her husband were both volunteers but what does she do? She goes and falls in love with one man and ends up under the patio. The man she fancied was Paul Beecham who'd put four bullets into his father, another nine in his mother and then shot his grandparents as well. That was back in February 1969. He kept the bodies in the bungalow and spread a load of fanny about how his father had had an operation and had died in hospital. It all come to an end when a window cleaner looked into the bungalow. He pleaded to manslaughter and got popped in Broadmoor. The doctors said he'd had a brainstorm, which sounds about right. Rita started holding hands with Paul on visits and kissing him. It wasn't surprising her marriage come to an end. They let Paul out after about ten years and he took up with Rita. Everyone liked him and it went well for years and years. Her kids liked him but she never told them what he'd done. Then she started to believe he was killing people and she went into hospital for depression. That's when she told the kids about Paul's conviction. When she come out in October 1997 he invited one of the kids, who'd grown up and left home by now, around for dinner and when they got there he'd blown himself away and there was no sign of Rita. Police dogs found her under the concrete about a month later. He'd hit her on the back of the head with a hammer. He'd been all right for eighteen years and then it all went wrong again.

I went back to see people a few times. Jack Rosa, of course, and later Ronnie Kray. That was after I'd done the twenty. I was going down with Stephen Berkoff when Charlie Richardson rang me up and said one of his old mates, an Eddie Jones who'd been an LF man years earlier, wanted to go. Could he come with us?

Anyway, things had changed a lot in visiting since I was there. No question of having to put your hand up to go to the toilet and when Eddie goes Ronnie follows him. They're gone quite a time and I get a bit worried because Ronnie could sometimes be a bit careless where he put his thin and thick so I go along too. When I come in there's Ronnie with his hand on Eddie's shoulder saying, 'Frank, I was telling him what a lovely day it was.' When we was leaving I asked Eddie was everything all right. 'No,' he says, 'When he come in, it went all down my leg.'

Eddie was on the box a few months ago in a programme which was slagging Reggie and Ronnie off. I couldn't bring myself to watch it really and I couldn't hardly recognise Eddie. He was described as a former gangster. He's put on a lot of weight.

EAST ANGLIA

It's always interesting to see who was topped or killed on your birthday. Mine was the 13 December 1922 and there was a couple hanged side by side at Lincoln Prison. There was Frank Fowler who went and killed Ivy Prentice in the White House pub in Market Deeping. She'd only been married three days and she went down to look at her wedding presents when Fowler turned up and shot her. He must have been an old boyfriend and he held a grudge. The second was another boy and girl romance which had gone wrong. George Robinson cut the throat of his girlfriend, Frances Pavey, when she broke off the engagement. He cut his own throat as well but they nursed him back to health so's they could top him.

Over the years there has been a lot of people who've been acquitted of doing someone by saying they was sleepwalking at the time. Round the world I suppose it's getting on for a hundred. It's often the case though that people say they've got away with it. It was like that in the Essex case in the 1960s when that American airforceman, Wills Boshears, wakes up on the floor and there next to him is a girl, Jean Constable, he picked up at a New Year's Eve dance. The trouble is she's dead. Not a good way to start the New Year.

Boshears' old woman was up in Scotland visiting her parents and what had happened apparently was that him and another man had gone home with the girl. They'd all had a skinful and they all fell asleep in front of the fire. The other man woke up and went home, and then a bit later Boshears wakes up and finds he's strangling the girl, and she's a goner. He then starts to cut off her hair, gets a touch of seconds and puts her body in the spare room and goes off back to sleep. He kept the body in the flat all day and then put it in a ditch a couple of days later. He burned her clothes but he kept her watch.

It wasn't what you'd call a good defence but some people have all the luck. The jury chucked it out inside two hours. There was no question of manslaughter. It was murder or nothing, and there was a joke going around that it should have been 'guilty but asleep'. It's not a defence for the likes of me though. If I tried to run it I'd be laughed out of court.

I suppose in a way it all worked out for the best. Boshears went back to America and got chucked out of the Force for something or other. It wasn't long before he was killed in a car smash.

Wartime was a good time for women getting killed. Soldiers was always on the move and you could be out of the country and maybe killed yourself, doing your duty for your country, before they ever found the girl's body. I suppose the most famous was the Wigwam case, like I've said, and there was that Canadian soldier who got topped after taking a machine gun to a woman who wouldn't go out with him. He was the longest there's ever been in the death cell. I was on punishment in Wandsworth at the time and he was opposite me.

There was a killing up near Beccles, which doesn't get too much in the way of crime usually. It was Winifred Mary Evans who was strangled in November 1944 at Ellough by Arthur Heys. She was only eighteen and worked as a wireless operator in the WRAF. It seems she'd left her barracks a bit after midnight. She'd been to a charity dance at an American base and she was already late for duty. The coppers reckoned that was when she ran into Heys. They was sure he'd been drinking and he wanted to have it off. They reckoned she fell in a ditch and whilst she was laying there Heys jumped on her back causing her liver to burst and begin to haemorrhage. Then he pulled her shirt up tearing the buttons, ripped off her slacks, got rid of the rags and had her from behind.

Her body was found the next morning by a special copper cycling along the Ellough Road. There was a girl who'd seen Heys in the area and when the coppers got to him he said he'd been to a dance in Caxton Hall, Beccles. He'd gone back to his barracks and fell asleep. There was a bit of scientific evidence that he'd washed his trousers around the crotch, and they matched some cat's hair from them with some on the body.

He tried his best. Whilst he was in the nick waiting for the Assizes he wrote an anonymous letter purporting to come from the murderer, saying Heys was innocent. In the supposed confession the man said how he had had an appointment to meet Winnie Evans shortly after midnight, that he had seen a drunken aircraftman [Heys] and that Winnie had arrived after that. The letter said the girl was 'unclean', which was the polite way of saying she was on, and the coppers reckoned only the killer could know that so, if the letter was genuine, it let Heys out.

They found out that he'd had access to paper and crayon and that he'd got someone who was being discharged to take the letter out. It wouldn't have been difficult. When I needed to get an authority out for my libel action to start against the *Empire News* that's what I did. Not that it did me any good.

As for the murder, they called up that fingerprint and handwriting expert, Fred Cherrill from Scotland Yard, to give evidence that the letter had been written by Heys, and that was just about that.

What was really interesting is he was working his way up to be a serial killer. On the file was the unsolved murder of a female in Colne, which is where he come from, before the War. Someone stabbed her in the back and it was reckoned to be down to him. He'd also been suspected of an attack on a LACW at the RAF station in Leuchars. This time he couldn't be identified and he said he'd been vomiting up booze. Heys had also been on site when another woman had been assaulted, this time it was at Thornaby.

There was a fellow put his wife under the floorboards in Newmarket and she didn't show up for ten years until a purchaser was looking the place over. In Field Terrace Road it was and the woman was Margaret Bennett. She disappeared back in the middle '80s. Her husband Frank reported her missing in January 1985. He told the coppers they'd an argument three days earlier and when he come back from work she was gone with a suitcase and a pony in cash. She'd gone missing before and it seems no one thought too much about it. Then three years later it looks like he topped himself. His body was found by the tracks at Welwyn Garden City and it seemed he must have walked in front of a train. There's a belief that people always leave suicide notes but a lot of them don't and Frank was one of them. The coroner returned an open verdict. There was all sorts of stories about how dogs wouldn't go in the house but it was another five years before the police got a tip and they dug up the patio. She wasn't there of course and the place stood empty until 1995 when this fellow buys it for thirty grand and starts to check for rising damp.

I didn't know Tony Maffia who was called The Magpie that well. I knew his mate Alfie Hinds much better. We come from the same bit of London and we did a lot of our bird together. I've written about him and his escapes a lot before. Tony did a good job getting him away from the Law Courts when Alfie had gone there for an appeal. They locked a screw up in the carsi and it was off and away.

Tony's body was found at the beginning of June 1968 in the front passenger seat of his Jaguar in the car park of the Midway Restaurant – it was midway between Southend and London. The staff noticed a smell and went to have a look. It's funny; if the car had been parked there nowadays it would have been clamped and towed away inside a couple of hours. He'd been shot behind the right ear and in the right eye, a proper professional killing you could say. There'd been a bit of a heatwave and the body was so swollen they could only recognise him from a ring he wore.

Tony had a car business, Justice Motors, as well as being one of the big receivers in England. There was nothing he wouldn't touch in the way of jewellery, antiques, a bit of porcelain, coins, currency, you name it, and there's no doubt he'd made a few enemies. He'd got a nasty tongue on him. I don't mean that unkindly but he could take the mickey out of people and they didn't like it. When the police searched his house they found it was just like a magpie's nest, full of stuff that shouldn't have been there including a bit of gold from a big robbery in Clerkenwell which had gone off the year before. He didn't get rid of stuff, he just seemed to hoard it, which is how he got his name.

Then a funny thing happens. A fellow called Stephen Jewell from Manchester walks into a nick to speak with that bent copper Kenneth Drury, who picked up an eight and got it down to a five when a load of officers from the porn squad went down. Like father, like son. Drury's old man was a copper I used to give money to when I was on the run at the beginning of the War. I've never understood quite why Jewell went in. There was plenty of other candidates and you'd think any sensible person would stay out of harm's way until at least the first heat had gone out of the fire. Maybe he wanted to get his oar in first. He said he'd been trying to sell Maffia a few forged notes and at the same time buy his place in Buckhurst Hill which he fancied. It wasn't all one way. Maffia was trying to unload a boat he'd got in a marina at Wallasey Island.

Jewell's story was that just after him and Tony left the marina after looking at the boat three men in a Zodiac stopped them and told him to go away as they wanted to talk to Tony about a deal. They was Essex heavies he said. When he come back both Tony and the Zodiac was gone and so was a pistol there's been in the Jaguar. Jewell had left his coat in the car and there was blood on it. So, what does he do? He takes the car and drives off to London and whilst he's on his way he throws the coat into a field. Then he parks the car at the Midway Restaurant.

You can see why the coppers might fancy him for it. Can you believe the killers saw the car and thought let's put Tony's body back in it? Anyway he went down on a ten to two majority. Of course, Alfie Hinds' name's been mentioned all through the trial – not too favourably either, and at the end Alfie's allowed to have a brief make a statement that it was nothing to do with him. The man he had was that Roger Frisby, who was wonderful until the drink got to him. I saw he'd died last year.

Whilst he was in the nick Jewell wrote to Tony's brother, Arthur, saying he wasn't responsible but I heard Arthur had a few friends ask about and it come back they was satisfied it was Jewell. Still when he come out there was a programme on the telly showing how it was a miscarriage of justice. He's dead now as well.

I never really knew what it was about. Maybe Tony legged him over and Jewell got upset and shot him. There was a lot of cash and coins on Tony when the body was found so it wasn't robbery. If it was a contract, well it wasn't the best done that I've heard of. The story which floated around most was that Tony had worked a little trick over Jewell with some forged notes and when he fell for it, Tony kept on baiting him till the man lost his temper. Like I've said Tony did have a spiteful tongue.

*   *   *

There was some funny hangings at Norwich Prison over the years. Well before my time, of course, but it was still part of legend when they hanged a man called Robert Goodale for doing his wife in. Back in 1885 it was, but the way people talked you'd think it happened yesterday. They'd just changed over to Marwood's method of breaking the neck in a hanging instead of strangling the man to death. It was all done on a table of weights. The heavier the man the longer the drop had to be. Anyway the screwsman decides he isn't going to go on the table of weights and shortens the drop. What happened was the drop pulled the man's head off. I think that people always had that sort of fear, not necessarily about being topped but having their head pulled off even though they probably wouldn't have known, nor would the family because it would be straight down to the prison graveyard and a report that everything had passed off all right.

There was another funny topping at Norwich much nearer my time. It was the case of Harold Bennett. He come from South London and there was real doubt about whether he did his wife, Mary, or if it was someone else who did for her. They made their living selling faked violins. It was just the old con game. She was the young widow forced to part with her late husband's most cherished possession. They were also at the badger game and a bit of insurance fraud thrown in. Good all-rounders they were. Somewhere down the line they fell out, and when it come to the trial there was the landlady saying she'd heard Bennett saying he wished his wife was dead and that if she wasn't careful she would be. Good stuff for a jury. She pushes off to Bexleyheath and now he's going out with a parlourmaid. He gives the maid a ring, but he doesn't seem to want to add bigamy to the other things he's been up to. Just like me. That's one of the few things I've never been done for. Then he goes and sees his wife and suggests she takes a holiday up in Yarmouth.

I've never been able to work out what they were up to but it was certainly something. Maybe they was putting the partnership back together because she's using the name of Hood. Then she tells the woman she rents a room from that she had been escorted by her dead husband's brother-in-law who was both madly in love with her and madly jealous. There's certainly some man she was seeing whilst she was up there. I think maybe they were going to work the badger game again with Bennett playing the brother-in-law.

Anyway the week after, Bennett tells the parlourmaid, Miss Meadows, that he has to go to Gravesend to see his grandfather who's ill, and off he goes to Norwich. Well, that's what the pros said. That night there's a courting couple on the sands at Yarmouth who sees another couple on the beach and hears the woman call, 'Mercy, mercy'. Then there's a moan but they don't do anything about it; simply get up and walk away. Later that evening, a man gets a room in the Crown and Anchor hotel, saying he had missed the last tram to Gorleston. The pros says that's Bennett.

They find his wife's body the next day. She'd been sexually assaulted and strangled with a mohair bootlace tied around her throat, but she wasn't identified for some six weeks when she got traced through a laundry mark on her clothing. Bennett was nicked and, when his room was searched, the police found a long old-fashioned gold chain together with men and women's wigs and a false moustache. There was also a bit of evidence that he had given a number of his wife's possessions to Miss Meadows. Just like Crippen gave away his wife's stuff to Ethel Le Neve.

Because local feeling was so strong against him the case came down to the Old Bailey. The evidence wasn't strong against Bennett. No one could agree whether the chain was the one she'd been wearing and Marshall Hall, who was defending Bennett, called an alibi. The real problem was that Bennett wouldn't give evidence himself. Some people say that you shouldn't give evidence unless you have to, and I don't think I've ever been acquitted after giving evidence. If I have it's only the once. But people I've been in the nick with have told me you really had to do it in a murder case when there was topping around. Anyway, he should have done, because the jury was out about 35 minutes.

They sent him back to Norwich Prison to be topped on 21 March 1901. They used to run up a black flag to announce the death in them days and as it was being raised the flagstaff snapped. People said it was a sign of Bennett's innocence.

Executions was regarded as one of the few entertainments the working classes could have. People took time off from work and women put on their best dresses to go and watch. After they stopped public executions people still crowded outside the prison gates waiting for the notices to be put up. Men would be called in off the street to be witnesses to the topping – a bit like how they used to put a coroner's jury together – and they'd get five bob for watching. It seems that people who worked in the neighbourhood would hang around the prison and hope to get picked so they could pick up the extra dosh.

The funny thing was that a few years after the Bennett case a girl, Dora Gray, was found strangled with a bootlace on the beach at Yarmouth in July 1912. Dora told a girlfriend she'd met what was called a gentleman friend in them days, and she was going to see him again. Her body was found just near where Mrs Bennett's was and the bootlace had been taken from her boot. The story went around of course that Bennett was innocent but I don't suppose too many cared. Her killer was never found and it got put down as a copycat but whoever it was it can't have been Bennett.

Of course overall, being a screwsman didn't bring out the best in people. Some of them couldn't take it after a time. One of them was Jimmy Ellis who went and topped himself. He'd tried to do it before in the days when attempted suicide was a crime. He was up in front of the bench and they just told him not to do it again. Many a person had been sent down for a few months for trying. He'd also appeared in a play when he was Marwood, the man who actually topped Charlie Peace. The climax was right at the end when he hangs Peace on stage. People loved it but there was an outcry and it got took off after a few days. I was about ten when Ellis started chasing his wife round the kitchen one day, threatening to kill her, before he did himself finally.

Talking of hanging people on the stage, I remember seeing Tod Slaughter at the Canterbury. It was amazing what value you got for your money then. Two films and a stage show often enough. He was always the villain in those Victorian melodramas. He'd be the Squire who got the local unmarried mother turned out of the tied cottage when he was the baby's father all along. Wonderful he was. People loved him. Great big man who was just as big a ham. Like Donald Wolfitt but he never got a knighthood. He was hanged on stage night after night. One night, in Derby I think it was, he's hanged same as usual and just goes back to his lodgings and dies. What a wonderful way to go. You can still see him in those old black-and-white films on the telly in the middle of the night.

I could see what a ham he was because St Patrick's, where I went to school, was more or less across the street from the Old Vic. When we was old enough groups of ten or twenty would be taken to see the matinées. Even if I never really understood what the plays was all about they got to you. I don't know that I saw anyone famous but I must have done because Gielgud and Olivier and the others were at the theatre then and whoever they were they was different from Tod.

Talking of hangmen, there was that Syd Dernley. He should have got the sack. He was an assistant when he goes to hang a man, Norman Goldthorpe, at Norwich for killing a brass; 1950 it was. He'd got a book with him and he starts reading that poem *The Farting Contest* whilst him and the hangman, Harry Kirk, are in the room over the condemned cell. They'd had a few drinks and soon they and the screw they're with are laughing so loud that the people in the condemned cell have to knock on the ceiling to get them to shut up. What made it worse was the next morning the poor sod gave Dernley the Woodbines he hadn't managed to smoke before they come for him.

Of course the biggest case come out of East Anglia in recent years is that Tony Martin who shot the burglar and got lifed off for it. People had been turning his place over regular and one night when some blokes come round he opens fire. A lot of people thought he'd get a not guilty. I think if he'd gone straight to the coppers and said, 'Look, this is what's happened', he'd probably have been all right but when it come to it he didn't. Then it come down to manslaughter in the Court of Appeal but he still got a five.

Mind you, there's always been a bit of vigilantism about. Take that case up in Darlington back at the end of the 1970s. A man screws a neighbour's house and they nail his hand to a railway carriage. Just like that film *Boxcar Bertha*. The nailer got three years and his stepbrother who'd given him a bit of help gets a three. It was a bit like pot calling kettle black. Both the geezers had a bit of form for screwing.

PORTLAND BORSTAL

I don't think I'd like to live in a village called Borstal but that's where it got it's name from – a bit like Dum Dum in India where they made the bullets. Borstal's in Kent, on the Medway near Rochester. They'd been talking about having an institution for young offenders for years before the first one opened. Around 1908 it was.

The early ones had a matron, a figurehead really but something to show how caring they was. If you was sick you reported to her, and if you had trouble at home she was meant to be an ear to wig. They looked good when the Commissioners come to do an inspection. They was wheeled out then but otherwise they was kept very much in the background. I've heard people say they was called Maggies but I never called them that. In fact, I was in punishment so much I don't think I ever spoke to one. They wasn't allowed near the punishment wings when I was in. They was mostly what you would call comfortable-looking women, female screws coming to the end of their service, that sort of person. The idea was that none of the boys – and remember they could be up to 26 by the time they left Borstal – would fancy them. One or two had a go at them and they was phased out. Nowadays, it's the other way around and you get some of the women who work in prison fancying the men all the time. They take up with them after their sentences but it doesn't work out all that often. There wasn't anything like that in my day.

The Borstal idea was to make it a bit like a public school and promote teamwork and self-sufficiency. The blocks were to be called houses and there was to be inter-house rivalry with football matches and things so you could feel proud. The staff wore civilian clothes and the inmates was called 'lads', but that soon became trainees. We all wore shorts. In Billy Hill's book there's a picture of him and some others in their kit. I was looking through a book on prisons the other day and there was a photo of a gymnastic display, everyone balanced properly like a display team at that Service of Remembrance. People said it just made young criminals fitter.

They might have a point. The grandson of one of my friends got a report from the probation office saying how well he'd done in the karate class. His brief said he couldn't use it. The magistrate would have had a fit. I've never gone for probation reports myself. I don't mean they don't mean well, but when you have someone who's bashed old ladies and threatened them with knives after getting in their houses pretending to be from the gas and it says, 'Henry has begun to show a real insight into his offences and I feel he will benefit from probation', that sort of baloney, it only annoys the beak. Does more harm than good.

The staff at Borstals in the early days was really being trained as well, before they moved on to proper prisons. Of course, not everyone thought Borstals was a good idea. There was plenty who still fancied the short sharp shock. There was good results at first but as the years went by that fell off. People realised that just like prison or probation, Borstal would do the trick for some people and not others. By the time I was there they wasn't doing as well as they had at the start when there was much fewer people in the country. Judges who sent people there were putting married men with families along with seventeen-year-olds in them. You heard it a lot. The judge would say 'I'm going to give you a chance.' You thought that here was a spot of probation until he added, 'You'll go to Borstal for three years. Take him down.' Eventually it was Maggie Thatcher had the courage to do what should have been done years earlier and that was to shut them down. It's amazing, it's over twenty years since they were closed.

One of the things we did at Borstal was breaking those stones. It was one of the useless tasks they set prisoners in them days. It was a sort of carry on from the treadwheel, which was before me I'm glad to say but the old men who was in the nick with me and had been on it said you could break a man. You had to do just under 8,700 feet a day. Like climbing up the Post Office tower a few times. If you didn't do your distance there was either a whipping or a cut back on your rations. Men use to cry when they was put on it.

One of the other useless things they did was to have you move stones. Not just pebbles but like the boulders they use in the Strongman competition on the telly. They'd keep prisoners at it all day. Moving a series of stones to one end of the yard and then back again, all day and all week and all year long. In fact once the stones come in useful because in the First World War a whole lot of prisoners was sent from Parkhurst up to Peterhead to build foundations for aircraft hangers. The idea was that they threw boulders into the sea to make a sort of platform. One of them was that fellow Charles Smith who shot Eddie Guerin, the man who escaped from Devil's Island, back in 1906. He was still inside and he'd only wounded him. When the men got there they found that there wasn't no tea served like at Parkhurst and they had a protest saying they wouldn't work without it. That did them a lot of good. Two months' remission lost all round and nine months for the Irish fellow who led them.

The treadmill and stones didn't stop crime, any more than Borstal did. The thing is that if you're a proper criminal you don't think you're going to get caught, and if you are you're not going to get a guilty, and if you do you're not going into the nick. That's the only way you look at it. And better than half the time you're going to be right. If you're going to do a job which will pull in twice what you'll earn in a year doing nine to five in an office, for one night's work and a bit of planning, you can see how people might fancy it.

When I went to Borstal the system was you were sent to Feltham for assessment to see whether you should go to an open one, but I tried to escape. I was never a great escaper. The time a few of us had a go at Feltham we never even made the wall so it doesn't count really in my mind but it meant I was sent to Rochester. That was where the other two escapes was from. At least we stayed out overnight then, not that it did us any good long term. They was within a month of each other. The first was on 8 October 1941. I sawed through the bars in one of the recreation rooms. You was mostly in there unsupervised to play cards or chess, things like that. If you were good the screws would put the radio on sometimes during evening association. There was a big window and one of the other fellows in with us had a job in a workshop. He took a hacksaw and smuggled it back in. It wasn't that difficult – no metal detectors then; the screws would give a man a pat down and if he was trusted they wouldn't even bother half the time. It wasn't properly planned. Eva never knew anything about it to try and get a car down but there was a chance you could make it in the blackout. A fellow named Cutler come with me. I can't think of his first name after all these years but he was a smashing fellow. I met him again in Wandsworth in 1948 but I never saw him after that.

We never got far that time and it was down the block for me. That's when I got out the second time. A good bit of the Borstal had been taken over by the Navy then and part of it was fenced off. When you was doing the pounding two screws would sit and watch. The Borstal had a back gate with big double doors, but not a second set like you get in most prisons. At quiet times it would be open for parties who'd been out bringing in vegetables and six of us just steamed at the screws and made a run for it. Three was nicked straight away but three of us got away. We were chased, of course, but we stayed out all night. Charlie Jennings was one with us. A big fellow he was, and then there was Tony Byrnes. I think he come from Lancashire. We was all in shorts and they looked pretty silly but because I was small and young looking I could pass a bit more easy. We screwed a small shop for some food but the coppers got us the next day on the banks of the Medway. Like I say it's easy enough to get out. It's staying out that's the trouble. It was down the block again and that's when I half drowned Holy Joe, the screw who was looking at me when I was having my bath. I wasn't having that. I tried to drown him but a couple of the other prisoners yelled for help and they pulled me off. So it was down to Portland. I went in a car with a special escort all the way across from Kent; 1942 it would be.

To get to Portland Borstal you had to go to Dorchester and then down to Chiswell Beach on a long road with waste land on either side. You'd come to Portland which was at the end of a peninsula and then it was uphill to the prison. In my day it was one of the four closed Borstals – Rochester, Sherwood and Feltham were the others. Before the War you were sent to Wormwood Scrubs for assessment but they shut it down at the beginning and MI5 used it. They still pretended it was open by having Black Marias going in and out but the prisoners had been transferred. It may have fooled the Germans but it didn't fool the likes of us.

I went back to Portland the other day to see my grandson, who was doing half a stretch for driving disqualified. He's the third of my five grandsons to have been away. Keeping the family flag flying. This time we took a taxi from the station. The building's just as forbidding. The prison visiting room's smarter but apart from that it's not much different from when I was there. The sea air doesn't half get into the fabric. That was when it all come back to me.

I remember when I was in there I was in E Wing, which was the punishment block, most of the time. All the wings had names after British admirals, Drake, Rodney and Benbow and so on to make us proud, but the block didn't have no name. If it did I suppose it should have been Claggart because it was really rough. He was the villain in that book, *Billy Budd*, I read. I've said before that was the one good thing about prison. The books I got to read, they was mainly classics. Nothing like *No Orchids for Miss Blandish*.

A lot of kids tried to escape but there wasn't really anywhere to go. The beach was mined and there was both Army and Navy in the area. Where was you going to go? I don't remember anyone even having a visit let alone escaping successfully. Of course, it wasn't long before I was in the punishment: chinned a screw same as usual.

In punishment we did stone pounding, out in the open and too bad if it was raining. The screws sat under a canopy and watched us. Two-and-a-half hours in the morning and another three in the afternoon. When you finished the screws would give you a little shovel and they'd watch while you put all the stuff you'd pounded into a sieve and shook it into a box. If you hadn't filled it up, then you was reckoned to be slacking and you did a bit more time on punishment to teach you.

In the punishment block there was a name scratched in the wall, John Lee. Babbacombe Lee he was called and I suppose he was one of the most famous people ever was in Portland. Everyone learned and remembered his name because he was the man who they couldn't hang.

He was meant to have killed the old woman who he worked for back in the 1880s. Even though he was only nineteen he was an ex-con then and she employed him as a footman. There was a bull about the way he did his work and she docked his wages down to ten pence a week. The pros said he did her with an axe and then cut her throat right through to her back. After that he set fire to the house. It was all circumstantial evidence and, in them days, Lee wasn't allowed to give evidence to tell his side of the story. That didn't come in for another ten years or more.

The thing was they couldn't hang him. He must have been the only person who stood on the trapdoor three times and it wouldn't open. In Exeter Gaol it was. Berry, the hangman who later got religion, was the one who mucked it up. They take Lee out of the cell and put the hood over his head, pull the lever and nothing happens. They take him off, stand him on one side and have a practice. It works perfectly. Put him back on and nothing happens. They take him off again and the door works. Then its back on and it still won't open. The reports all say how calm he was. Not so the prison chaplain. He can't take any more and walks off. They took Lee back to his cell and a reprieve come through in a matter of hours. He served 22 years and then when he was let out he went off to America. He married and died there in 1933. After he come out he wrote a book, *The Man They Could Not Hang*. He'd got a bit religious and well he might. He said things like it was the Lord whose hand stopped him being topped. He kept on saying he was innocent, and I suppose he might have been.

There was many stories about what had happened including one that there was a convict underneath who shoved a wedge in every time Lee stood on the trapdoor. Berry thought that the iron catches of the trap doors weren't heavy enough and they bent with Lee's weight. Most likely the doors had become warped. Apparently there'd been a lot of rain over the weekend before he was to be hanged on the Monday.

There was another got religion in the punishment block at Portland. A fellow called Fred Lemon so the story goes. One day he sees Jesus. I suppose it's as good a place to see Him as any but there's not many who do. Anyway Fred gives up crime and becomes a vicar. He wrote a book as well. It didn't go down too well. The phrase 'a right lemon' is meant to refer to him but I don't know if it's true.

As for me, one day I just put down the pounder and said, 'Bollocks to this' and chinned a screw. Even though I was officially too young the Home Secretary, Herbert Morrison, had me sent to Wandsworth and then on to Chelmsford, which is where I first met Billy Hill.

It was whilst I was at Wandsworth that I was taken in front of the medical board and that's where I made a mistake. They asked me if I was fit and instead of saying I'd had a fractured skull and suffered from memory loss, I said 'Of course I am.' I was really a bit angry because they could see I was keeping myself fit. I got a Grade 1 instead of Grade 4 which I was entitled to. It was true I'd had a fractured skull. I'd been knocked down outside on our street when I was about six, running into the road to blag cigarette cards off of the lorry drivers. I was in hospital weeks.

So more or less the minute I come out I'm meant to be in the Army. I wasn't having that.

WEST

What happened to us all after Parkhurst? Well, we was dispersed all over the country and I never saw some of the fellows again. That same afternoon I was taken off the island and transferred to Wakefield into the hospital there. Billy Blythe, no relation to the good man who was with me over Spot, was eventually released and took up with my niece, Shirley, but he turned out to be a wrong 'un. Martin Frape did a couple of years in Leicester. I heard of him a bit back when I was doing a signing. He was out and about. Had been for years. Andy Anderson mixed with the Scots mob in King's Cross for a time but I haven't heard of him in years. You've got to remember that what with the couple I got for receiving, I did over twenty after that before I finally come out. You lose touch.

One of us who had it hard was Timmy Noonan. He went to Liverpool and he was put straight into solitary. He'd been in solitary since well before the trial even. In fact one of the reasons for the protest on the island was the treatment that Timmy and others had had in the punishment cells. There'd been a round robin signed by 120 prisoners complaining about what was happening to him.

As I say he'd been in Broadmoor with me but there wasn't much talk of sending him back, even though he did a dirty protest and found a moth in his cell to talk to. By January 1973 he'd been in solitary for 1,041 consecutive days, which people said was a record. I thought I'd had the record myself but I'm happy Timmy should have it. The authorities said that when he come back into the prison proper he got into fights with the other cons, but if he did it was with the screws. And can you blame him? Three and a bit years banged up on your own 23 hours a day. He'd made himself some playing cards out of lavatory paper but they'd taken those away from him as well. They could keep you on Rule 43, which meant you could be kept out of prison proper for 28 days at a time, and then the magistrates had to reconsider things. That meant they'd considered it forty times and still wasn't prepared to allow him up.

That MP Ernle Money, who was meant to defend in the riot trial before the election came and ruined it, took up his case but it didn't do no good. By then there was a special wing at Parkhurst for cons who was violent. The idea was to give them a bit of controlled association but they never took Timmy there. Whilst he was in Liverpool in 1971 he had a heart attack and he was only 35. He lived in fear he'd have another and no one would notice. Of course, poor Timmy did have another attack and this time it was fatal.

It's funny how some words last in slang and others come and go. People make it up, particularly rhyming slang, as they go along. Very often it's done on people who are famous at the time. Some of it lasts, and we still say Oscar for cash, but who remembers that Oscar Ashe was the star of *Chu Chin Chow*? Nowadays people is saying Britneys for beers but I don't suppose that'll be around in a hundred years. Some of it's quite clever. Bill Wyman for hymen, but I don't suppose that'll last any longer than they do. But take Sweet Fanny Adams. How many people know where that comes from although it's been around for getting on for 150 years and it's still as popular as it ever was?

She was a little girl who was done by a solicitor's clerk, Baker, down near Alton sometime around 1860. It was about the time that tinned beef was introduced in the Navy and there was a joke that what they was getting was Sweet Fanny Adams, and it went on from there.

You hear all about it when our sort of people kill others so it's quite good when a copper goes and does it. I was thinking about it the other day after that copper who went and killed his whole family and then topped himself. Absolutely wicked it was. There was all that rubbish about his suffering from depression but I reckon that's a load of fanny. You go and top yourself, not everyone else, kids and all.

Still, I suppose it wasn't as bad as that copper down in Worcester a few years after I was born. November 1925 it was. Herbert Burrows was his name. He'd been a probationary copper and he wanted some dough to go on leave, so what does he do?

He stays drinking after hours in The Garibaldi, the pub opposite where he's got his lodgings, and then goes and shoots his friend Ernie Light, who was the landlord, in the back. Then, when the man's missus goes to find out what's happened he does her too. He's ransacking the house and the baby starts crying so he kills him as well, strikes him over the head and fractures his skull. He lets the six-year-old daughter alone but then, when he's got about seventy quid, he tries to set fire to the place. Throws paper all around the cellar and sets light to it. Then he goes back across the road to his digs and goes to sleep. Next morning he's back on the beat as though nothing's happened. It was only when he dropped into the nick for his breakfast and starts opening his gob that people get suspicious. He makes a fanny of a statement saying how he's brought disgrace on the force and apologises to them.

After that he pleads not guilty, saying he's got the pox and that was what made him do it. He doesn't seem to have cared much whilst he was waiting to be topped either, sang to himself and played cards until his day come on 17 February. They didn't hang about then so to speak. Good riddance.

Funny how sometimes things runs in families. Ignatius Lincoln was the son of Trebitsch Lincoln, who'd been an MP and was a spy. The boy, whose mother was German, enlists in the British Army and then with one of his mates decides to do a drum in Shepton Mallet on Christmas Eve 1925. Him and the other fellow, Ian Stewart, can't find any money in the house, so instead of hopping it they start drinking the man's booze and piling it up by the front door. Of course what happens but the man comes in and tells them the game's up. Lincoln just shoots him stone dead. Fifteen minutes was all it took to find him guilty, and about a third of that to top him.

I know my niece Shirley got found with a head in her fridge, a bit like John the Baptist, but she'd been forced to keep it there. Anyway it wasn't on the shelf more than a few hours, but I don't understand how people can have bodies on the premises for years. Not that I'd be afraid of having one there but surely it's got to be the first place for the coppers to look if the person's a relative. Yet people do it time and again. And sometimes if they've got enough front they can get away with it. In the past if they did it long enough there was no evidence how the relative had died and they ended up getting convicted only of things like drawing their social security for ten years. Look at Christie, the Notting Hill murderer. He had half the brasses in the neighbourhood walled up in his kitchen. When the next tenant took over and started re-papering he near enough died of fright.

Then take that family down in Weston-super-Mare, that small town in Somerset. They lived on The Boulevard and Joy Mayes was a mother who did everything she could for her boys. One of them went to university and the other to a good school. She took a job waitressing to put the money together. Then one of them, Roderick, gets himself hooked on LSD and she thinks he's in for a long drawn-out death, so she tops him in his sleep. She puts a handful of sleeping pills in a mug of cocoa as he lay in bed and when he's become unconscious she fractures his skull with an iron bootscraper and cuts his throat. The other boy, Sean, is with a rock band off touring abroad when she done it. April 1972 it was.

Understandably when he comes home, the boy says he wants his brother to have a decent burial and so him and his grandfather, who's been a Commander in the Navy, helps take the body which she's hidden under the bed, wraps it in a candlewick bedspread and plastic sheeting and they dig a shallow grave in the back garden. Friends were told that Roderick had gone to live with hippies. No one took that much notice.

The old boy dies a few years later and then Mrs Mayes pops off in 1992. That leaves Sean and by 1995 he's got HIV and he's on his way out too. It's then he tells the coppers what's happened to Roderick and there he is in the garden. This time, because of the plastic sheet they wrapped him in, the body was well preserved and they could prove who it was from the teeth. No charges were brought against Sean. Quite rightly, no one thought it was in the public interest to prosecute him.

The Commander had left a diary with entries which looked like he was referring to the killing. That got read at the inquest. Within a couple of days of Rod being topped he'd written 'Terrific operation'. They thought that meant the burial. He doesn't seem to have minded too much about the loss of his grandson. He'd also gone and written, 'Such a relief with R and friends not popping in and out.' So I suppose when it come to it things was a bit quieter and everyone was reasonably happy. Though if I'd been Sean I'd have been a bit worried when me mum asked if I wanted a drink before bedtime.

You could get away without being topped if you did yourself badly enough. That was why they made you keep your hands above the bed clothes at night when you was in the condemned cell. Stop you spoiling their fun by doing yourself first. In the last 24 hours they increased the number of warders in your cell. Still some people managed it. There was a fellow Ernest Wood, up in Durham nick, cut his throat very badly. It wasn't that he was going to die from it but the thought was that the rope would pull his head off and it would make so much mess that he got a reprieve.

A long time ago that was, but then there was the fellow William Gray, who made a good end to the year by shooting his wife Una on New Year's Eve 1948. He's quarrelled with her and she's round at her mother's in Andover. He'd had it in mind for a bit because he'd talked to a friend who'd told him not to do it, but he'd gone ahead and put a down payment on a gun, gone and paid the balance and bought some cartridges.

He went round to his mother-in-law's and as Una leaves the house with three friends and mum he comes up, calls out, 'Is that you, Una?' and then 'Stand clear' to the others and blasts away. I suppose he's in a third category of my murderers. The ones who plan, the ones who do it on the spur of the moment, and then those who try and top themselves straight away. You can never tell with those who fail if they was just making it look good, giving themselves some sort of an excuse – in which case they go straight back into the planners' category, or when it comes to doing themselves in they think life's going to get better and they bottle out. Whichever it was Gray's found later that day laying on a bank beside the road. He had blown part of his face away with the gun. He put his hands up to it at Winchester Assizes but now his jaw was so brittle the noose would have been likely to break it and so slip over his head when they tried to top him. So his sentence was commuted to one of life imprisonment.

That wasn't the only time when a fellow had been saved from the gallows because he couldn't be hanged properly. Back before the long drop one fellow who was done for killing a gamekeeper had a bent neck, and so to strangle him, which is what happened in those days, would have caused him too much suffering. He got reprieved, which was just as well because whilst he was in the nick another bloke came along and admitted he'd done it.

Another deserter from down West in the First World War was Percy Toplis and he went on to do a string of blaggings. He'd started off life with a conviction for fraud at the age of seventeen and then he did a couple of years for attempted rape. There were stories that he had been in the RAMC but he'd deserted during the Somme campaign. He was found in a little village outside Le Touquet, Rang des Fliers, and was arrested, but when him and another was taken to a guard camp, they dug out in the sand and got away. The other fellow was nicked but Toplis made it to Paris and there he hung out until he was able to get back to England.

I don't know if that's true but certainly it was after the War when he was at his peak. He was a master fraudsman. He'd got an Oxford accent by now and he could persuade people he was a half colonel. He'd even got the nerve to dress a couple of subbies down for not saluting him properly when one of them had been an officer in Toplis's regiment.

He worked the West Country mostly and that's where he shot a taxi driver near Andover in April 1920. He'd already thrown another cabbie onto the pavement in Bristol. He made his way to Wales and then came up to London. By this time there's a full hue and cry and in the six weeks he was out there was more people reporting they've seen him than saw Lord Lucan. There was 1,097 different sightings and he was meant to have gone to the Derby as well. He even went back to the camp he'd deserted from.

He tried to get back to Paris and he was a bit unlucky. He'd been staying at the Union Jack Club in the Waterloo Road near where we lived and no one had sussed him then. But when he was waiting for the boat train at Victoria station he sees some coppers. He thinks they're after him but in fact they was there for another reason; instead of holding his bottle he panics and goes off to Skegness and works his way up to Scotland, where the coppers find him in Upper Banffshire. He holes up in a gamekeeper's hut and when the man and a copper come to see why there's a fire burning he shoots the pair of them.

Then a couple of days later he's on his way back down south when near Penrith he runs into a copper who recognises him and sends for help. There's a gun battle in which he's shot. Best thing for him really.

It's amazing how often it happens. You see coppers and think the worst and they probably haven't even heard about you. It was the same with that brilliant housebreaker right at the beginning of the last century. A foreigner he was. He's done countless big houses in London, got the nerve of the devil, and he's sitting on the promenade in Ramsgate when a copper sits down next to him. He thinks it's all on top and instead of just saying 'Good Morning' or something and walking off, he starts to run. The copper follows him and the man turns and shoots. He misses and then turns the gun on himself. He was a better burglar than he was with a gun because he didn't top himself, he just took his own eye out. It didn't stop him getting a fifteen at the Assizes. Later he got out of Portland, I think it was, and for a few days he's on the run before the gentry turns out on their horses and they get a pack of hounds and run him down.

There was another soldier who swung for a killing in 1952. He'd been a bit lucky he hadn't swung before. John James Alcott his name was. He hadn't learned from a previous time when he was done for the murder of a caretaker in Germany in 1949 when he'd been in the Grenadier Guards. The conviction was quashed, because no one it seems had told his mother he was on trial. This time there's no mistake. He killed a railway booking clerk, Geoffrey Dean, who was known as Dixie of course. It was at a station called Ash Vale near Aldershot where the barracks are. He was topped on 2 January 1953 so I don't suppose he had that good a Christmas. Still, there can't be that many people in this country who've offed two people by the time they was 22.

You wouldn't think Bournemouth was the place for crime, but you'd be wrong. The Twins had interests down there, sort of supervised by Bill Ackerman on their behalf. There were stalls at markets which had a bit of protection and a couple of clubs here and there. You've got to remember, where there's people making money on the side there's always someone stronger or who's got a bit more clout who's going to take a nip out of them. Bill came a tumble once or twice in the '70s. There was one case when he was asking for bail and the copper told the court that Bill was the No. 1 Criminal in Bournemouth, which must have caused a bit of a laugh to those who didn't know better. Bill tried to turn the Twins over once. I don't rightly know what it was about but I do know they didn't half have the facts of life explained to him.

Bournemouth was a useful town. There was a good bit of protection going on and there was a lot of jewellers to blag. The trouble was if a job went bad in the town you had to have a stow, someone who had a place where you could bake-up for three or four days until someone sent a motor to collect you. Bournemouth wasn't the only place like that. If you were doing a small town, say Scarborough or Blackpool even, then it was essential.

I wasn't the only person who walked out of barracks during the War but some people who did caused a lot more damage than me. There was that fellow Leslie Goodall down in Bournemouth, who ended in Broadmoor in my time. He didn't want to be a soldier anymore than I did and he wasn't any smarter with the fitness board than me. He went and told them that he was a Communist, and when that didn't work he said he was a conscientious objector. All that did was get him a sentence for refusing to be medically examined and the moment he was released they had him in again. He got sent to the Royal Fusiliers and he didn't last long there. He got away as far as Scotland where he was picked up, and he got another spell inside before they took him down to Bournemouth where the regiment was. It's funny, no one ever thought he was completely bats because the next thing he does is go absent again. I suppose they thought he was just trying to work his ticket. He lasted two days on the outside this time. At least I did a bit better.

He's found in the centre of the town and handed over to the military, and he's put in barracks at Wimborne Road where he's left to scrub some floors. Only a few hours later he's off again but now he's got himself his rifle and some ammo's missing from the barrack room. He just shoots two soldiers dead. A couple of NCOs go after him, and one of them gets through the ceiling and into the room where he's hiding and persuades him to give up the gun. There's no question of anything but guilty but insane, and he had that really good brief, J. D. Casswell, for him.

Casswell was really big in his day. He defended in a lot of murder cases and didn't lose many. The pros said that Goodall just didn't like authority, but Casswell ran it that Goodall was suffering from a split personality and the jury agreed. They took less than half an hour when it come to it and off Goodall goes to Broadmoor. He's there for years and eventually they let him out on the proviso that he'll go back up to where his father was at Morpeth and become a patient at a hospital up there; 1964 that was. He did all right. Then his father died and he started causing trouble, having fights with other inmates. Goodall had a sister in Hampshire and he wanted to get back to Broadmoor so she could get to see him. He even went to see his MP about it but nothing come of it quick enough for him.

It seems that the patients at St George's hospital got a good bit of freedom. There was one nutter who thought himself the store detective at Woolworths in the town. He just walked up and down the aisles all day. He never arrested anyone and he didn't cause trouble, so they left him alone. There's shops like that. They're good that way. They let people alone if they don't do any harm. I was signing one day in London and a fellow dressed up as a Highlander kept coming in, walking round the shop, shouting at a couple of people and then leaving. He must have been in half-a-dozen times in the couple of hours I was there. Seems he thought he was security as well.

Anyway Goodall gets a knife and back at the hospital does the man who thinks he's a store detective; stabs him in the neck. When he's made sure the poor fellow's dead he goes down to the police and tells them what he's done. He pleaded guilty up at Newcastle Crown Court in 1977. They couldn't have him back at Rampton or Broadmoor at first because there wasn't any room, but I think he got moved out of the nick fairly quickly. The judge said he hoped he'd never be in a position to go and buy a knife again.

I suppose the most famous case which Casswell defended was Neville Heath, although there was a lot of others. There was the porthole murder where that man James Camb pushes the girl he's had it off with through the porthole when she dies when they're having sex. That was one of the cases where there was a question about not convicting him because they couldn't find a body. They did though. Then there was Mrs Rattenbury. I was in the nick with the man who did her husband. She got a not guilty but she went and topped herself all the same. The man got a reprieve. There was those Russians at the end of the War who killed a blackmarketeer, and there was also that girl, Elizabeth Jones, who took up with an American deserter and did a taxi-driver down Hammersmith way. I've mentioned both of those cases in *Mad Frank's London*.

Anyway Heath, after he's done a half brass in London – flogged her to death and bit her nipples off – comes down to Bournemouth to hide out. This time he's pretending to be an officer and a gentleman again. When he did Margery Gardner in South Kensington he'd been Lt Colonel Heath, but now he'd demoted himself and was Group Captain Rupert Brooke. There was a big search going on for him at the time. Anyway he stays at a hotel near the sea and that's where he meets a young girl, Doreen Marshall, in July 1946. They go out for a walk in the chines, those zig-zag paths down to the sea, and that's the last anyone sees of her alive. Something like five days later she's found with her throat cut and a whole lot of injuries in Branksome Chine. In the end he was done for the murder of Margery Gardner rather than her.

There was a whole lot of talk that Doreen needn't have died. Some of the top coppers wanted a photo of Heath circulated as wanted, but because there was a question of an ID it was decided not to do it. If they had he might have been nicked before he got the young girl.

One fellow from down there was in the condemned cell a bit longer than his marriage lasted. That was Reginald Woolmington. He was another who was defended by Casswell. Poor devil, he was a 21-year-old farm labourer. His wife Violet, well she was only seventeen and she was well in the club when they got married in August 1934. The kid was born a month after the marriage. It wasn't like it is today when it's a sort of competition for young girls to have a kid as soon as they can and get a council flat of their own. This pair lived for the first few weeks with his parents in Milborne Port where, of course, everyone knew just what everyone else was up to.

Then they moved into a farm cottage at a rent of three shillings a week. A week later their son was born and from then on it was the usual story. The cottage was tiny; the baby cried; Reginald was out working long hours; he was only earning 33 shillings and they didn't have enough money. Thank God, I've never been in that position. When I was out I was always able to earn good money, even if we never had a bath of our own.

Violet had worked with her mother making up gloves at piece rate for local manufacturers and so mum come round bringing work for her to do. He started to think she was trying to get Violet to go back home and of course that's what she did. They hadn't been married three months when he comes home and there's a note saying Violet had asked her mother to have her back and she was going into service. If that had been all, I suppose he might have worn it, but it was a bit worse than that.

A fortnight later he meets her brother who tells him there's a new Mr Woolmington on the horizon. The next day he get a double-barrelled shotgun from his governor, saws the barrels and cycles over to his mother-in-law's. He pleads with Violet to come back and when she blanks him off he shoots her. Of course even the local coppers could work out who to look for and there's a note in his pocket, 'Goodbye all. It is agonies to carry on any longer. I have kept hoping she would return. This is the only way out . . . Have no more cartridges, only two, one for her and one for me.' Of course, he didn't use the one for himself. He's also written a note for his employer, 'I shall not be coming to work today. I have shot my wife.'

When it come to it I don't know if he was lucky. The first jury at Taunton couldn't agree and the second was told it was for him to show he hadn't acted maliciously. That's where the pros come unstuck. It got all the way to the House of Lords with him in the death cell and they say the judge was wrong. He shouldn't have had to prove anything. First rule of British law and all that; it's up to the pros. Out he went. Not even a manslaughter over him. But he'd been 81 days in the condemned cell.

The further west you get the less real crime there is. For a start it's a long way and there's always the trouble of getting out. There's not much in the way of motorways in Cornwall and there's always the danger of a road block. Even so there's been one or two good little cases – more domestic than professional really. One was that boy Miles Giffard in 1952. His father was a solicitor and the Under Sheriff of Cornwall, and when it came to it he had a bishop come and plead for him so he'd got good connections. He'd been to Rugby. He topped his parents because they didn't approve of his playing around in London. By the time he was in his mid-twenties he was a remittance man. Those were the days when things like all-night jazz parties were happening at places like Cy Laurie's club in Windmill Street and people was fearful what their kids might be doing. I remember reading in the linens about a girl who was suing the man she claimed was the father of the baby, and when she was asked where she'd fallen pregnant, she said in a box at the Chelsea Arts Ball at the Albert Hall.

Giffard come down to his parents' place on a cliff top at Porthpean near St Austell, and there was a big row. He was in love with a girl in London but his parents wanted him to come back to Cornwall and make something of himself. So he did them, just battered them to death with an iron pipe and then tipped them in the ocean. His mother was still alive when he did it. Then he took his father's car and drove to London to see his girlfriend in Tite Street and popped his mother's jewels. He took his girl to see that Charlie Chaplin film *Limelight*, and as they come out of the cinema there was the coppers waiting.

His brief, who was John Maude, ran a defence that he'd been unstable since he was a kid and that a cruel nurse had locked him in the cupboard, but that was never going to work, even though a doctor had said he was bats at about the time he was fourteen. He got topped in the November. He might have thought that a bit of class prejudice would work in his favour like it had for Ronald True all those years earlier but it didn't.

THE MOOR

It was interesting reading at the beginning of the year the coating Dartmoor got over conditions there in a report. Screws calling the cons 'vermin', wire cages for exercise, things like that. It's funny because it isn't the end of the prison road where all the villains are sent as it was in my day. It's been down graded to something like a C class prison since I've been there. Even so, whatever it's like it can't be as bad as it was when I was there. I know every old con is going to say things like 'You youngsters haven't half got it cushy', but it was really tough back in the 1950s and worse before that as well. There were people who inspected prisoners but they didn't get notice taken of them.

If you was in the punishment wing, which I was mostly, you were meant to get an hour's exercise every day but it could be cut to half an hour for what they called special circumstances. And that could mean anything – staff shortages, sickness, you were the type of prisoner who'd cause difficulties, anything they could drum up. You were never told what it was. When it come to it you got about twenty minutes.

When you did get your exercise it was in a small cage about ten foot by ten foot. You couldn't see who was in the next one to you. You'd be let out of your cell and the first would be taken to his little pen before the next was let out and so on. One side was open so a screw could walk up and down and see you weren't doing anything wrong.

You had ranks in those days. When you'd done four years you got a blue circle sewed to the sleeve of your coat and that meant you went in D wing on the Moor. This was what they called special stage and there was two landings. There was about twenty or more prisoners at any one time. Now you could have a radio, but of course you had to have it sent in. I was lucky, I'd got family and people like Billy who was looking after me, but of the twenty or so men I shouldn't think ten had family. Remember, they'd already done four years and by now they'd be half forgotten. They'd have had a Dear John letter that their wife's going to have a baby by some geezer, if they had a wife that is. And those whose wives were still faithful, well the girls probably didn't have the money to spare anyway. You got released straight out of Dartmoor in those days. Just before their release one or two lucky guys got sent to Wakefield where there was a sort of camp but the only open prison was Leyhill and it wasn't for the likes of me or anyone else who'd been sent to the Moor.

The trouble with prisons in the old days was that it wasn't the Governor who ran it, it was the screws. From the reports it looks as though in some nicks it's still the same.

There was always someone who could make alcohol in prison and when I was in Dartmoor, Wino Richards was the man. He worked out on the Moor itself and he distilled the stuff when he was on a work party. Remember how lax things could be with Frank Mitchell just drifting off to the pub when he wanted to. There was also another lag whose wife wanted to get in the club, and she'd drive down in a van with a mattress in the back and he'd get in and have it away. I never knew if she fell. I reckon Wino used to make some of the drink for the screws and that's why they turned a blind eye.

I suppose the reason they let us see the film *The Blue Lamp* in the nick at Dartmoor was because it was meant to be a warning to us. Shows there is life after death for coppers. Dirk Bogarde, who's the little tearaway, goes and shoots honest old Jack Warner who's PC Dixon. Bogarde gets topped but Jack comes back for a television series. That bit was filmed just near the old theatre, the Metropolitan in the Edgware Road where Max Miller used to appear so regular. I remember in the film 'Two Ton' Tessie O'Shea was meant to be topping the bill there. Big Welsh girl she was, looked a bit like Diana Dors, played the ukelele and sang smutty songs. Well, smutty for those days you know. Some line would end with 'witch' and you know what the end of the next one would be, except she'd smile and give a clunk on the uke. Bit like a female George Formby.

Anyway, the film wasn't that much of a warning as Harold Thirkettle found out. He was stabbed to death during a showing of *The Blue Lamp* in the prison chapel at Dartmoor, the middle of June 1961. He'd got a number of convictions and was doing twelve years for the manslaughter of the woman he'd been living with. When she said she was leaving him for another man he'd attacked her with an axe. A black guy, Matthew Nwachukwa, was charged with his manslaughter. There must have been more knives in the audience than on the screen that night. Nwachukwa was reckoned to be a grass and someone had stabbed him during the film already. He got the knife out of his back and went and stabbed the two men nearest him. Neither had been involved in the attack. It all got chucked. Who cared what cons did to each other back then?

BIRMINGHAM AND THE MIDLANDS

The first bit of work I ever did outside London was in Birmingham. It was during the War. People all over the country was on the run, deserters, and a couple we met in London had stuck up this firm. I was on the run myself. I looked young and I was small. People wouldn't really give me a second look. The job was the usual story. The bosses would send a couple of men to the bank on a Friday morning for the wages and the workers would get their dough by four that afternoon. There was no question of cheques. Nor did they ever think it was a good idea to vary the time the men went or the route they took. Dead on nine or ten whichever it was. It was a piece of cake. As far as I can remember we took two grand, which was serious money.

How did we get there? Well, petrol wasn't that difficult to obtain. Billy Hill had the market in forged coupons and we had a hooky man who ran a garage just off the Waterloo Road. We'd give him a drink and he'd fill us up. Sometimes he'd take Billy's coupons, others he wouldn't bother. Birmingham was good because you could be back in the day. We used to take two motors. One was hooky and we'd use that for the job; we'd probably dump it and come back in the straight one. But if the job was sweet we'd bring it back and keep it for another day.

During the War I was hardly out but, when I was, I was an enthusiastic thief. I was living at home and of course my mother would be given something. By now she must have realised what I was up to but we still went on pretending. Eva was dividing her time between my mother and our Gran, and she was the one who looked after my dough for me.

One of the big rivals to Darby Sabini, who I worked for on the racecourses when I was a kid, was the Brummagem Boys who was led by Billy Kimber. What it was all about was a struggle for control of bookmaking on the racecourses. You could make real money if you had the bookmakers in your pocket. You could make them buy chalk for writing the odds on their boards, the paper with the runners and riders, you could have them employ a kid like me going round with a bucket to sponge down the chalk between races. Of course, they could have done all these things themselves, but if they didn't want cutting or rows in front of their boxes and people calling out welsher at them then they paid up and looked pleasant about it.

All through the 1920s there was trouble over who ran the racecourses. There'd been fights in London and Bath and Doncaster as well as Yarmouth and at some of the trotting tracks which were popular then. But the biggest set-back for the Birmingham boys come on Derby Day 1921 when nearly forty of them got nicked after they'd attacked the wrong people.

They'd been put up to it by that crooked financier, Horatio Bottomley, who'd got the magazine *John Bull*. He was sounding off about how it was all wrong that Italians and other foreigners should be running the courses when good Englishmen back from the War wasn't getting a look in. A meeting was arranged in a hotel off the Bull Ring and instructions were given to attack London bookmakers taking taxis back home from the races. It didn't matter if the Sabinis wasn't among them, it was going to be a lesson who could protect them. The idea was to ambush them in the Ewell Road. After the big race the Birmingham men left and blocked the road with their charabanc and attacked the first cab in sight. One of the men inside lost three fingers to a meat cleaver. The cabs were overturned and the occupants routed. Unfortunately it wasn't the Sabini bookmakers who was in the taxi; it was people from Leeds who wasn't at all pleased.

Of course, the coppers heard of it pretty quick and they seem to have thought it was a Sinn Fein riot, but when a Sergeant Dawson arrived on the spot he did for the lot of them single handed. First, he took the sparking plugs from the charabanc and then he threatened to shoot the first of the men who moved. That way he kept 28 of them under control until other coppers turned up. In all 17 out of the 28 was found guilty and there was some good bird handed out. After it was over people wrote suggesting that Dawson should get a subscription set up for him but the police didn't seem to think that he deserved anything. A vote of thanks was about all his reward. One of the blokes who went down was Edward Banks who'd been involved in the shooting of Darby Sabini at Alexandra Park the previous year, and there was talk he had been going to get some Mills bombs, so you can see it was getting to be heavy stuff.

But a bit after that there was a big alliance between the Midlands and London. It came about through 'Brummy' Sparkes, who was Maggie Hill, Billy's sister's first husband. He might have been her only husband for all I know. She was much older than Billy and so was very much older than me. That sort of cemented things because Maggie was a big shoplifter going all over the country. Maggie Hill really took over the Forty Thieves as they was known, from another Maggie who was married to Ted Hughes, the one Billy called Odd Legs in his book because he was gimpy. Maggie was only 25 when she picked up a three at the Bailey for lifting back in 1923. It was reckoned that she and her team had cleared over £100,000 in the previous twelve months. She used to go down to Brighton a lot where the coppers reckoned she had a receiver, but if she did he was never picked up. She was good with a knife as well. The previous year she'd done a girl real bad but she was never prossed. Brummy Sparkes was a big burglar in his day, good for country houses.

Lord Woolf never did me any harm. In fact he did me good. When I went down for three years over receiving coins a bit after I'd come out from the twenty, he wouldn't quash the conviction, but him and two others knocked the sentence down to two years. Good man, known to be liberal, so I did wonder what he was saying earlier this year about people who mug mobile telephones getting a minimum of four. Still, I suppose that what they're doing is knocking women and kids about to get the phones so they deserve what they get. There was that Judge Michael Argyle at the Bailey. He'd been the Recorder of Birmingham and there was a rash of stealing from telephone boxes so it got that you couldn't find one which was working. He started potting people for long stretches and the word soon got around. It was the same back in the 1860s when there was what was called garroting going on. You put a chokehold on the neck of the man and nicked his kettle. Apparently if you didn't know what you were doing you could kill the bloke. People got the bash for that. Twelve strokes as you went in the nick and another twelve just before you came out, so you had something to look forward to. That stopped it pretty quick. So maybe Lord Woolf's right.

I suppose that what Argyle'd done in Birmingham earned him promotion and that was when he went to the Bailey. I read a couple of years ago that Argyle had died. I was never in front of him but enough of my friends was. He was a funny man; dead keen on racing. He'd go out to the betting shop in the lunch adjournment. His wife's racing colours were nigger brown and black cap and he couldn't for the life of him see what was wrong with that. He was the one who remanded that Richard Neville and his mates over the magazine *Oz* and said the prison authorities should make sure they had a short-back-and-sides before they came back to court. He chucked a kid's bicycle in the river as well. No question of charging him with criminal damage though. He got his come-uppance in the end. The people who'd run *Oz* did very well in business later on and Argyle libelled one of them in an article he wrote. The man sued and got a lot of money for charity.

People don't remember how the cinema was before there was television. You'd get what they call a B picture, something like a Randolph Scott Western, then you might get a travelogue, you know the sort of thing, 'Now as the sun goes down over the island, sadly, we leave the land of bare-breasted women.' Of course you never saw the bare-breasted women except at the other end of the island. It was like those nudist films they had in the 1950s, you never got a shot of anything at all. They were always playing beach ball with the ball covering up everything. Anyway, then there'd be the news with a good bit of sport; one of the boxing matches or cricket or a big race like the Grand National. They used to rush it out for the Monday and there'd be queues round the block even though we all knew the result. Then there'd be the main film. But what they also had was advertisements for people who'd gone missing and the police wanted help finding them. Sort of an early version of *Crimewatch*. The War was about the best time to get rid of a wife or girlfriend. You could say they'd gone away to the country or gone off with some other bloke. People would accept it and the police was too busy to go searching for every wife who'd gone off.

Even when they found a body they couldn't always link it up to anyone. That's what happened in November 1943 when one turned up at the water level at Osborne Bridge Road in Luton. They had the pathologist Keith Simpson and he reckoned she'd been done within the past couple of days. He reckoned she was in her early thirties and she was well in the club. She was missing a few teeth and all. She'd been put in sacks and they came from a local potato merchant.

This was when they used the cinema and, like usual, a whole lot of people come forward to try and identify the body but it didn't do no good. It was sheer luck that they found out who she was. It was some months later when a dog nosed out a shoulder-pad from a woman's dress off a rubbish tip. The copper in the case was nearby and it was given to him. There was a dyer's tag on it and it was traced to the Sketchley dye works in Luton. Once they'd made that step it was only another to Caroline Manton who lived in Regent Street. In fact there'd already been a house-to-house enquiry and the two kids there had been shown the photograph but had failed to recognise their mother.

When the coppers asked her husband, Bertie, about Caroline he said there'd been trouble over her going with soldiers; she'd left him to go and live with her brother in Grantham and had then moved on to London. He was another like that man down in Hampshire who got caught because he couldn't spell. He'd been writing letters to his wife's mother saying they come from Hampstead, but when the coppers got him to write the word he left out the 'p' just the same as on the letters. Then they started to turn over the place in earnest and there was some blood splashes and a fingerprint. That was more or less it for Bertie.

It was the usual wartime story. She complained he did nothing but work and had thrown a cup of tea over him. He'd hit her with a stool and it went on from there. The trouble was he was a boxer and even if he has to hit her, there was no need for the stool. Then there was the usual fanny about how he had a blackout and wakes up to find she's dead. He put the body in the cellar and that evening, when the kids are out, he put it on his bike and pedals off to the river. He'd gone and smashed up her false teeth because the kids knew their mother always wore them.

There was a big petition to save him being topped. I think it was something like 30,000 signatures, and they reprieved him. But he didn't last all that long. He died in Parkhurst in 1947. Funnily, if he hadn't tried to get rid of the shoulder pad he'd probably never have been caught. What made it worse for him was there wasn't even any blood on it.

Over the years I got to know a lot of murderers who'd been reprieved. They'd all had the pressure in the condemned cell to make them think they were going to be topped. Condition them so that when it came to their being swagged that last morning it would be easy. Once they got the verdict and was back to prison they'd be taken straight in to the cell and there was a wall with a screen just like you'd have your photo taken against. They never realised that on the other side was a door and that's where the handle was.

If they was reprieved then the sheer joy could last a few years. I know it sounds silly but that's what happened. By the time they got their act together maybe they'd done three or four years, sometimes longer, and they'd become a proper prisoner. Then they could start to sail through their bird because they'd got that number of years behind them.

These were straight guys. In their wildest dreams or maybe nightmares they never thought they'd be going to prison. They was the kind who wouldn't steal an apple in the market. Then they'd found their old woman was having it off with the bloke two doors down the street and they'd lost it. You had to be wary of them. They were straight mugs and the screws could lay a cherry in front of them because they didn't know any better. They thought if they brown-nosed they'd be let out earlier. 'Anything you hear you've got to tell us. That's the rules.' And they'd go on, 'That Fraser, anything you hear about him . . .' Poor sods, there was a perpetual carrot. Their probation officers would be the same, 'Anything you hear let the screws know . . .' At that stage they'd shop their own mother.

Of course some turned out to be terrific guys. They'd tell you how the screws had approached them, but unfortunately they was rare. Little did they realise that if they kept out of trouble and had someone on the outside to look out for them and give them a home they'd no need to be grasses to get out after a few years.

You tend to forget that the IRA has been active for years. When I was in the nick in the 1940s there was still a lot of the IRA in prisons here left over from before the War. There'd been a lot of IRA activity in the '30s. When people of my generation talk about the Birmingham Bombing they could as easily be talking about the one in August 1939. What happened was a bomb was planted on a bicycle left in Broadgate. Five people was killed. The coppers was able to trace the owner from its serial number and five people were charged. Three of them got off but two of them, James Richards and James Barnes, were found guilty. There was no question of a reprieve for them and they got topped in February 1940.

One thing that's changed crime is DNA. Not so much in what was my line of work, because there was always fingerprints and palm prints, but in rapes and what you call domestic murders. It's changed things so much.

The first time it was used in England was in a case in the Midlands. There was a very nasty rape and murder in a village, Littlethorpe near Leicester; back in 1984 it was. It's amazing to think it's nearly twenty years ago. Then there was a second one two years later. The chances are in something like that it's someone who knows the area well enough. One, maybe it's a stranger, but two – that's pushing coincidence.

They had one kid in who confessed, saying he'd probably gone mad when he done it. Here's the good thing about DNA; the samples they took from him and the girls proved he couldn't have done it. He still did three months in custody though whilst they was sorting things out.

The next thing they did was to try and get samples from all the young men in the neighbourhood, well up to the age of 35. Of course you couldn't make people give samples but if they didn't you could go round and have a look at them. It had been done with fingerprints before then. They got a good turn out of people.

You had to take some ID to the local hall and give a sample there and then. Of course, these things can go wrong and it did in this case. One fellow goes and gives a sample for another. The man who should have turned up was called Colin Pitchfork and he persuaded his mate that he should give the sample for him. Of course what happens is that the fellow talks about it in the pub and one of the women in the group knows a copper and reports it to him. Not surprising that Pitchfork didn't want to give a sample. He'd got a couple of convictions for indecency already.

It was only a matter of hours before the coppers went to see him and straightaway he says he's done it. But really it was the girls' fault. He intended just to expose himself but they'd seen who he was and could identify him so they had to go. That's what his sort always say. It was just like that man in Bradford caught having it off with a bull terrier. The dog made the first approach he said.

Apparently in one case Pitchfork's taken his wife to evening class, killed the girl and then gone and collected her. The baby had been on the back seat of the car in a carry cot when he'd done it. He said he'd exposed himself to over 1,000 women, which shows people don't report this sort of thing as they should. I can see why they don't but if someone had then maybe he'd have been locked up before he got to the girls. He got life, of course, and the bloke who'd taken the test for him got a bender.

I was looking at the linens the other day about the chef, also from Leicester, who's been done twenty years later for killing a young girl. It seems the pros' evidence is all DNA. The fellow says there must be some mistake. I wonder if this DNA thing is all that it's cracked up to be. In a way it's just like fingerprinting was a century ago. The scientists said your little finger print matched something found on a cup and you put your hands up. Now, a hundred years later, there's doubts creeping in. Briefs didn't know how to deal with it. If the scientists said it was a match, well then, a match it was. Juries simply lapped up that sort of evidence. I remember that case when the brief John Platts Mills said that a copper had lifted a fingerprint and planted it. The judge, who was that Melford Stevenson, was so cross he tried to have his fees taken away from him. I reckon in ten or twenty years' time it's going to be the same with DNA, and there'll be a whole lot more people queuing up for the Criminal Review Commission. Platts Mills acted for me in my libel trial against the *Empire News*.

There was a really funny case in Peterborough a few years ago and the bloke was lucky he didn't swing. A few years earlier and it would have been a posthumous reprieve, which doesn't do too many people much good. One day in October 1973, around lunchtime, Albert Taylor calls on his girlfriend, Gillian Seaton, in Mountsteven Avenue to tell her how he's got on at a job interview, and he finds her fifteen-year-old sister, Jackie, stabbed to death and with a dog-lead around her throat. She had seventeen stab wounds and someone had interfered with her.

Instead of calling the police he panicked and ran, caught a bus and went back to his room at the Great Northern Hotel in Peterborough. He noticed he had blood on his trousers, from the time he had knelt by the body to see if Jackie was alive, and took them to the cleaners. Not the most sensible thing to have done. He then met Gillian as she left the local technical college but he didn't tell her of the murder. She went to another class and Taylor went to her home, but by then the coppers had already arrived.

He had an alibi. What he said was that he'd been on Peterborough railway station buying a newspaper at 1.15 p.m. Then he went for his interview which lasted half an hour and then he went to his girlfriend's home. He said he knew it was 1.15 p.m. when he was at the station because of the peculiar ticking noise of the station clock. The pros wasn't having that and they called evidence to show that the clock was electric and didn't tick. Guilty, My Lord.

Taylor wasn't having it though and he managed to get the case re-opened and coppers from another force to investigate the thing. The man in charge managed to trace the clock which had been removed when they'd done up the station. He found that it did tick, but only in cold weather and then at certain times of the day. It would have ticked at 1.15 p.m. on the day of the murder.

Taylor explained the reasons why he had not told his girlfriend of the death of her sister by saying that he thought he had imagined it. As to the cleaning, he said if he had killed Jackie he would have burned his clothes, and anyway, there was blood on his coat which he had not had cleaned. So far as running away from the scene of the crime was concerned, he said both that he had had trouble with the police before and that he had seen a cyclist killed under a bus as a child. After that he couldn't stand the sight of blood.

Very often, the Court of Appeal is grudging when they allow an appeal against conviction. It's never a straight, 'We think he's not guilty'. It's more usual that they say 'The conviction's not safe', which means we still think he might have done it. They did that a lot in the Irish terrorist convictions. They wouldn't come right out. It was the same here. 'Not clear where the truth is.' That sort of thing.

Taylor'd served five years and five months of his sentence and he got £12,000 compensation for the wrongful conviction. It doesn't seem much nowadays, what with people getting hundreds of thousands, but then the pay-out rate was about two grand a year and there was no guarantee you would get it. He was always hoping he'd get back with his girlfriend after he was freed but it didn't work out. She'd married someone else by that time and said she'd told the local papers she didn't want to see him again. So he changed his appearance and put an ad in the local linen for a new girlfriend.

Things seem to have gone better for him after that, until May 1980 when the house he was living in with his new girlfriend and their four-year-old daughter, Donna, caught fire. He didn't panic this time. He caught their three-month-old baby when it was thrown to safety, and then he went back in to try and get Donna. He got very badly burned. Brave thing to do. You like to think you would do it yourself but until it happens you never know. There's many a person would stay outside waiting for the fire brigade.

Birmingham was the place where Ray Rosa and Dido Frett got caught when they was off to Ireland after they did the Carters with me back in 1955. I was off there as well but I was travelling separate which was good for me. It wasn't their fault neither. What had happened they was travelling with Patsy Lyons, who'd been such a good man in his day. He was the one who did a jewellers in Victoria with me at the end of the War. Later he mixed with the wrong people. He was with Charlie Mitchell who turned against the twins when Mitchell has a bull down Fulham way and ends up prossing the pair who did him. Patsy shouldn't never, ever have been in the same car as Mitchell.

Anyway, Patsy's driving Ray and Dido up north. In fact they're on their way to Leeds when they get a pull. What's happened is that Patsy had done a jewellers in Birmingham the previous year. What people didn't know is that in them days jewellers used to buy wholesale and a lot of them belonged to a chain. The suppliers would drive round delivering fresh stuff and taking away the stuff which hadn't sold, moving it around. It was a routine just like sending a couple of men to the bank at the same time on a Friday. Anyway Patsy was in his own car and he got nicked. He was in Winson Green a few months before he got a not guilty.

In them days you had to wait for Quarter Sessions, which in the beginning was just that, every three months, and if you missed it you generally had to wait for the next one. Sometimes there was a bit of compassion. There was one case in the north, Durham I think it was, that a woman got arrested for killing her old man on the Friday and appeared at the Assizes the next week. It was the quickest there's ever been. If she'd missed it she'd have had to wait for months. I seem to remember it was some sort of mercy killing and although she got sentenced to death everyone knew she was going to be reprieved.

Patsy's in his own car again and the coppers see it and bang. This time it's the jackpot for them because there's warrants out for Dido and Ray over Carter. Patsy gives them a story, says he didn't know they were on the run and they have to let him go. Jack and Dido weren't so lucky. They was brought down to London.

Like I say I'd been in another car and I got to Liverpool and over to Dublin. I was met off the boat and stowed away safely in the suburbs. Bill had arranged it all. I stayed very quiet but when it come to it I wasn't there long. If I'd stayed there longer I'd have made myself useful, done a bit of work, but when I heard they'd been nicked, I was gutted. I felt responsible and I come back to London to see if I could help straighten things out. That was me gone as well. I wasn't out of the baggage hall at Heathrow when I was nicked.

Birmingham was a lucky place for my friend Ruby Sparks, the great smash and grab man and escaper, though. He knocked down a woman after a smash and grab raid in New Street in November 1924 and she died. For a time there was a chance he'd be done for murder but he stayed away and by the time he was nicked there was no chance the witnesses would pick him out on an ID. The coppers never managed to trace him or the other two who was with him. They'd left behind a load of stuff in the Buick when they abandoned it, including a Van Heusen collar with laundry marks on it. It was the first smash and grab raid there'd been in Brum and they nicked over a grand's worth of jewels.

Funnily, two days later there was a second smash and grab. This time a couple of fellows did a pawnbrokers. They was chased by a man on a bicycle but they got on a tram and he couldn't pedal fast enough.

It's amazing what ordinary straight people kill over and how you never know your neighbour's a schizophrenic until it's too late. Look at that case in Birmingham a few years ago. Jeffrey Gould couldn't stand his neighbour James Bourke, playing classical music and so he battered him to death. He thought Bourke had been sent by what he called the Divine Lord to spy on him. Then there was two people on different occasions when neighbours killed each other over the gardening. One of them happened quite recently in Leicester. A fellow called Sandor Bata goes and kills his neighbour Mick Willson because he was dumping his clematis cuttings on his allotment. He says Willson was abusive so he goes and gets a shotgun. He was lifed off in September 1999. The most amazing bit of the story is that Bata was 73 when he done it.

What with modern science I don't suppose now there'll be too many more cases where girls have been cut up and put in parcels all over the railway and no one can find out who they are. But I expect people will still have a go. There was a girl a few years back found in a suitcase on the Wolverhampton train from London. Well, a bit of her was. Her head and legs was missing, but they soon worked out she was Asian. Then a bit more of her turned up and then, finally, her head was found in a duffel bag over

Wanstead Flats. It turned out her father had done it. She'd been going out with a married man and got herself in the club. She wouldn't give the man up and her dad hit her over the head with a coal hammer.

Whenever I watch those news bits on TV with grieving boyfriends and husbands saying they can't think who'd have killed their girls and someone must be able to help, it's then I start to wonder. Of course a lot of them are genuine but sometimes I think the police have people on so they can see how they behave. It's not that rare to see them weeping on the telly one week and the next being hustled into the magistrates' court with a blanket over their heads.

Look at that Gordon Wardell back in 1994. His wife Carol's body was found in a lay-by near Nuneaton. The building society where she worked had its branch robbed after her code had been used to get in. There he was in a wheelchair weeping on the box. Then there was him throwing a personal note into the grave at her funeral. What had happened, he said, was that a gang had broken into the house, and had been waiting for him to come home. They'd tied him up and taken Carol off to the building society and killed her after they'd got the money. What the pros said was that he'd suffocated her and gone and done the building society himself. After that he'd tied himself up and he'd been in the house for fourteen hours before the police broke in and found him, but he hadn't even wet himself. The jury agreed. The last I heard he was still saying he was innocent and the coppers had made a lot of mistakes in the enquiries.

NOTTINGHAM

Sherwood Borstal near Nottingham was for older boys. You could still be sent to Borstal at the age of 23 and so some of the so-called boys was grown men with families. Kenny Strickson got topped for doing the matron there. Mrs Phillips was her name, and she was only 46. In 1949 it was.

She must have been quite good looking for a matron and it seems like he'd made a remark about her figure and she hadn't put him down hard enough. She'd said something about it was a good job she was broadminded. He told another inmate that he fancied his chances with her. He was told he'd get three years, but he went to see her back up near the chapel, locked the door and did her. He didn't touch her sexually but he didn't half bash her about. The doctors reckoned most of the blows had come when she was on the floor and he'd broken up a couple of chairs to use. He goes and confesses straight away. He'd have been better off sticking to Widow Palm like the rest of us.

The trial was over in a day. The pros called the boy he'd talked with to prove he'd done it deliberately. The fellow had done eighteen months for rape, which shows what lenient sentences there were then. Kenny's brief tried to show that the fellow had made it all up and was trying to get an early release but, of course, the bloke denied it. The brief didn't call Kenny and relied on a medical report that his father had been in a home and had epilepsy, but it didn't do no good. The jury can only have gone out for a smoke. They were back in 25 minutes. But by then the big story in the papers was of John Haigh, the acid bath murderer, who'd done that Mrs Deacon down in Crawley and a whole lot of others it turned out. I was the hospital in Brixton with him before his trial. All murderers went in the hospital in those days so they could get a nut and gut report on them. I'd just been nicked over a torch but because I'd been in the hospital at Cane Hill they had to have me under observation. Haigh seemed perfectly normal to me.

It was a fellow from Nottingham that went and confessed to a newspaper reporter. Newspapers were really big on crime a bit after the War. Each of them had their own special reporter, often more than one, and they had good contacts. There was people like Tom Tullett and Peter Earle. Like I've said before, Edgar Wallace knew an uncle of mine and he was always down the Elephant picking up bits of gossip. Anyway this bloke, Herbert Mills, telephones Norman Rae, the reporter on the *News of the World*, in August 1951 to say he'd discovered the body of a woman and it looked like murder. He said he'd read a poem when he found the body while he thought about what he should do. It's funny how often the killer reckons he's discovered the body. That way, in the past at any rate, he's got some sort of explanation for how blood got all over him.

What had happened was Mills had strangled the woman after trying to steal her necklace. He seems to have been one of those committing the perfect crime, or so he thought. He fancied himself as an artist and poet and took this middle-aged woman out to the cinema and arranged to meet her the next day, which was when he did her. He went and made a long confession, which he wrote out himself, and the paper gave it to the police. He was on the blower trying to get the *News of the World* to buy an exclusive of his story when the coppers traced the call to a coin box and they give him a tap on the shoulder whilst he was still talking with Rae. That was the last time he saw daylight. He'd wanted £250 for the story.

He tried to run the defence he'd discovered the body. If there'd been only blood he might have done better, but there was fibres from his suit under her nails. That was a bit too much to swallow. They topped him at Lincoln even though he was only nineteen. There was a report that his heart beat on for another twenty minutes. It must have been a bit iffy whether he was all there.

Paddy Meehan got out of Nottingham prison with three others in August 1963. It was the same month I was bombing the screws' houses in Pentonville and Wandsworth and when it come to it the Nottingham local paper give that more coverage than the escape. But Paddy's was a story and a half. In 1961 he'd come down to London to do the Co-op Store in Edmonton along with Billy Gentry, and it looked a million to one that someone grassed them.

I think Paddy was trying to put money together so's him and his family could go to Australia.

Paddy was just the explosives expert and when he looked at what they was doing he reckoned there was enough jelly bobbling about to send them and half the neighbourhood to kingdom come. That was why the English boys had to get in expert help. If you didn't know what you was doing you could blow yourself up. That's what happened in Liverpool one time. Some fellows were trying to blow the safe at the Bootle Dock Board which had got the dockers' pay in it. They must have used too much. I don't think they killed themselves but there was blood all over the place. It's at times like that you've got to have a tame doctor. You don't want to be booking into the local casualty department. Anyway Paddy's taking the jelly out of the lock with a knitting needle when Old Bill arrives. He got an eight at the Bailey under the name Patrick Carson. Judge Maude was the one put him away; a very aristocratic man he was. Good sense of humour if you wasn't on the end of it. He once told two top of the roofs who'd been caught plating each other not to do it again, but if they felt they couldn't control themselves then not to do it under his favourite bridge.

Paddy tried to get out in December 1962 and all he got for his troubles was six months' loss of remission and some bread and water. Then in August 1963 he tried again. There was a diversion set up when they was meant to be watching a cricket match in the nick and they was away through the fence. There was a car waiting for them. That's what I mean when I say it's no use just getting out. You've got to stay out, and for that you need help. They all come down to London and go round to Eva who's only too glad to help them out and give them some clothes and food. Paddy and a man called Hogan go back up to Scotland and then, if you believe what he said, and wrote for that matter, Meehan had the most amazing time.

He went over to Dublin and then went on to Frankfurt. After that he took a train to a place called Badhersfeld and then he got a bike and cycled over into East Germany. It was there he got nicked. It seems like he'd been to some Communist meetings in the past and he'd run into one of the men there a few months before he'd been nicked over the Co-op. According to Paddy his name had been put up as someone who might help spring a spy – there was a few of them in the nick at the time – and when he'd got to East Germany he was pulled. Once people started interrogating him, he told them that he could spring a spy and gave them details of the lay-outs of some of the nicks and so forth. It didn't work out too well for him because by the time he'd given all this info, the East Germans simply took him to Berlin and at Checkpoint Charlie handed him over. After that it was back to Wandsworth to finish off the sentence. MI5 interviewed him and what he used to say was that he told them the Communists wanted to spring the Krogers and George Blake. According to the Mountbatten Report into how Blake got sprung, Paddy had said there wasn't much interest in him. By that time Paddy had got sent to Parkhurst, which was where he met Jimmy Griffiths.

What I wonder now is why more people didn't try and escape in the old days. There was the great prize. If you stayed away until the end of your sentence the authorities sort of called it a draw and you didn't have to go back. It didn't do you no good if you failed to go the distance. You didn't get any time wiped off for the days you was out. Got a bit more, more like, but if you kept away from them then the sentence was scrubbed. I suppose the reason there wasn't more escapes was that you was watched so much. There were so few prisoners at the time. No question of two or three in a cell. Half the time there weren't enough cons to fill them. There wasn't much work and so you was locked up most of the time except for exercise. You could expect a cell search every ten days and, since when you was out, all the cell doors were open the screws would be able to look in. There was no question of other cons stealing because there wasn't anything in them to nick. Anyone who was even suspected was branded a cell thief and could expect a very bad time. There was no Rule 43 then so people couldn't ask to go into isolation. Rule 45 it is now, but I don't suppose it'll be known as anything but Rule 43 for years. Even though a man who was thought to be a cell thief might have been innocent, it stuck and it would follow him around.

If you got caught trying to escape you'd be put on special watch even though that wasn't much. You had to put your clothes outside the cell door at night. Not that that stopped Charlie Wilson getting out of Winson Green and that was years later. People also had to wear patches. They refused at first and there was a tear up in Wandsworth but, of course, it was like trying to stop the tide coming in.

I don't know about women who marry men who are doing life or a long sentence. If I was a psychiatrist or a miracle man maybe I could give you the right answer. To some of them the man represents something different. It sounds silly but it's a bit of glamour. Dead straight women are never going to meet men like that in their lives. There's also a theory that for some of them, they do it knowing the man's not going to be out for years so there's no pressure on them. Some of them do it just for the publicity. The more famous you are the more interest you get from the outside. A guy gets the headlines and women write in. Years back Ruby Sparks used to tell me women wrote in after his escape from Dartmoor and the news of him being in the riot there. As I've said you usually weren't given letters from people you hadn't written to in the first place but sometimes they'd let them through. By the end of my twenty even I at my age was getting a few bits of love mail. Of course by then it was easier to get letters.

Then there's the women who think that, despite all the evidence, they're going to reform them. Love of a good woman and that sort of thing. They're the ones who are going to make the men change. Sometimes it works out really well but as often as not there's problems. Stands to reason there's going to be. It's difficult enough when someone comes out after a long stretch to readjust to life on the outside with people he knows, let alone with someone he doesn't. All these years he's been under pressure to keep his cell tidy and clean and now he finds his new wife, however tidy and smart she is when she comes to see him, doesn't make the bed or leaves the toothpaste all over the bathroom.

Of course a lot of men who've had long stretches will come out with nothing. The Discharged Prisoners Association would give them something in my day but it was a real problem. You haven't got any dough. This woman you've married, and who you've only seen outside the warehouse for a couple of days, is on at you to get work and so there's a real temptation to do a job. If you get away with it that's good but you don't really care if you get nicked and it's back in the warehouse. It's an option. If a Chap comes out that's different. He's going to get help and cash from his friends.

As I've said before it was never any hardship for me readjusting. The moment I was out I'd forgotten what it was all about. If someone said after I'd been out 24 hours, 'What were you doing this time two days ago, Frank?' I'd have to think, and then I'd go, 'What's the time? 2.30 p.m. Well, I'd have been banged up.'

It's difficult enough for the woman who's already married and then discovers her husband's a murderer. Is she going to stay with him? Does she send a Dear John straight off or let him down as the years go by? A lot of women start working for the man's release. There was one who got her bloke's release almost by accident. The fellow was a vet and he'd gone down for life. She was Catherine Crooks who'd married Ryan James from Burton on Trent whilst he was in Gartree. She'd known him before and in fact they'd been having an affair before he was put away. What the pros had said was that Ryan James had given his wife, Sandra, an injection of Immobilion, which they drug horses with, to clear off his debts with the insurance money. The jury gives him a guilty and the judge says what an evil man he is. How wrong can you get? Catherine's going through James's old papers and she comes across a note from the wife stuck in between the pages of one of his books, saying that she wasn't leaving him anything except the note, and she'd added, 'If you find it in time'. It really confirmed she'd done herself. You wonder how many other cases like it there are.

Mind you, marrying a man you know's committed a murder and done his time for it must be better than marrying a bloke who's done a girl 24 hours before your wedding and you not knowing it. That's what a fellow David Blake did in Leeds back in 1934. Strangled a waitress, Emily Yeomans, and tried to rape her as well. He was done because he kept her powder compact and the girls she worked with recognised it because it had a torn lid. He'd already done time for attacking a girl and stealing her necklace, which he gave to the girl he was going out with then. There was a big effort to get him a reprieve but he was topped.

* * *

Taking little girls off the streets and killing them isn't really anything new. Frederick Nodder was one of those nonces who do that. His was a bit of a legal case, like the one in London I've mentioned.[1] It was straightforward in a way; a little girl, Mona Tinsley, disappeared in January 1937 and Nodder'd been seen with her at a bus stop near Retford. When she never turned up he was done for abduction and got a seven. It was really one of those no body cases where they reckoned they couldn't pros for murder without one. The judge was convinced the kid was dead, saying things like '. . . may be that time will reveal the dreadful secret which you carry in your breast'. It's amazing to think that they actually spoke like that in them days.

Anyway, three months after Nodder's been potted, Mona's body is found in the River Idle and so they try him for murder. In fact the only reason she was found was that a medium predicted where the body was. There was no doubt she'd been strangled. His brief tried the defence that he'd been tried once and so couldn't be tried again. When that did no good they reckoned she must have met a stranger. That didn't wash either, and he was topped at Lincoln just before the year's end.

Nottingham was where the judge, Mr Justice Watkin Williams, dropped dead in a brothel. He'd been touring on Assize in 1884 and he was having a bit of relaxation in the evening when the dinner and the port and then the effort was a bit much for him and his heart give out. The place he copped it in was on Low Pavement. They got him back to his lodgings and tried to cover it up but these things never work. Then they tried to hide the inquest away as well. Coroners could hold inquests any hour and wherever they wanted, even in their own front rooms, so as to keep people out. But again it did no good. The linens got hold of it. 'Corinthian pleasure' they called it. The girl he had been with, who was called Nellie Banks, said the old gentleman had given a sort of grunt and she thought he'd come, but he'd gone. He wasn't even that old, only 56.

---

[1] See p. 17.

NORTHAMPTONSHIRE

Sometimes I think the killing's the easy part. It's what to do with the body that's the trouble. Billy Hill was all right when he had the man at the crematorium squared. Drop the body in, give it the military salute and that's that. They don't come back from the ashes. But over the years a lot of good people – and bad ones for that matter – have come unstuck trying to be too tricky about what to do with bodies. Epping Forest's always been a favourite place. That was where they found Jerry Hawley, the so-called tattooed man who starred in his own porn films, as I've said in *Mad Frank's London*.

Then there was that copper who liked to take pictures of girls tied up. The man had been on duty outside Downing Street once upon a time, guarding Mrs Thatcher. He started off with them prettily enough, little pink ribbons on their wrists, things like that. Then it was a bit more serious, and eventually he got done over an eighteen-stone lesbian brass in leather and chains, who was blind drunk and went and suffocated in the mask he'd got her to wear.

This was down in his place in King's Cross and now he's got problems. He can't hardly go to his superiors and say 'I've got this eighteen-stone les in an armchair in the flat and I can't move her', because, for a start, coppers aren't meant to be going out with brasses. So what does he do? He gets her in the bath and starts sawing. It's summer and the neighbours think there's a smell, but he gets her in moveable bits and it's off to Epping Forest where there's every chance she won't be found until the foxes have had a good go. Bad luck on him. Some kid sees her bum and starts using it for target practice. The kid goes to see if he's hit anything and now it's all on top. He got done for murder and went down for it, but the Court of Appeal said all he should have had was a sentence for hindering an inquest and he could have five years.

Other people have tried to burn the victims. It certainly won't work now when even the smallest bit of bone is going to be identifiable, but Alfred Rouse, who was a commercial traveller, tried it in the 1930s.

It was a really big case, not just the murder itself but the trial. He just got himself in a terrible mess. He had women all over the place and I think what he really wanted was to disappear. He'd been in the First World War and he'd been injured, so you have to give him credit for something; they'd operated on his head. I don't know whether it was what made him a bit funny but he couldn't keep his hands off women. He's got to have been a charmer because they reckoned he had eighty illegitimate children, and there was always some bum bailiff knocking on the door with another court order. He also went and had a bigamous marriage which, I suppose, is about the only thing I've never done. He was a right Hans Christian Andersen as well; said he'd been to Eton and Cambridge when he'd been to the local council school. When he decided he had to disappear he was meant to be getting married to yet another girl, Ivy, who was in the club and thought he was going to move her to a big place down in Kingston. More fool her.

What he does is set fire to his car in the middle of the night in a place called Hardingstone in Northamptonshire. November 1930 it was, and it was big stuff in the linens. Remember, there wasn't all that much murder in those days. No Yardies opening fire in a club every second night in some drugs battle. A murder was headlines. It was bad luck for him that two men was walking by and saw him climb out of a ditch. What was more there was a body in the car and the coppers traced the plates back to Rouse's home in Finchley. They had his wife go to Northampton, and she had a look at what was left and said it looked like her old man's stuff.

So far so good, but this is where Rouse went and made another mistake really, and I've never been able to work out why he did it except that Ivy was in a bad way with the baby. Instead of getting out of the country, which was the only thing for him, he goes to Glamorganshire to see her. Her father went and showed him a picture of the burned out car and all. There was also a description of him by the two men who'd seen him in the ditch. He must know his number's up and he gets on a bus back to London. He's nicked at Hammersmith bus station. By this time he's thought he's got up a half-way decent story. What he tells the coppers is that he'd given a lift to a man who was hitch-hiking and he'd stopped to refill the petrol with a can he had. After that he'd gone over to the ditch to have a jimmy and suddenly when he looks back the car's in flames. He thought the man must have struck a match and that was when the car went up. It wasn't the best story but it wasn't a bad one in the circumstances. Remember scientific evidence wasn't like it is today. What the pros said was that he'd set fire to the car with the man still conscious.

What really did him was his own expert. He called a man who said he was an engineer and tried to explain that there'd been a spark and it was all an accident. Norman Birkett, who was doing the pros, asked him, 'What is the co-efficient of the expansion of brass?' When the man said he didn't know Birkett just ripped him to pieces after that, making out he wasn't an expert at all. People said it was an unfair question, but the brief said he'd got it out of a pocket diary for engineers and if it was in there then the man should have known. It didn't matter much because Rouse went and made a confession to the *Daily Sketch* who'd put up the money for his defence. That was the rules. They'd pay your brief but if you was topped you was expected to have left them the story of how you'd done it so they could get their money back through selling more papers afterwards.

They had a waxwork of him in Madam Tussauds in the Chamber of Horrors there. There used to be a sort of jury box where all the great murderers like him and Seddon and Charlie Peace were sitting like they were doing the deciding. There was also an exhibit of torture through the ages and a man hanging on a butcher's hook. I used to think that was much the best.

The copper who did the Rouse investigation got called in a few years later to have a look at a murder in Dunstable even though it wasn't in his county. The reason was it was a girl who'd been the fiancée of a Bedfordshire copper who was done. Ruby Keen was engaged but she was still quite happy to go out with other blokes when the man was on duty. She was done back in 1932, strangled with her scarf, said Spilsbury. The reason they was being a bit discreet was because she'd been seeing another copper, as well as a fellow called Leslie Stone. He'd been out with her and then done her. Although there was no sexual assault he got topped at Pentonville and the other copper was booted out the force. The girl's fiancé was asked to resign, which seems a bit hard. Losing your girl and your job at the same time don't seem really fair.

Funnily, the day they topped Stone was the same day of the year they'd had the first private hanging in the country. Back in 1868 it was. A young fellow, Thomas Wells, got the sack from his job with the London, Chatham and Dover Railway and he went and shot the stationmaster. It was the first time a hanging hadn't been done in public, although there was plenty of reporters there. It seems it was a botched job and the boy just strangled slowly.

MANCHESTER

Manchester was a good place to be just after the War and one of the best of the men there was Bobby Critchley, who had a bulletproof car. I've no idea where he got it. He was a large man, distinguished looking. There was a big Jewish population in Manchester and Jack Spot came to the city in search of a nightclub to mind. The club Spot fancied was Critchley's Jacaranda in the Stretford Road, but Bobby saw him off. Over the years Bobby had been involved in racecourse protection and he'd done a bit of bird in his youth, but when I knew him he'd got some property and he was more of a putter-up. The Mrs Post job I've written about was one he gave us.[1]

There was plenty of others though. A good man who wasn't a villain but who mixed with us was known as the Aga because he looked like the Aga Khan. He was a brilliant card player, straight as well as hooky. Very often there was no need for him to cheat. If he went down a spiel you could see the punters lining up to play cards with him or have their man play with him. It was like that Paul Newman film, a card player would have backers who'd stake him out and take a percentage of his winnings. Sometimes the Aga'd string them along, let them win a bit and so the next night they'd be back for more, thinking he wasn't as good as he was cracked up to be – then Bosh. There was big money floating around both Manchester and London. No disrespect but the better players were in London. Up there they wasn't quite up to the mark and it was like having a baby over for him. As I say he wasn't a villain but he admired villains. To him anyone could play cards – of course they couldn't, not like him – but it was a different thing going out and risking your liberty. A couple of times when I come out he slipped me a few hundred. He faded away. He needed to be smart and he got ill and was never the same. For a time he played in a spiel Billy Howard had in Brixton but he went right down the pan.

Then there was Bobby MacDermott, a really good man – King of the Barrowmen, and a good thief and receiver in his time. He

---

[1] See *Mad Frank*.

was probably the king of them all, linked up with Billy Hill and Arthur Thompson. I don't think people realised quite what a network there was even back in them days. He'd come and see me in the nick when I was doing the rounds and when I was up his way. He didn't drink. He'd done a bit of bird in his youth after a fight when he'd been drinking and he just give it up.

I'm not sure Manchester was a good city for me or for many of us. I was never nicked there but all the jobs I did didn't exactly pay for the trouble. There was that job we did with Jock the Fitter, a tie-up on Mrs Post which come to nothing. Jerry Callaghan and Jimmy Robson lost a load of jewellery in Manchester, along with Danny Swain. He was the wheelman, of course, in a smash and grab but what Jerry and Jimmy do in their hurry is not shut the door properly as they're getting in and the stuff goes all over the pavement. They couldn't stop and pick it up but at least they got away all right. It was the same with the Aussie, the one they called Joe the Bash, when he did a job in St James's before the War. It shows there's more to a blagging than breaking a window.

In fact the more I think back, in my earlier days Manchester wasn't a good city to me. The info where Jack Spot was the night I did him and got a seven came from a contact in Manchester, though I don't suppose it was Manchester's fault for that. Then in a way it was down to a fellow from Manchester that I got the five which led to the twenty. Not his fault, of course, but he came from Manchester.

There was some good clubs up in the place. Not as good as say Churchills or Winstons, but good clubs and Owen Ratcliffe had one. Cromfords it was, a lovely place. If I remember rightly Jack London, the old heavyweight boxer, was on the door. There was also a lot of what they called Sporting Clubs. Nice places they was in the main. You could take your wife and there'd be a couple of bouts of all-in wrestling, not people on the big circuits, but those who was billed as The Fighting Irishman versus Red Mask, that sort of thing. Then there'd be a cabaret, someone like Wee Willie Harris, and a bit of Bingo. All for just a few quid. The ex-wrestler 'Big' Bill Benny, who was massive, owned clubs including the Cabaret Club; he used to advertise it as 'The South of France comes to Manchester', and Chez Joey with roulette and blackjack tables at the back. When the police come the doorman would try and delay them a bit to give the punters time to clear up. The story was always that Big Bill died in bed and had to be sort of winched off the girl.

It was Owen who set me on my way to the twenty. Not that it was his fault, but Owen and his partner Paddy McGrath had opened Mr Smith's in Catford and were having a bit of trouble there. That was when me and Eddie was asked to look after the place and put a few of our machines in. The very night we signed up there was the fight with the Haywards and Dickie Hart was shot.

It was funny how reprieves went. Sometimes you couldn't see neither rhyme nor reason. Look at that fellow Patrick Monaghan who killed a woman in Swords, near Dublin just before the War. Beat her, raped her and then suffocated her. The jury recommended mercy on the grounds that he hadn't intended to kill her and he got a reprieve. He only served eleven as well. When you think poor Charlie Richardson got 25 for a spot of GBH in a case they wouldn't even bring to court today. I suppose that Monaghan case was in Eire so they may have done things differently there.

Contrast that with the case of James Makin who does a brass, Sarah Clutton, in Manchester in 1925. She was only 24 and she'd been poxed up before; now she thinks she's got it again so to cheer herself up she goes and buys herself a new green hat. The pox isn't going to stop her working though, and she picks up this Makin fellow in the city centre. They start having a few drinks and she insists he takes her to his home. He's married and living with his wife's uncle out at Cross Street in Newton Heath which is four miles away. He must have been mad to agree but off they go on the bus. His wife and the uncle are out working but there's plenty of neighbours twitching the curtains, so to speak. They see the pair go in and notice her hat in particular. Usual thing, they thought they'd been drinking but wasn't drunk. Then an hour later he comes out alone. When the uncle and his wife come back from work, under the bed is what's left of Sarah, who's had her throat cut and whose legs is sticking out. Makin meets a pal and tells him what he's done before he goes and gives himself up.

What seems to have happened is that after they've had it off the brass starts crying and asks for a bowl of water. He realises he may have caught something and does her.

It turns out that his eldest brother had died in the asylum and that Makin begun to get depressed after the War. He'd thrown himself in the Rochdale canal three times. His sister said she'd had to turn him out because of his moods and the threats he made against her and her husband whilst he'd been living there. His wife said he'd threatened to kill her and she'd hidden his razor but it didn't do no good. The jury was only out twenty minutes, and he didn't bother to appeal. It was all a bit of a waste really because it comes out there was nothing wrong with the brass after all.

It was in Strangeways when I saw a Flying Saucer. I was in my cell one night and it just came past the window. Fortunately Stan Cahill saw it from his cell too, otherwise people would have thought I really was mad. I hadn't liked to say anything until Stan mentioned it first. I think there was word of it on the radio the next day. Stan was a good boxer in his day. He trained well in the nick and was allowed out to take part in the ABAs as a light-heavyweight – under escort of course. I don't think he won but he did quite well. His trouble was he couldn't get the real training you can outside. He turned pro when he come out but he wasn't really up to it. I think he opened a couple of clubs in the North. He was big in Liverpool.

I think the last time I saw him was when he came to my seventieth birthday at Jack Trickett's place in Stockport. He brought a half dozen of champagne over to our table and we had a good chat. That was a good evening. I remember seeing a whole party of dwarves at one of the other tables and I couldn't think what they was doing. I don't think I'd ever seen as many at the same time. The comedian had a good joke with them and they loved it. Then I realised they must have been up for the pantomine, *Snow White*. Poor old Stan, he's doing a long stretch up in Scotland now; something like a twenty.

Mrs Van Der Elst reckoned she spent more time protesting about executions in Manchester than anywhere else. When she first went up there in 1935 it was over the killing of a girl called Amelia Nuttall who was known as Milly. It was her boyfriend John Bridge who was in the frame. He was only 22. He'd known her most of his life but then he'd met a girl, Eileen Earl, at work and he got himself in a right mess. More or less engaged to both of them. Eileen breaks it off and starts going out with another fellow; then she breaks that off because she realises she's in love with John, and he reckons he's in love with her. So he makes an appointment to break it off with Milly, but he's late and she starts a bull with him and comes at him with a poker. He takes the poker from her and bashes her with it and then he takes a bread knife and cuts her throat and pushes off. He's nicked when he comes back later. The coppers say it was to see what he'd done because there's plenty of people like to come back to the scene of the crime. That's why coppers turn out at funerals, just to clock the faces of who's there.

The jury recommended mercy and that's where things went wrong. The lawyers decided there shouldn't be an appeal and they'd go straight to the Home Secretary, but he wouldn't wear it. Mrs Elst was on the blower day and night it seems and sending telegrams but it did no good neither. She held a rally at the Free Trade Hall the night before the topping and 2,000 turned up. She was urging them to protest outside Strangeways the next morning and a lot of them did go there as well. In fact they say it was the biggest crowd ever to go to a non-public hanging. I don't suppose it would have made Bridge feel any better even if he'd got to hear of it. Mrs Elst had a row with the people there, shouted they was like the French Revolution, and they said they was mothers and what about poor Milly. She went to the inquest on Bridge and the coroner got quite sniffy. He said 'this matron' would be better off if she devoted herself to saving souls, which, I suppose, in a way is what she was trying to do all along. Then one juror pipes up that he agrees and there'd be a lot more killings if there wasn't hanging.

Brasses have a hard time. It's said you're most likely to get done by someone you know but in their case it must be the reverse. I saw a bit in the papers a few months ago saying there was a survey amongst brasses in Glasgow and at some time or another 80 per cent had been attacked or raped or knocked about in some way. I should think if you did a survey they're killed more than anyone else. That's one reason some girls don't mind working for pimps. There's a bit of protection from the punters knowing there's a bloke round the corner who's there to look after you. That and they always think the ponce is going to marry them and they can give up the game just as soon as he's become a lawyer, or written a bestseller, or gets a try-out with Man United. There's always some excuse.

The danger is you can just meet a psycho. Look at that girl Annie Riley who meets a Jewish boy, Solly Stein, just before he's 21. Back in October 1931 it was. He'd never been with a girl and he thinks he ought to give himself a treat for his birthday. He's been out celebrating with his mates and he meets her in New Bridge Street just by Deansgate. They go to the Station Temperance Hotel and he puts down ten shillings for a room. He asked for a knock on the door so he wouldn't be late for work. Next morning, when he wakes up he looks and sees she's a right old scrubber, and I suppose he's a bit ashamed at what he's done so, instead of just walking out and writing it off to experience, he strangles her with his tie. He put in granny knots so the poor girl can't undo them. Stands and watches her apparently. Then he wanders around Manchester and stays out a second night just when his family is preparing to have his 21st for him; he gives himself up the next day.

When he comes up at court he pleads guilty. His brief can't understand it and tries to get the judge to disallow the plea because he knows it's a topping matter, but the judge won't have it. After the case the boy won't see anyone but his father and then only once, and he won't appeal. He just kept on saying he was guilty. I think he was only the third Jewish man ever to be hung at Strangeways.

There was a story that the hangman James Billington was in the Fox Tavern in Wigan at the end of the nineteenth century and he's introduced all round and shakes hands with people. One fellow, Elijah Winstanley, says he wouldn't like to meet him in his official capacity and there's a good old laugh. Anyway Elijah and his mate go out to do a screwing at the local railway depot which goes wrong and a copper's stabbed. The man who gets topped by Billington is this Winstanley. It a bit like that story of Albert Pierrepont, who was called Tish by his mate in the pub he had, and he calls him Tosh. One day he's called to do the job and he finds it's Tosh he's going to hang. Pierrepont was the man I did at Wandsworth when he came to hang Derek Bentley.

If you were in punishment and reported sick, the doctors came to see you, but on the morning of an execution you were taken over to the hospital. E wing was just a few yards from the hospital. They tried to discourage prisoners from going sick on the day of an execution. On E1 you had to have two screws unlock you if you were in the single cells; this day, a mug screw did it on his own and told me to wait at the end of E2 landing. I said, 'Which end? The hospital end or the centre end?' He said the centre end. I went down the corridor as he'd said, there were two other prisoners already there. Patsy Lyons was one, and a fellow called Spiro. Now it's a bit after eight and out of F2 wing come Pierrepont with two burly prison officers on each side. One was Jack Manning. I'd already lost my remission after doing Carter. I did Pierrepoint – *bosh* – and kicked the door of the cell, shouting out, 'God bless you son, I know you're innocent.' It was only a few seconds before they was on me. Next day I was charged with assaulting a servant of the prison.

Like I've said before, it's not too often a man goes on to do a second murder. My friend Jimmy Essex was one and another was a fellow, Walter Rowland. Just after the War it was, in Manchester. He'd been in the death cell before for killing his two-year-old daughter. That was well before the War, back in March 1934.

The second time was in October 1946 and it was a funny sort of case altogether. This time he stood trial for doing a Manchester prostitute, Olive Balchin. There was no doubt as to his guilt in the killing of his daughter, but there were considerable doubts over the verdict in the Balchin case.

In October 1946 she was found battered to death on a bombsite. A blood-stained hammer had been left by her body and the evidence against Rowland was a witness, MacDonald, who said he had sold the hammer to him on the day of the murder. There were also traces of hair which could have been that of Olive. There was human blood on his shoe but it was impossible to type it with the tests they had then. What was in his favour was there was no blood on his shirt, nor were his prints on the hammer. On his arrest he'd asked, 'You don't want me for the murder of that woman do you?' Nowadays you'd reckon that was a typical verbal.

He pleaded not guilty, but he went down. Whilst awaiting his own trial a prisoner in Liverpool, David Ware, confessed to the murder of Olive Balchin and the confession was the big ground of the appeal.

The Court of Appeal wasn't going to call Ware like Rowland's brief wanted. Goddard was saying how often people made confessions when they'd nothing to do with a case. If anyone was to re-examine the case then it was for the Home Secretary who had infinitely more resources. As he was taken down Rowlands really went beserk, shouting out how innocent he was. There was a KC appointed to head an inquiry and he acted fast. There was another ID and MacDonald failed to pick out Ware. Ware went and withdrew his confession and it was reckoned he'd learned most of what he wrote from the newspapers. Rowland was topped at the end of February. He'd been in the same cell after he'd done his daughter before his reprieve.

It didn't end there because in November 1951 Ware turned up at Bristol Assizes, charged with attempted murder. He'd told the coppers, 'I have killed a woman. I keep having an urge to hit women on the head.' It was off to the bin for him. If you're the one the police fancy then the confession must be right.

There'd been another case like that before the War when George Armstrong, who was manager of a Manchester clothing store, was beaten to death at the beginning of May 1929. The man they had up for it, George Fratson, was nicked a bit afterwards in a brothel in Preston. He made over a dozen statements to the coppers but at last he come up with the one the police said was right and that was when he confessed. At his trial he tried to take it back, saying he made it only because he was despondent and wanted to die. He was convicted at Manchester Assizes in the July and he got a reprieve in the August.

After his trial it turned out that a cardboard collar-box in the shop was stained with blood and it had a finger or palm print on it which matched neither Fratson nor Armstrong. So his case came before the full five-member Court of Criminal Appeal. A senior copper gave evidence that he leaned towards the view that the impression had been made by the hand of a police sergeant who had visited the premises in the course of the investigation. I don't know why the sergeant was never printed so it could show things one way or the other. A second ground of appeal was that the pros knew that a raincoat belonging to Fratson and sold by him shortly after the murder showed no traces of blood. The Court wasn't having it and knocked out the case, saying there was nothing in the prints and he might not have been wearing the coat. Whilst he was in the nick Fratson became insane and was hauled off to Broadmoor.

Even then it wasn't over. In July 1934 Walter Prince, who'd been found guilty of murdering a young woman and had been sentenced to death, confessed to the murder of Armstrong. He got a reprieve and slung in Broadmoor. If he was insane his confession couldn't be right, now could it? I don't know if they ever met. Fratson's conviction was never overturned but if that new Criminal Cases Review Commission ever runs out of work they might like to have a look at both it and Rowlands' as well. But they never will, run out of work that is, and there's no one to keep pestering on Rowlands' behalf, or for Fratson for that matter.

It was like that case in Wales when Stephen Miller was convicted in 1989 of the murder of a brass, Lynette White, in Cardiff. He was questioned for hours and hours before he said he'd done it, but the Court of Appeal's had a bit of a change recently and they said it was oppressive and threw the conviction out. They've come to realise if you question someone long enough they'll say what you want just to get you to stop.

People generally had a lot more respect for the police years ago and so that's why when the Mayor says the coppers wanted to take everyone's fingerprints in Blackburn back in 1948 and they'd be destroyed when they'd been checked, people believed him and they come forward in their droves. Mind you it was the killing of a little girl who was in hospital so in a way it's not surprising. If someone had killed me and they wanted to check fingerprints I don't suppose there'd have been the same response.

What had happened was the kid, June, had been nicked out of her bed in the children's ward at Queens Park Hospital. Poor kid had been in there with pneumonia and she was due out the next morning. A nurse had checked the ward at 11 p.m., seeing to a child in the next bed to June's; half an hour later she had been working in the kitchen when she thought she heard a child's voice in the corridor.

She went outside and saw a door to the garden open. There'd been a wind that night and she thought it had just blown open so she shut it and went back to work. A quarter of an hour later she makes another round and this time she sees what looks like adult footprints, either barefoot or with thin socks, on the polished floor. I don't suppose nowadays anyone would notice in most hospitals but back then things was always highly polished. You could literally eat your dinner off the floor of a ward. She started checking and she could see June's bed was empty and under it was a bottle of distilled drinking water. She went to see if the little girl had gone to the toilet and when she wasn't there she raised the alarm. They found the body up against the hospital wall in some long grass about three hours later.

They had that copper John Capstick, who liked to be known as Artful Johnny and who'd tangled with Eva and the rest of the Forty Thieves, down from Scotland Yard. They fingerprinted everybody in sight and the only print they couldn't match was the one on the water bottle. It was the same with the files at Scotland Yard. There wasn't a match and the print got sent abroad in case it was a sailor or foreigner, but that didn't do no good either.

That was when they decided to see if they could fingerprint every male in Blackburn. They reckoned they'd need to take about 50,000 prints. In the May the Mayor made a public announcement saying that the prints would be just used against the bottle only. They'd not be checked against a list of wanted men nor would they be used to solve any other crime. Now people wouldn't have believed it. The work would be done on a house-to-house basis. There would be no need for anyone to attend a police station. By the September they'd got around 45,000 and there still wasn't a match. Then they decided to have a check on who'd been sent ration cards, and there was still another 800 people to be printed.

In the middle of August a copper calls a place in Birtley Street and asks if a Peter Griffiths, who's nineteen, will give his prints. If he hadn't I suppose they could have made some excuse to nick him but he gave them willingly and this time they check out. Once they've got him things fall into place and they matched up fibres from a suit he'd popped with some found on the body and there was bloodstains as well. He didn't even try to say it wasn't him The briefs said that he killed June whilst suffering from schizophrenia. His old man had been in the bin, but the jury wasn't having it. Less than 25 minutes they was out. A couple of weeks before Griffiths got topped all the fingerprints were shredded in public at a local paper mill.

Blackburn wasn't the only place where there was mass fingerprinting. There was more claims for nationwide fingerprinting when 'Aunt Polly' Mary Ornesher and her sister Margaret got battered to death in Ormskirk, Lancashire in May 1956. Fifteen thousand fingerprints were taken over a period of six months of every male over sixteen years of age, but none matched with the prints left behind. It happened again in Reading and also in Beeston over the murder of an elderly shopkeeper, Lily Blenkarn. There was fingerprints on a toffee tin and also on the backdoor latch. Something like 24,000 prints were taken in 1974 but they still couldn't get the man. Then a seventeen-year-old fellow, Anthony Hunter, threw a brick through a window and he was fingerprinted. It turned up a match. He'd managed to get round the big fingerprinting by getting a mate to practise his signature and do it for him. Just like Pitchfork did all those years later.

Not everyone reckoned everyone should be fingerprinted after 73 year-old Florence Gooding was found battered to death in Oxted. There was a bit of a straw poll and there was just as much objection from older people as from younger ones. It wouldn't matter to me since my dabs have been on file since the 1930s.

Back ten years ago contract killings weren't as popular as they've come to be nowadays. Of course, like I say, there was always work to be had if you were in that line but husbands and wives didn't go out looking for people in pubs who'd do their loved ones in for them. Looking back I don't think there was that much killing of straight people in business. Just like solicitors, provided they didn't meddle accountants were safe as well. It's only when people like them run up debts or start to get into business with the likes of us that there's generally trouble. That's what happened to David Wilson from Chorley in March 1992. He got involved in a cigarette smuggling scam. He was big in debt and he wanted to clear the books but it all went on top.

The people who done it must have been watching for their opportunity because when it came there was only Wilson and one daughter left in the house one evening. The others had gone off visiting. It's always easier to control just a couple of people at a time. If there's too many in a place there's always the chance someone will manage to slip off and bell the coppers. This time the Wilsons hadn't been gone for five minutes before a couple of men in balaclavas burst in and did a tie up. Then when the others came back they was tied up as well and made to lie on the floor. David Wilson was taken outside and they thought he was being kept hostage because that was about the time when kidnapping and hostages was making a bit of a show in this country.

Eventually they managed to get loose and then they find that the telephone wires had been cut and they drove to get help from a neighbour. When they came back they found David Wilson's body face down. He had been shot point blank. When they'd heard it earlier the family had thought it was a car backfiring, but it wasn't.

At first the coppers said things like nothing known to his detriment but it began to leak out in the press. It always does. There were suggestions it was the IRA and that Wilson was a bit too close to some drug gangs. He'd also been a bit close to a shipping fraud for his own good.

Then a year and a half later most of the story come out when Stephen Schepke, who'd been an art restorer, was charged with conspiracy to murder him. The shipping fraud over a non-existent cargo of fags had involved £26.5 million and the original plan had been to pass off cheap Mexican cigarettes as Marlboros, but Hector

Portillo, who the pros said was really Michael Austin, and who'd been Wilson's partner, pulled a double cross. There were no cigarettes nor was there any gold which Wilson was buying for an Isle of Man company from Portillo. Instead of keeping stumm or trying to get someone to make a deal for him, what does Wilson do? He goes to the CPS. He was also sending off faxes to Portillo complaining and saying he'd never forgive nor forget. Portillo decided he was too dangerous and talks to Schepke.

In October there was a bit of a funny verdict. Schepke was found guilty of aiding and abetting Wilson's murder but the jury was unable to agree a verdict that he had conspired to have Wilson killed. It didn't make no difference – he was lifed off.

The rest come out at Carlisle Crown Court in early 1995 when Hector Portillo, who was a top-class fraudsman in the States and was reckoned to be worth around £60 million, and who'd paid £1.5 million in cash for a suite in the Trump Tower in New York, got convicted of conspiracy to murder Wilson. He got life as well. All it had taken to organise the murder was a series of telephone and fax messages. It was a bit like that film *The Thomas Crown Affair* with cut-outs so that no one knew who anyone else was and all you did was leave messages on an answering machine. Once the number was changed, something which frequently happened, the contact was broken for ever. I'm not sure that the actual killers was ever caught.

The trouble with drug wars is that innocent bystanders cop it, far more than in our day. For a start we didn't spray whole areas with bullets. Really guns was not that common and there was no such things as drive-bys. When you think, when Babe Mancini got topped in 1941 he was the first so-called Soho gangster to be done for over twenty years. Now, if the death penalty was in force they'd have to have a dozen hangmen working several days a week to cope with the deaths from shoot-outs. Take the case of that girl in Old Trafford. By 1993 the drug wars had moved out of Moss Side, and Old Trafford, where the cricket ground is, was suffering. In April that year five houses got sprayed in one go and in one of them was a young student, Andrea Mairs. All she did was pull back the curtains in her bedroom window and she gets a stray bullet in the stomach. She lived, which is one thing, but there's many who haven't.

I know I keep on saying it but we did what we could to keep our bits and pieces well away from innocent people who could get hurt. I know the Carters turned up to do me when my wife and kids was in the flat that Christmas after the War, but there's no way they would have kidnapped her and set fire to her. That's what happened to that girl in Blackpool. She was just another in the wrong place.

The really bad case I've always thought is that little kid, Dillon Hull, killed when people opened fire on his stepfather John Batts, when they was walking in Bankfield Street, Bolton in August 1997. He was only five but he saw what was happening and tried to jump in front of his dad. He got wiped out and Batts was hit in the side. There'd been an attack on Batts earlier in the afternoon and someone was laying in wait. Batts had run drugs in Blackburn and had moved out to Bolton when things had got a bit warm. He'd upset someone there as well, wouldn't co-operate and so a contract was put out on him. They got the fellow who took it up. The man was Paul Seddon and £5,000 was the price. They got around £4,000 of the money back but they never got the man who took the contract out. They don't too often. Seddon got lifed off, of course.

Some women do have all the bad luck. Look at the woman whose son was taken off by Brady and Hindley. She adopts a little boy, Benjy Stanley, and he gets wiped out when he goes to the local takeaway to get a goat pie or something like that. He was wearing a scarf showing he was a Manchester United fan and the first story was he ran into a turf war. Like in America the Crips and the Bloods have blue and red colours – I forget which is which – so did the Gooch Gang and the Pepperdines over Moss Side in Manchester. Afterwards people said he wasn't all that innocent and he'd got over twenty grand in his building society account which hadn't come from baby sitting, and what was he doing with a £900 mountain bike?

Just before my seventieth birthday party at Jack Trickett's good hotel in Stockport there'd been a double killing just down the road. A couple of MoT inspectors was shot in a garage, Chestergate Auto Centre. Whilst they was talking to the manager a fellow in a mask come through the door and just blew them away. There was all sorts of talk that they was investigating a big ring of stolen certificates and it was a gangland contract which had got the wrong people, but it turned out nothing like that. It was the owner of the garage Tommy Burke. They called him the Milky Bar Kid. He'd had his brief to do MoTs taken away and he'd just lost an application to get it back. He took the men out as revenge.

LANCASTER

There's a saying that if a wife gets topped, look for the husband and if the husband's a doctor don't bother to look any further. Of course it's not always a hundred per cent. Look at that Dr Sam Shepherd in America, accused of doing his wife years ago and now it looks odds on his story he was attacked himself is true. Not much help to him though, he's been dead years as well.

But one which shows the rule's often right is the fellow Buck Ruxton from Lancaster who did his wife in the 1940s. Did the maid and all because she walked in at the wrong moment, and then chopped them both up and distributed them in Scotland at Gardenholme Linn between Moffatt and Edinburgh. Sometimes I wonder how people think they're going to get away with things but, in a way, it's as I say. Murderers do it on the spur of the moment or they think they're so clever they'll never be caught. But it's not enough to tell the coppers that the wife's gone off to see friends or run away with another bloke but he doesn't know his name or where he's gone. The Bill must be thinking, 'Pull the other one' as they nod and say 'Sad for you, sir', whilst they wait for him to cock it up like Crippen, who had Ethel Le Neve wearing his wife Belle's jewellery whilst she was still just about warm in the cellar. Wrapped in his pyjamas, she was. They'd got a label on them. He said it wasn't his wife and the body must have been there before they bought the house. The coppers showed the local shop didn't sell those sort of pyjamas until well after he'd moved in.

Ruxton was a Parsee and he'd met his wife, Isabella, when she was working in a restaurant in Edinburgh. She'd been married to a Dutchman but she set up housekeeping with Ruxton in Dalton Square, Lancaster. They were quite well off; they'd a live-in maid, Mary Rogerson. He always reckoned that when his wife was out of his sight she was having it off somewhere and he'd give her a good tongue-lashing or, if he felt like it, a beating. He'd got some French phrase which would appeal to Women's Rights nowadays, 'Who loves most, chastises most.' It all came on top in 1935 when he's convinced himself that she's having an affair with someone from the Town Clerk's office. She wasn't, but there was no persuading him otherwise.

She goes over to see the Blackpool Illuminations in the middle of September that year and there's no doubt she came back because the car's there, but there's no sign of her. As far as anyone can tell, since Ruxton said it wasn't him, what happened was there was a big quarrel when she went up to bed and he started strangling her. Mary hears what's going on and comes out of her room and he does her too. It was a Sunday so there's no patients and no one around and he spends the day cutting them up. Then he goes to one of his patients and says the decorators are coming in the next day, would she mind helping out scrubbing the stairs. There's a lot of blood about as you might expect and he says she can have the stair carpets. He tells her he's cut his hand opening a tin of peaches.

Then of course he's got to explain where his wife and the girl is and he makes up a lot of stories. Her and his wife have gone to Scotland for a holiday; the girl's in the club and Mrs Ruxton's taken her to see someone; his wife was on holiday; she'd gone off with another man. But once the bodies turned up, even though at first they was said to be a man and a woman, the tongues were wagging. His real mistake was that he used part of the *Sunday Graphic* as wrapping and there was an insert with details of the Morecambe carnival which was only distributed in the Morecambe and Lancaster area. Then Mrs Rogerson identified one of her daughter's blouses, and he'd used his kid's rompers and they were recognised as well. The trial lasted eleven days, which was a long time in those days. Norman Birkett defended him and Ruxton was in the box for two days. He wasn't a good witness, shouting and weeping, but it didn't do no good. He got topped at Strangeways. Apparently he left Birkett a set of fish knives in his will, which Birkett sent back, but the brief made sure that Ruxton's kids were educated.

Some people get away with it for years though and it's just bad luck when it comes on top. Look at that airline pilot Peter Hogg, who reported his wife Margaret missing back in 1976. He'd been a bit of a hero when the airline he worked for in Halifax, Nova

Scotia went out of business. It looked like the aeroplane was going to be impounded and all the passengers trapped so he made a daring escape with them. He said he thought his wife had gone off with another bloke, which seemed quite likely because one of the neighbours said that she ate men for breakfast, but I don't think they meant it the way it sounds today. Anyway it's nearly ten years later before her body's found, and then it's by accident. A French girl, who had been walking near Wast Water in Cumbria, had gone missing and they was dragging the lake to find her. It's the deepest lake in the whole of England. They don't find the girl but wrapped in a carpet and weighted down is Mrs Hogg. They can work that out from the wedding ring which has got the date of the marriage on. What had happened, he said, was that there'd been a quarrel and he'd strangled her. He'd driven north and dumped her body from a dinghy. If he'd rowed just a few yards further it would have been the deepest bit. He was defended by that wonderful brief Patrick Back who did so much for us at Parkhurst, and he got a four for manslaughter. It was a couple of months after he was weighed off they found the body of the French girl. She'd just fallen about 300 feet.

There was another body turned up. This time it was in Coniston Water not that long ago. It had been there 21 years and was found by some amateur divers in some plastic sacking and weighted down. The woman had vanished after she'd said she wasn't feeling too good and wanted to stay at home, not go away with her husband and their three kids. When the family comes back she's not there. Once the body turned up the coppers arrested the husband, but there was no evidence against him and although he was charged, the CPS soon chucked their hand in.

One fellow who come a long way to end up in a lake in Lancashire was that Marty Johnstone. He was found by divers in Ecclestone Depth back in October 1979. Someone had taken his hands off but what they should have done is taken the Chinese long life pendant from off his neck. Not that it worked. Johnstone had been a founder member of what was called the Mr Asia drug syndicate which ran out of Australia and the Far East; huge it was. Eventually it was run by a fellow called Alexander Sinclair who was also known as Terence Clark, and when Johnstone'd been caught skimming money to set up his own syndicate he had been killed on Clark's orders.

Clark persuaded Johnstone to go to London to set up a Scottish deal and another bloke, Andy Maher, was to drive him. Once they got near Carnforth Maher had asked him to take over the driving and as he got out of the car he was killed with two bullets to the head. His body was then mutilated but Maher and another man with him, James Smith, forgot to remove the pendant. The body was taken to Ecclestone Depth and rolled down the bank into the water but it caught on a ledge under the surface. When the aqua club members found it they thought it was a tailor's dummy, until they learned better that is.

Clark went down in July 1981, after a 121-day trial and the judge, who was that Rose Heilbron, was told he was worth £25 million, give or take a million or two. During the trial one of the fellows in the dock at Lancaster Castle complained it was cold. 'Not as cold as Mr Johnstone is,' says the pros. Roars of laughter.

Clark was another of those who died in prison. He had a heart attack in Parkhurst. He'd been ducking and diving and there was a story that he'd been taking drugs to try and get himself into the hospital wing so he could get out from there. He might even have been the second man off the island. With his money there'd have been no problem in having a helicopter come for him. The dough was said to be invested in restaurants in Sydney, a silver mine in Indonesia, and Swiss bank accounts. But he won't be using them now. Funnily one of the others in the case got nicked again and was put away last year after a big drugs case.

There was some more people who was cold in Lancaster Castle. Most of a family got wiped out inside a year. It seemed that the first was old man William Bingham, who'd been a sort of caretaker and guide to the castle. He suddenly started having diarrhoea and sickness and he died within the day at the end of January 1911. But when it come to it his daughter Annie had gone the previous November. Then his son James took over being the caretaker and he invited his half-sister Margaret to come and do the housekeeping. She lasted only a few days and died in July. The doctor said it was a brain tumour. James next got hold of his sister, Edith, to do the housekeeping but she was not a success. She's missing a few sandwiches in the picnic basket and she's mucky and stays out all hours, so he gets a Mrs Cox Walker to came and replace her. But before she can do so, down goes James. This time the doctor says it's arsenic. They dig up all the rest and only Annie doesn't have arsenic in her. In them days a coroner's jury could say who the actual killer was and they nominated Edith. There wasn't much against her though. She didn't actually get any benefit from the deaths of her family and she wasn't exactly being put on the street when Mrs Cox Walker come. In those days the pros had to nominate which murder they was going with and they picked the one of James. They could bring evidence of the others in to show method but there was also a bit of trouble showing how she'd actually done Margaret in. Everyone had had some of the same tin of beefsteak for breakfast that day and it hadn't harmed the others. The judge, Avory, was on her side, which must have been about the one time he ever helped anyone out, and she got a not guilty. Most people think she was very lucky at that.

BLACKPOOL

Blackpool was a town and a half, going back. There was a man there, Henry Starr, who got a not guilty first time he was charged with murder, but he never learned his lesson. He did his wife in when she wanted a separation after finding out he'd been seeing other women. Back in 1903 that was; topped in Liverpool. Then that fellow George Joseph Smith, who drowned all his brides in the bath. Did one of them in Regents Road back in 1913 and got £600 insurance for her. His landlady chucked him out but all he did was come down south and swindled a girl in Bournemouth. She was lucky; a century and her clothes and jewellery was all she lost; then it was on to Bath, which was quite appropriate, where he did another.

There was a bit of a sad case a few years after that. A fellow called Frederick Holt killed his sweetheart, Kitty Breaks; shot her on the sand hills at St Annes on Christmas Eve 1919. He'd left his gloves and a revolver near the body and it was easy even in them days to trace his footprints. Next day he called at the hotel where he'd been staying and asked for her. The pros said he'd done it for £5,000 insurance and going to see if she was at the hotel was all part of the plan, but Marshall Hall who defended him reckoned he was off his trolley. He tried to get a verdict that he was unfit to plead but that didn't work. The pros said he was faking it. It didn't help that his family tried to give him an alibi. He got a guilty but then a doctor wrote in and said he'd treated Holt for the syph in Malaya and that he'd thought he was shell-shocked from the War even then. They brought that up in the Court of Appeal but it didn't do any good; the Home Secretary wouldn't give a reprieve. You didn't get reprieved where you'd done someone for money. The story is that after the verdict he just folded the evening paper and put it in his pocket. When he got back to the nick he said, 'Well, that's over now. I hope my tea won't be late.'

Another fellow who passed through the town years later was James Hanratty, the one there's all that fuss over whether he killed Michael Gregsten and shot the girl on the A6. He'd dyed his hair so he wouldn't be recognised but a couple of coppers grabbed him. Last space he walked as a free man. Peter Manuel, who killed all those people up in Scotland, was another. He came to Blackpool to try and make a name for himself just after the War but he didn't last. He got chucked on a burglary but he wasn't trusted there anymore than he was in London. He couldn't keep his yap shut.

It was for a job in Blackpool that James Griffiths got his four following a tie up. He was working with three men from Rochdale and one of them falls over when they get in the house and the gun he's carrying goes off. Griffiths' got a bayonet and he stabs a couple of men but after that he gets a bandage for the man's hand. They cleared £700 but a couple of guns was found in Griffiths' flat. When you think of it four years wasn't bad even though conditions in the nick were so much worse. A ten would be more likely nowadays. As I've said he went on to get off the Isle of Wight.

Just as Brighton was to London, so Blackpool was to both Manchester and Liverpool, although the Liverpool boys really preferred Southport. Blackpool was a short drive away and at one time, just like Brighton, there was a dodgy Chief Constable which meant it was an open town. Stanley Parr, that was his name. There'd been trouble about him being appointed and then he wound up on something like thirty disciplinary charges in the 1950s and got the hoof. I knew him, not well, but he'd drink with the Chaps, just like Ridge did in Brighton, which isn't a good idea when you're the top copper. Good for us mind. He'd straighten things out. Back then top coppers could go hooky without much risk. There wasn't that investigative journalism in them days. The top crime reporters was interested in murderers and there was no TV investigations. Coppers had reporters in their pockets. Look at Percy Hoskins from the *Daily Express*. He used to travel with Fabian so there wasn't much in the way of what you might call critical reporting going on was there?

Blackpool was a town you could work. There was always a lot of punters on the look out for a bargain. I remember in the early 1960s when watches were a bit more scarce than they are today there was a whole lot of Swiss watches on offer. They was smuggled into England, sealed into car bodies or people wearing special waistcoats like they used for gold smuggling a few years later. Then they was dumped in Blackpool and unloaded on the punters. The watches was sold at a fiver each and was worth thirty bob top whack.

There was a hotel there, the Norbreck Hydro. It's very fashionable today. In the '50s, when I'm talking about it, it was reckoned to be the place to go with someone else's wife. You had to sign in and strictly it was an offence if you did it in a false name. There was no sharing rooms then. If you wanted to go case it was a walk along the corridor in your slippers and dressing gown. It wasn't all that odd because in a lot of hotels there wasn't private bathrooms so there was always plenty of people wandering up and down with their spongebags. The story was a bell was rung at 5 a.m. for you to go back to your own room. If it was I never heard it but then I've always been a good sleeper.

One of the best pubs in London for the Chaps was run by Ruby Mancini, one of that big family. They all seemed to be cousins or half-cousins, straight people and all, and they was all over the place. Ruby'd got a pub off the Tottenham Court Road. I can't remember its name. No one ever called it the Queen of Hearts or The Admiral's Head, to the Chaps it was always Ruby's. He used to play the piano marvellously. I think he'd got another place over Paddington way. Then he suddenly sort of retired and went to Blackpool. Bought himself a small hotel there and he was gone.

I met him again after I'd had a bit of an escape. It was after I come out from the receiving of the coins and I was still working. Some of us had a van in our sights over Waterloo way but somehow the coppers got wind of it and nicked two of us. Brian Perry was one of those with me and we were just over there having a look. If it had been right we'd have done it and we'd have slung caution to the winds but it was still really in the planning stages. I wasn't sure the law hadn't seen me and all so I was off. I rang Wally Downes, he's dead now – God rest his soul. He got hold of Louis and Vinnie up in Manchester and I was on my way. When something comes on top like that speed is of the essence. Speed for us and speed for the coppers whilst it's still warm. It's all right if two are nicked but if two more get nicked then someone's bottle may go.

I didn't even go home for a change of clothing. Fortunately I'd got some dough on me. I didn't let anyone drive me. I just got the train and got off the station before Manchester and Vinnie and Louis sent someone to meet me. I was away about three and a half months but by the end I'd started coming down, trying to gee things up for the two who was nicked. If you don't do things yourself and rely on other people they get slack. They think they'll do something the next day when they should be doing it right now. I'm pleased to say the boys got chucked. Billy always used to say that a thief's best partner was himself and he was right. Anyway Vinnie mentioned that Ruby had this hotel and when things was all over Marilyn and I went over there for a break and he remembered me. We had a really good time.

I liked Abie Tobias. Abie come from Manchester and then he went to Blackpool. He was a top man in the town. One of Abie's daughters had been walking out with a copper and the man got called in to say he shouldn't have no more to do with her; not because Abie was a villain, which he was, but because he was Jewish. Think of that for prejudice.

It was Abe who had good connections with London and he put up a lot of screwings. He had the Continental Café in the town at the time. He come undone with one at the end of November 1953 though, when he had Alfred Curtis from Waterloo and Siddy Golder from King's Cross come up to Blackpool with Danny Swain and another bloke, to do the wrestler Jack Pye's drum in Cornwall Avenue on the North Shore. Danny was the driver, of course.

Jack used to wrestle most Friday nights at the Empire Stadium in Liverpool and they knew he'd be out of the way. After that he'd look in on his club, the Horseshoe, in Dickson Road. What they had to do is make sure his boy Dominic, who lived in the same house, was out of the way as well. They knew he'd go to Leslie's Bar at the Metropole and they found out he was wrestling over in Rochdale so he was gone as well. He was a big man, bigger than his father, and he was strong. He was dangerous when he'd been drinking as well. He turned a man's car over on the promenade once because he was annoyed with him. It was Dominic that Owen Ratcliffe was chasing when he fired a shot in the ceiling of the Horseshoe. Poor Dominic, he topped himself a few years later.

Abe and the others piled tyres in the place and coats to muffle the sound and they got the safe with Pye's money and savings certificates out. They also took a mink stole with them. What they didn't know was there was a bottle of haircream in the safe. The trouble was Abe's car had been seen by a copper who wrote the number down. Abe's brief come a tumble over that at the trial. He asked the copper why he'd noted Abe's number down in particular and the copper replied that all of them was under instructions to make a note of where they saw Abe or his car. Danny did the 19 miles to a farm near Preston, where they was to unlock the safe, in 36 minutes, but once they go there they couldn't get any keys to work. They had to rip the front off and the fellow whose place it was noticed the bottle of haircream. Pye always had long black hair and he'd put the haircream on in the ring to annoy people, and make sure it never got pulled too strong as well.

Anyway Pye gets the word that Abe's had something to do with the screwing and he takes Dominic and a couple of brothers and the old boxer, Paddy McGrath, round to the Continental for a chat. You can imagine what that was like. Abe gets humpy and says Pye isn't going about it the right way and that if he'd approached him properly he might have been able to help. At the court Pye was asked why he'd gone mob handed and that's another mistake. He says it's because Abe runs with the London mob and they've always got guns. After that it's all on top. Abe's in custody and he and Siddy get sent up the Assizes for the screwing, and Alf goes up as well on a conspiracy charge.

Danny was never nicked and he did what he could whilst he was out. One of the pros' witnesses was in the nick and Danny posed as his brother and got to see him at Lewes. Said there was a cow's calf down and another £50 after the trial if he changed his evidence. It didn't do no good. Once the trial was running you could see where was it was going. There was just too much for Abie to get over. He said the copper couldn't have seen his car because it was parked at the café. That was about the strength of his alibi. The judge asks him how many witnesses have been wrong about him during the trial and Abe says 'About six'. He got a seven and Siddy a six. Alf got a three. I was in the nick at the time but it wasn't long after I saw both Abie and Siddy in Dartmoor, where I heard all about it.

Another of Abe's daughters, Sheila, married Georgie Porritt and she got herself in all sorts of trouble. Georgie had a great escape when in May 1961 he killed his stepfather and was nearly topped for it. He'd got involved with Florence 'Fluffy' Copeland, who was the former girlfriend of Edwin Copley who we called Cadillac Johnny. Poor old Johnny had killed himself when he crashed at 75 mph in a chase over Tower Bridge. She'd taken up with what the Copleys saw as one of their rivals. There was a quarrel between her and one of the Copleys in the Manor House Club near Wrotham down in Kent and later that night, so the pros said, six armed men came to the Porritt home. George had always been keen on guns and he's got quite a few. He reckoned they was attacking his stepfather and so he shot at them, missed and topped his dad. And, of course, they did him for capital murder.

He got convicted at the Bailey but the jury recommended mercy. George was sentenced to be hanged at Wandsworth Prison in the July. Thankfully, when it come to it, the scragsman didn't get his fee. Fluffy did a lot of good work collecting signatures for the reprieve and the Copleys, give them their credit, joined in. They said they hadn't nothing against George and it was his stepfather who was the trouble.

In fact his appeal was allowed on the day before he was due to hang. Neither the pros nor the defence had raised the question of manslaughter and the court said that was no reason why the judge shouldn't have done it himself. So George got a manslaughter and ten years to go with it.

Fluffy went back to her own people and whilst he was on the Moor in March 1963 George married Abie's Sheila. That didn't turn out too well when it come to it. She was later convicted as the driver in a wages snatch back in Manchester. What she'd done was taken her kid from a former relationship along with her because she could not find a childminder. Later she did find a minder for an evening and paid her £2 out of some of the stolen money. It was traced and she picked up five years whilst others in the team drew up to fifteen. One of them, Albert Reddans, one of the brothers from Canning Town, collected ten years and this got made consecutive to another ten he'd collected the previous month. Albert put it about on that television programme *Hard Bastards*, which Kate Kray ran, that he'd chinned me in the nick. His memory must be going. Albert wasn't really a great credit to himself. He got stabbed. I thought it was in Reading, which made it appropriate but Charlie Richardson said it was Gartree. Anyway he went and gave evidence against the people who done him. He chinned Charlie in Durham in the security wing but it was in front of three screws so Charlie never got the chance to retaliate. As for chinning me it never happened. If he had done it would have been the talk of the nick.

It was George Porritt's brother, Roy, who worked with us in Atlantic Machines, the one-arm bandits Eddie Richardson and I ran. I still think that fight in Mr Smith's Club in March 1965 was because one of the Haywards had been having it off with Roy's wife. Seeing me and Eddie and Roy in the club together with him meant we was going to have some words over it. I'll never know now. What I do know is that I wasn't the one who killed Dickie Hart. I know who did but I've never said and I still won't; though I was charged I was found not guilty. Good luck to the man.

I haven't heard of Abe Tobias in years. There was a story he'd gone to Israel and it might be right. All I know is he'd be nearly ninety if he's still alive.

I knew Freddie Sewell quite well. A few years earlier and he'd have swung, no questions asked. He came from South London and he got life for killing a copper in the town. It was meant to be a routine job. He and four others go up North to do a jewellers in The Strand, what they call the Golden Mile; 23 August 1971 it was. They reckoned they'd get around £100,000 but one of the staff in the joint manages to set the alarm off and from then it's all on top. They hadn't noticed the sales manager get into the back office. They was still just about putting the jewels in bags when the coppers arrived. There was a chase and one copper was shot in the leg and another in the chest. Then a Superintendent Gerald

Richardson goes after Freddie and pulls him down. That's when the gun goes off and the copper is hit in the stomach. Freddie managed to reach the getaway car and was driven off in the boot.

Fred gets away down South but, of course, half the country's looking for him and there's rewards all over the place, including one from one of the newspapers putting up ten grand so its only a matter of time before he's given up. People didn't get out of the country then as they do now so someone was always going to lolly him if he stayed here. Lolly him they did. The coppers found him in Birnham Road, Holloway at the beginning of October and it was back to Blackpool. He got a recommendation that he do thirty years. The story was that a club owner put him away hoping to get a bit of rest from the coppers but you never know. There's another story that it was the well-known grass, Philly Herbert, who put a handful of people away including his parents over the years. That's the sort of son you want to have.

Of course, Fred wasn't going to get any sympathy from anyone and there was reports in the papers about how he was looking bruised when he comes to court the first time but no one said anything about it. Just a few days before he was nicked Arthur Skingle had picked up life, and the judge said that should mean life, after he went down for shooting a copper in Reading. Peter Sparrow who was with him got a recommendation of 25 years. After his conviction Fred ends up as a waxwork in the Chamber of Horrors at Louis Tussaud's on the Central Beach.

Years ago if you was a good murderer and you was convicted you went straight into Madame Tussaud's in Baker Street in the Chamber of Horrors. There was a sort of jury box with all the old villains like Charlie Peace and others who'd been topped in it; all looking out and serious, as well they might. Many of them was in their own clothes because the firm used to try and buy them to make it more realistic. There was one fellow who sued for libel when they made a waxwork of him. He was a con man, William Monson, and he was well connected. Back in 1893 he'd done in a fellow called Cecil Hambrough whose investments he was meant to be looking after. Hambrough was suspicious Monson was helping himself, and first Monson tipped him out of a boat but the man swum to shore. The next day the pair and another fellow went out shooting; the target was Hambrough. Monson got that funny not proven verdict you can get in Scotland and when his figure was put in the Chamber of Horrors he sued. He won but he got a farthing damages and had to pay the costs. I've said before that when the likes of us sue it generally doesn't do any good. Anyway, it was a couple of years later Monson turns up at the Old Bailey and gets a five over a share fraud.

It's amazing how many people do for themselves by opening their traps. I suppose it's human nature to boast but if you're thinking of killing someone it doesn't help you if you go around spouting away before you've done it. I can't think how many times the pros has brought in evidence remarks about how husbands was saying they'd do their wives and wouldn't mind swinging for it. Which as a rule is just what they did. That Louisa Merrifield was one. If she hadn't opened her big mouth she might be alive today. Well, hardly since she'd be just about a hundred, but you know what I mean.

In March 1953 she'd only just got married – the third time it was – to a man much older than herself. She'd been married before the War to a Joseph Ellison and they lived quite comfortably – an eight-room house near Wigan. She was some-thing of a party girl because she had four kids and they all got took into care. She'd done a bit of bird just after the War, something to do with ration books. The authorities liked a few convictions for that sort of thing. It kept everyone toeing the line. Then her first husband died in 1949 and she starts talking to old Alfred Merrifield who's 79. He was a patient in the same hospital as Joseph, but he's not husband No. 2 though, because she marries a fellow called Richard Weston who's a year younger than him. It seems she wasn't after him for his money, only his pension, but he didn't last long. Ten weeks later he's had a heart attack and now it's Alfred's turn. They got jobs as housekeepers and caretakers and it was about job number twenty in Blackpool when she latched on to a Sarah Ricketts in Devonshire Road in the town.

The old girl must have liked her because within a fortnight she made her will in favour of Mrs Merrifield and Alfred. Next thing is Mrs M. opens her trap and tells a friend she and her husband have come into the bungalow worth £4,000 and the old girl has died leaving it to them. The trouble was she wasn't dead for another three days. Mrs Merrifield kept on though. She told a friend she has to lay the old girl out and when the friend asked how long she'd been dead Mrs M. replies she isn't but it won't be long. Mrs Merrifield was all for trying to get her cremated but the doctors called for a postmortem. You've got to give her credit for a bit of style. She had the Sally Ann band come and play 'Abide With Me' outside the bungalow. Rat poison was what the doctors said, and not only does she open her mouth but she kept the spoon in her bag. It's like I say, people are so confident they think no one will find out.

The funny thing was that poor old Alfred gets nicked. He's allowed to see her in the cells when she's waiting to be committed and next thing he's in the dock with her. From what I heard and read she made a bad witness, arguing and boasting. There was the question of why they hadn't called a doctor and Mrs Merrifield said she didn't like going out on the streets late at night and Alfred said he was crippled which he wasn't. She never fancied she was going to get a guilty but she did and she was topped in the September. The jury failed to agree about Alfred and he was let go. He stuck it out, claiming a share in the house and eventually he got a sixth of its value, provided he left the place straight off. The story is he told a reporter, 'The old bugger was going to do me next.'

NORTH

The more I think back to the people who was reprieved and who wasn't, the less I understand how the decisions were reached. There was a couple of cases up in Lancashire just about the same time which could have gone either way. It was in 1964 and first there was Joe Masters who got done for the murder of an old age pensioner in Clitheroe, a bit outside Preston. Straightforward robbery it was. He'd got a bit of form for violence as well. Knocked the old boy down and he hit his head. At the trial he said he was only there to borrow money, not to steal anything, but since he was wearing gloves that didn't do him any good. Then suddenly he gets a reprieve. It was just about the time that topping was coming to an end and people thought if Masters wasn't going to swing then you wouldn't put money on anyone swinging ever again. Maybe what saved him was he was only 22. Not that over the years many people younger than that haven't gone down.

But there was a couple more. Peter Allen and Gwynne Owen Evans swung on the same day – 13 August 1964; unlucky for them. They'd done a man John West in Kings Avenue, Workington, not far from Carlisle where the pubs used to be owned and run by the Government. Again it was a robbery. They were behind with the rent and they'd got to pay fines of a tenner each in Preston. Evans, I think it was, knew the old boy and thought he'd got a bit of money. They went to see him in the middle of the night. Evans got the man to let them in and then they did him with an iron bar and stabbed him. Completely botched job it was. Just as if they'd said come and find us. Evans left behind his mac, together with a Royal Life Saving Society medallion with his name on it. They didn't get any money even, although there was a fair bit hidden. It was only a question of time before the coppers picked them up. Each blamed the other for hitting him with the iron bar but the jury convicted them both.

You'd have thought they might be reprieved because they weren't much older than Joe Masters, and Allen had young kids.

You were never told you hadn't been reprieved until right near the end. There was some baloney about it being kinder to let people go on hoping until the last possible moment. Allen was topped at Walton and Evans at Strangeways.

From what I heard, at the last meeting Allen had with his wife he really went berserk and smashed the bullet-proof glass, just like my friend Nicky Carley did when his girlfriend came and told him she'd met another man. Mind you, I don't like giving that Governor Lawton credit but he did good then. Carley was doing something like a ten and Lawton could have sent him outside for punishment which could have added another five, but he didn't. He kept it to the Visiting Magistrates. Just about the only bit of compassion he must have ever showed.

Everyone had closed visits in them days. Screws would pace up and down outside the booths. You were meant to get half an hour but they'd shave it down to twenty minutes or even less if they could. You might get an open visit if someone had died. Dartmoor and Parkhurst was the only places you got open visits. You might be allowed a kiss and a cuddle at the end. After all, when Doreen come to see me she'd had a three-day journey, there and back. It was expensive and all. Princetown Station had closed down and when you got off the stop after Exeter you had to get a cab. It was a thing for a man to get a visit. Outside working parties would wave and cheer it was so rare.

Evans and Allen went in the record books as the last men to be hanged in England but, of course, they didn't live to know it. Funny, the hangman in Evans' case was also called Allen.

I read the other day there's a proposal to sell off the old prisons to raise money for modern ones. The idea is people will buy them for lofts and things. I wonder what they're going to do about the bodies. There's got to be around a hundred each in most of the prisons where there was topping. I suppose they'll have to notify the relatives. It's only, what? a bit under forty years since Allen and Evans, and there were a good few just before them. It's likely the wives of some of these men will have moved away from the area and maybe re-married. Some of them may have changed their names. They'll have kids by new partners and there'll be grandchildren. It's going to be a bit embarrassing if they get asked what they want done with the bodies. The grandkids may have been told Grandpa was lost at sea. Now they'll find out he was lost at Swansea, or wherever.

LIVERPOOL

The only time I put my flame thrower to use was over some people from Liverpool who was troubling the James's and their Kingsway Club in Southport. Not that the James's knew I was going to use it, nor anyone else for that matter. They'd have said 'Lay off Frank'.

We'd had a bit of trouble before with local people throwing their weight about at the James's. That was when there was a fight with Peter Ioannides in a club up there. He got a bit lippy and Eddie had to sort him out. As we was driving off some heavies chased after us and set a dog on us, but we sort of kidnapped it, put it in the car and only let it out when we'd gone a few hundred yards. As I've said before Eddie was nicked over it and John James was nicked for a thing a bit earlier when I'd done a few people. Fortunately it all blew over at the magistrates' court.[1]

I'd got the flame thrower from a friend, a real craftsman he was. If you couldn't get a silencer for a gun he could make something which would cut the sound, make keys, that sort of thing. He never charged me; he just wanted to know it would be used well. So when there was people causing trouble at the club I said I'd come up and meet them on the seafront late one night. They turned up and there was just me and my flame thrower. I didn't talk to them, it was just bosh. It stopped them in their tracks. Monty would have been proud of me. A couple of them was quite badly singed but they was straight up people, good men really. It was between us. They didn't go to the bogeys and after that they left the club alone. I think they spread the word because we never had any trouble again anywhere in the North.

The James's looked after us when we was in the nick over the Torture Trial and the Parkhurst Riot. Every month there was my money on the table and that's how Doreen was able to pay for the house in Hove and keep herself and Francis all those years. They was good. They could easily have said, 'On your bike', and I couldn't have done nothing. In fact it wouldn't have been fair for

---

[1] See *Mad Frank*.

me even to think about it; I wasn't doing anything for them in return. When Eddie got out before me they suggested they give us a lump sum and I agreed, but what good people.

It was even funnier because years earlier Bert Marsh, who was Darby Sabini's right-hand man for years and who organised the bullion raid at Croydon Airport, had stuck up a caravan for us at Porthcawl, but when me and Billy Blythe – God rest his soul – got there we found the place deserted. Just as well because we didn't know it belonged to one of the James's. In fact it was Bert Marsh's mate Bert Wilkins who put them in touch with us later when they was having their trouble.

There's been some good men from Liverpool over the years, including the Grimwood family. It was Billy Grimwood who did for Amies in the Crow's Nest in the city. Amies was a right dog. He wasn't called The Snake for nothing. He was that copper Tony Lundy's man and he was one of the first supergrasses. Amies was a half iron and he was a really nasty robber. He was into what you'd call home invasions and he'd threaten to cut the victim's balls off or to rape the guy's daughter. He got nicked up in Liverpool with a hardman from there, John Tremarco, and back in October 1977 he pleads guilty. Then he comes to London and starts grassing everyone in sight. After that it's back to Liverpool to be weighed off with thanks from the judge for all his help. He's with some coppers and the night before he's due in court he wants to go and have a drink. It was quite usual with grasses. Keep them sweet was the motto. He and the copper who was actually with him went to the Crow's Nest and got a right beating. When it come to it Tremarco drew a fifteen. They brought Amies back to London and he only served something like a two. The last I heard he'd disappeared and was dead of natural causes, whatever that may mean.

There's been lots of dodgy cases in Liverpool over the years going right back to that Mrs Maybrick who was meant to have done her husband in 1889. A few years ago someone found a diary which was meant to have been written by him and they reckon it shows he was Jack the Ripper. But then there's people who says it was done with the wrong ink and anyway it doesn't really give no details which someone couldn't have got from the papers. Poor old Mrs Maybrick was one of them women in Victorian times who's meant to have killed her old man by giving him arsenic. One of her problems was they found out she'd been having it off with a bloke and that was put up as a motive. It didn't matter that Maybrick spent a good lot of his time with brasses; Victorian women didn't do that sort of thing, and if they did and was caught, well it was too bad for them. It was a funny case because most people thought she was going to get a not guilty and crowds turned up to cheer her, but at the end the judge, who was called Stephens, went against her and swayed the jury. She got a reprieve but Queen Victoria wouldn't have her released. It seems she was still in love with Prince Albert and thought that women who topped their husbands should suffer like she did. Once Victoria was dead they let Mrs Maybrick out in 1904 and she went to America. Funnily the judge went into an asylum within a couple of years of the case, and there's some people who say it was his son who was Jack the Ripper. It goes round in circles don't it?

It's funny how you could get topped because someone's hat got knocked off but that's what happened just before the First World War. December 1913 it was. A seaman, Walter Eaves, was standing waiting for his girl outside a shop in Old Hall Street and the wind caused a blind to come down and put a dent in his new hat. The next thing an assistant, George Ball, comes out to put the blind back up and Eaves demands compensation for his hat. Ball goes back and comes out with two shillings. Later Eaves sees Ball and another man pushing a cart with something in a tarpaulin and they look like they're making heavy weather of it. Next morning the owner of the shop, Catherine Bradfield, is found in the Liverpool–Leeds canal and Eaves puts two and two together. The coppers got onto the other assistant, Samuel Eltof, and he coughed straight away. Said it was because the woman had been always on at them. Ball disappeared and there was all sorts of advertisements on cinema screens asking where he was.

He was found as he left a football match a week later. He put up a wonderful fanny. Him and Sam had been threatened by a man who'd killed the owner and who was going to kill them if they didn't get rid of the body. The only trouble with that was that Eaves, who was a big man, was right outside the shop and they could have asked for help. In fact Ball had come out and paid him the money for his hat whilst the gunman was supposed to be in the shop. It didn't help that when Ball was nicked he was wearing the woman's watch. They topped him of course. The other kid, who was reckoned to be simple minded, got a few years as an accessory.

The Court of Appeal's never done me any good in the way of quashing my convictions and the only time I ever got any time off was when they knocked a year off my receiving the coins after I come out from the twenty. Sometimes I think, and I'm not alone, that they're there to try and uphold as many convictions as they can. They had that rule called the proviso which allowed them to do just about anything they wanted. They could say that the judge shouldn't have allowed the confession to come in or should have warned the jury about taking the word of a grass more strongly than he did; but when it come to it they applied the proviso – said it wouldn't have made any difference and you'd have been convicted just the same. Look at some of the things the judges have said. Take Lord Denning, who was meant to be the most humane judge ever. What does he say in the Birmingham Six case? It's better that a few Irishmen stay in gaol rather than it turns out the police have been corrupt. And that Lord Lane, who said that the longer they went on hearing the Birmingham Six appeal the more convinced they was that the men had done it. Then, of course, it comes down like a pack of cards on their heads.

Still it must be better than nothing. It all started out with that Adolf Beck at the beginning of the last century. He got convicted a couple of times of getting money out of women by false pretences. Someone was picking up these high class brasses and swindling them out of their money. He couldn't persuade anyone he wasn't the man even though the fellow was Jewish and Beck had never had his thin and thick snipped. He did over five years in the days when sentences really was sentences. We've all got to be grateful to him because after what happened they set up the Court of Criminal Appeal. That's what it was called then.

There's one man must have been really grateful and it's funny how the Court went his way. That was William Wallace who got convicted of killing his wife, Julia. I suppose it's just about the classic case in Britain; people are still writing books about it. In the early 1930s it was. It was really big; all over the papers. He was an insurance agent, a sort of the man from the Pru. who lived in Woolverton Street, Anfield. He was a member of the local chess club which played at a café in the city centre. Anyway, one night there's a phone message left for him at the club. Would he go the next night to Menelove Gardens East for a bit of business? The man said he wanted to arrange some insurance for his daughter. He gave the name Qualtrough. Sure enough, Wallace goes off the next evening but he can't find Menelove Gardens East. He asks around, including a policeman, and he makes a remark about the time. Later the pros said that he was setting up the alibi. There were a West and a North but no East, so he gives up and goes home, where he finds someone's bashed Julia to death and stolen £4 from the house.

Like it usually is, it was a question of look at the husband. The coppers, who were known as Jacks in Liverpool in them days, sets out to prove that he'd made the phone call himself to set up an alibi. One of the things they was able to prove was that the call to the club come from a box near where Wallace lived. The coppers said that as a local man who went round the city on business Wallace should have known there was no Gardens East and he'd set the whole thing up. The coppers were given the name Springheeled Jacks after *That Springheeled Jack*, a well-known Victorian melodrama that Tod Slaughter used to put on and tour with, about a man who could leap over walls and attacked people, because of the way they ran round Liverpool trying to show he could get to Menelove Gardens and back and do his wife in the time.

Anyway, he come up at the Assizes and the great thing was the pros couldn't really show a motive. There wasn't a bit on the side, and no one was saying she was having it off either so there was no story of revenge. There wasn't any blood all over the place, only a tiny bit in the lavatory pan. There's no question that forensics was as good then as they are now but you'd have expected to find some traces. There was theories that he'd done it naked and then had a bath or he'd wore a mac but no one ever found any wet towels and they never found the murder weapon. There was a kid who said he'd seen Mrs Wallace half an hour later than the pathologist said she died, but people said that was Wallace dressed up in her clothes. There's no doubt a lot of the town was against him.

He goes down but the Court of Appeal did something they've never done before, and that's say they wasn't happy with the verdict. Nothing wrong with the summing-up or anything but they just wasn't happy and they let him go. People in the neighbourhood didn't like it though and he moved down the road to Fleetwood; he died a couple of years later. He always said he knew who'd done it. There was a fellow called Parry who'd worked with him and who Wallace had got the sack after the fellow was caught nicking some of the money. He always said it was revenge. Parry denied it when people asked him and he'd got an alibi, but a few years later that fell a bit apart. He died a bit ago and so I suppose we'll never know, but it's not often you get a murder with two good suspects like that. There's been plenty of books and stuff been written trying to prove it was Wallace or that he was innocent and it was Parry really.

The most famous copper in Liverpool a bit before and after the War was probably Herbert Balmer. He'd been in the Navy before he becomes a bogey. He had three big cases and there's still trouble going on about one if not two of them. The third was much more straightforward.

There was still some racecourse trouble going on. The Sabinis wasn't as interested as they had been but there was always money to be made and, of course, the Grand National was the big thing at Aintree. There used to be flat racing there but that was stopped after that jockey, Doug Smith, nearly got killed in a fall. There was also motor racing but that was stopped after a couple of years. That was after the War of course. Just before it there was protection going on up there, according to Balmer.

He reckoned there was a gang of Australians, which was a bit funny, and another gang led by a Colonel from down South –

Colonel in the criminal sense like Ronnie that is. Balmer reckoned that any trouble would occur after the National was run at a time when the crowds would begin to leave the course without waiting to see the remaining races. He was right. Him and his men found a couple of bookies been slashed. One had eighteen stitches and the other fifteen. Apparently at first they was staunch, saying it was their own fault and they should have paid, but he leaned on them a bit. Then nicked the Colonel and there was a big fight with Balmer's coat getting slashed. After that the Colonel asked him if he couldn't make it a case for the local beaks, which would have made six months max, but Balmer got him four years.

I don't know if that story was true but I do know that Charlie Wooder, who was from Little Cross Street in Islington, Jimmy's older brother I think, got six months in 1937 for being at the bottle. That was more or less the standard sentence. A carpet or half a stretch and you could reckon on the second if you was caught working on Derby Day or the Grand National. There used to be special magistrates' courts set up behind the stands to deal with the dips.

In fact there don't seem to be as many at the bottle today. It's become more a black crime. Them and foreigners. You'd think people would still fancy it what with the stuff the mugs carry on them. In the old days the bottle mobs like the Titanics from Hoxton would go out twenty handed and work trains or football crowds. If they're caught it's only three or six months and it's worth it. What ripped the arse out of the bottlers was the Criminal Justice Act 1948 when if you was over thirty and had three previous you could get eight years PD at the snap of fingers. The law come in April 1949 and it slowed people down, but a lot of the bottlers worked until middle age and later. Old Dodger Mullins was working until he was well in his sixties.

It was never my game although I went out once or twice. It was during the War and the bottle mob would come into the 21 Club in Clapham High Street or The Bungalow of an evening and when I'd had a drink I went with them, more or less for a laugh. I was the stall. The person who'd bump into them or stand behind them, but it wasn't for me. You needed long fingers and the best were the ones whose first and middle fingers was just about the same length. Bottling was at its peak then. Every big city had at least one good bottle mob. There was no unemployed so wallets was full, and there was the blackout to help you, but it wasn't for me.

Of course just like London and the other cities with docks which got blitzed Liverpool was fair game for the likes of us. There was food shortages and it was easy to get rid of stolen goods. Then because of the poor street lighting it wasn't too difficult for the dippers and the rollers to work. There was a lot of gang fighting around Park Lane, Paradise Street and Back George Street. Sailors was being lured out of the safe haven of milk bars and the YMCA with the offers of visits to illegal drinking clubs and, as a result, being rolled on the way to a girl's flat.

There was a lot of gangs after the War as well. If you've got docks you've got brasses for the seamen, and there was one lot used to work near the Adelphi hotel – that place they had a series about on television a few years back. Big Victorian pile it was but it's been done up now. And of course Lime Street was famous worldwide amongst sailors I should think. There was that song 'Maggie May' about a brass who worked Lime Street. Just like Piccadilly down South. If you wanted a cup of tea at a stall outside Lime Street station at the end of the War you had to pay 5d deposit on the cup. There weren't any saucers. Even so the geezer that run it reckoned he lost about sixty a week.

There was thought to be 200 gangs in the city just after the War but of course they might just have had two or three people in them. It was the conviction of George Kelly which broke a lot of them up, but even so there was still a good few about. One was called the Peanut Gang, which started off nicking peanuts from bags on the docks and went on from there. They became big in muggings. There was also a good network which smuggled a wanted man from family to family keeping him on the move the whole time. Then there was the Throstles, into mugging sailors having it away with the brasses. What's got to be remembered also is that people in Liverpool didn't like the police. They remembered when they was charged by police with batons in motorcycle sidecars. There'd also been a lot of religious trouble up there as well. I never really worked with the Liverpool boys. It was much more Manchester for me, but since I was in the nick in Walton with them for so long over the years I heard a lot of what had gone on.

One crime in Liverpool which never really caught on down in London was taking grids off the Nat Gonellas and getting in through them so as to screw the houses. It must have run for forty or fifty years from the 1920s. It seems the householders either did not have them mended when the grids rusted or that coalmen failed to put them properly back in place. You have to think some of the coalmen was in on it. Of course it wasn't very different from the time when 'Tom Thumb' Brindle and the others got done when they bashed the coppers after they found them getting into the cellar of the Duke of Clarence in Walworth. There was Whippo Brindle and Jimmy, Eva's husband, and there was Billy Holmes and Jimmy Robson. They took their chance when the road was being done up. The nick was only just up the road and someone must have had a dog and belled them. Jimmy Robson got a two and Jimmy Brindle, Borstal. 'Whippo' Brindle got eighteen months; he should have had the biggest because he had form but he wasn't fool enough to call out 'I think you've made a mistake'. The Clarence has been closed a few years now but it was big in its day. We never screwed houses like that though.

In those days if you got two years you had to accept that you was going to lose a month's remission and it was no use getting the hump. Petty things, talking in the workshop, not doing your sewing in your cell. Five days here, three days there, it all added up. If you got a three years' PS then you had to reckon on at least three months' loss. It was par for the course.

The first of Balmer's big cases was the Cameo Cinema murder which broke the so-called Kelly gang; there's still an argument about it today. George Kelly was a local face who'd deserted from the Navy. He'd been the barker for an escapologist before he took up running a string of girls. There was the usual game of getting a girl to go with a fellow and whilst the man was having an upright or thinking he was going to get one in an alley, doing him. Usually the girl was in on it but later in the 1980s there was people who'd just frightened the girl and make her go along. Cocky Warren was one of them. Funny, he sent me a card a bit before he got nicked in Holland over a load of drugs. By then he was stone rich, one of the richest faces in England the papers said.

But going back to Kelly, he'd done a three for desertion and also a bit for assault and receiving as well. He was a bit like me. His first conviction came when he was ten. He was always good with his fists as well. He had another line with his girls; he was one of the first to get them into cars. He took about three-quarters of their earnings and the brasses was also expected to steer punters into clip joints where they would be overcharged for their drinks. Unlike the near beer joints in Soho the men could get what they was paying for because there was often a couple of rooms at the back of the joint. He was in the nick with me when I was in Walton just after the War.

Kelly was always putting up jobs, a bit of a blagging here, what they'd now call a steaming at a funfair over in New Brighton there, that sort of thing – doing over a cab driver they thought was a grass. But what he and a fellow Charles Connolly finally settled on was a snatch at the Cameo Cinema, Wavertree.

It seems like it was Connolly who originally suggested nicking the takings from the picture place. They wanted a gun to put the frighteners on the manager and Kelly went out and got one. There was a raft of them floating around at that time what with the end of the War. The next evening Kelly and Connolly went to the cinema. Connolly remained outside and Kelly goes up the stairs to the office and tries to blag the takings from the manager. He's having nothing of it and Kelly shoots him, and the assistant manager and all. Now he in a panic and he drops the bag of money he's snatched. On his way out he was seen by Patrick Griffith, the cinema fireman.

Connolly was long gone by the time Kelly got down the stairs. He's gone at the sound of the first shot. So Kelly's now got to start to put an alibi together and he goes into the Leigh Arms and buys a drink for a fellow he hardly knows. If you're going to do that sort of thing you've got to pick a fellow you know's going to stand up and is one of the Chaps. Of course this man isn't. He's straight and he tells the court Kelly was so out of breath and nervous he asks him if he's been in a fight. Kelly says he had. By now Connolly's pushed off to meet up with his wife and sisters in a local dance hall.

The next day the papers were full of the news. Connolly's bottle has more or less gone because it's a topping matter for him as well and he says he wants to get out of the country. The real trouble, so far as they are concerned, is there's a few hangers-on who really don't have any bottle either. One of the girls who was around Kelly was a Jackie Dickson who was with a fellow, Jimmy Northam, known as Stuttie. He'd got a speech impediment; he'd been hit on the head when he'd been rolling servicemen. Another fellow I knew who had an impediment after being hit on the head was Bobby Maynard who went down for the Torso case in the 1970s with Reggie Dudley. He really could hardly speak for years but I'm pleased to say he's better now, and best of all the court threw out their convictions this July.

Then there was a girl Marjorie Dawson, called Norwegian Marjorie. Kelly'd been flashing the gun around in a pub and she'd told him to put it away but he'd loaded it there and then. She'd given over a green apron for him to wear as a mask and Stuttie had put up his raincoat. You can see where it all went wrong. Far too many people involved who don't have to be and who may not stand up.

Now Kelly's got to put the frighteners on Stuttie Northam and Jackie Dickson and he says they'll get a seeing to from his brothers if they should open their traps. Shortly after this is when Norwegian Marjorie tops herself. It's then Northam and Dickson decide to write to the police and although they don't put up names that gives Balmer something to go on. They wanted immunity and that's what they got – if they agreed the police was to put an ad in the local paper saying 'Promise' or something like that, and they did.

Even before the letter Balmer's been rounding up the usual suspects and he'd had Kelly in but he's put up an alibi from his girlfriend and for the moment it's stuck. One thing the fireman was sure was that the man had very dark eyebrows and that's what Kelly's got. Meanwhile Dickson and Stuttie have pushed off to Manchester. Not all that far but far enough for the moment, and it wasn't for six months that the coppers found them and Stuttie put up the names Balmer wanted.

If ever a brief fought hard it was that Rose Heilbron, who later became a High Court Judge. It was the first time a woman had led in a murder case but there was a prejudice against women briefs in them days. There really still is now. Kelly's meant to have said 'I want no Judy defending me' but when it come to it he couldn't have done better. If anyone ever tried, she did.

There really wasn't much evidence against Kelly and even less against Connolly. There was a bit of ID and of course Jackie Dickson and Stuttie. But out of the woodwork comes a prisoner who says both Kelly and Connolly had talked about the murder and how Connolly said he'd run away and Kelly had put up a moody alibi. All three witnesses, Northam, Dickson and this fellow Graham, told the court how frightened they were of reprisals from Kelly's family and friends, and Stuttie and his girlfriend wouldn't even write down their addresses for the judge. It makes it look good for the pros when something like that happens.

Then it all comes on top for Connolly and his alibi was broken. He said he had been at a dance hall from about 8.20 in the evening and that his wife had joined him twenty minutes later. He also said he had entered a rumba competition and his wife, two of his sisters and their friends all put him in the dance hall before the murder was committed. What happens is the MC is sure that Connolly hadn't arrived until after the pubs closed. He remembered Connolly because he'd been wearing his hat on the dance floor and had been told to take it off.

For the time it was the longest trial they'd had in Britain. It lasted thirteen days and after four hours the jury said they couldn't agree. Now, of course, they could have thirteen nights in a hotel. It was then the prosecution had the bright idea of trying the men separately and the re-trial was fixed for a week later. One of the reasons was it was said that Jackie Dickson was dying.

This time the jury was only a bit under an hour before they put Kelly away. It often happens in a re-trial. It looks so good the first time round but the pros has learned by its mistakes for the second go and there's nothing to surprise them with. You're stuck with what you've got. Kelly was found guilty of murder – a decision in which the judge said he heartily concurred. Northam and Dickson each received £20 reward from the court.

Miss Heilbron did what she could. She went to the Court of Criminal Appeal saying that because there was a juryman who had a felony conviction the trial was a nullity and the conviction should be quashed. It come before Goddard and it certainly wasn't going to work with him. Kelly was topped in March 1950 at Walton Prison. Connolly pleaded to the robbery and got a ten. They dropped the murder.

There's been a lot of trouble over that case with allegations that Balmer leaned on and then coached his witnesses. There's plenty of briefs and a few old time coppers up there who would say Balmer wasn't straight, and I reckon they'd be right.

In a way the fact that Kelly wasn't too pleased to get a woman brief wasn't surprising. There just wasn't any around. I think Miss Heilbron was about the only one doing big crime. There was a few that did civil work – divorce and things like that – but otherwise the chances were that the solicitor you had might have a girl receptionist but even that wasn't always the case. I think if I'd had a woman brief turn up I'd have had the wind knocked out of my sails. I'd have said politely, 'No thanks, I'll wait until Mr Smith can get here.' It seems ridiculous when you think now how many of the top briefs are women but that was how it was in my day. You'd imagine the beak and the pros would have been treading all over her. It was bad enough having a really experienced man for you, let alone a young woman who didn't have the experience. The coppers would have been sneering at her. The brain trembles at the thought of it. Now, if you said no, they'd do you for discrimination. That's where the world's changed.

There was one woman magistrate appointed about that time and that was Sybil Campbell, who used to sit at Tower Bridge; she was a terror. She'd really hand it out to shoplifters but she must have liked the Chaps because she gave me and the others bail after we'd done the Town Hall in Dagenham and there'd been a chase through the Rotherhithe Tunnel. I turned up, of course. It was a matter of honour but, if I'm honest, there was also a question of finding the dough to give the fellow who was standing surety and who'd have to pay up if you went on your toes. If he couldn't pay then it was often him who went away for a few weeks.

Getting back to Balmer, his second famous case was the killing of Beatrice Rimmer, a middle-aged widow who, the SP was, had a load of dough put away in her house. The fellows involved were

Edward Devlin and Alfred Burns and they'd known each other for some years. In August 1951, when Burns was on the run staying with Devlin, they put up the job to a couple of girls. The idea was a straight-forward con trick to get in. One of the girls was to make sure the woman was in and then she was to keep watch, knock and keep her talking whilst the others broke in at the back. A fellow they was going to use got himself nicked a couple of days before it was due off.

Eventually they decided not to use the girl and just break in and that's where it all went wrong. The woman showed up and they knocked her about with a piece of wood. The fellow they'd left out then sees a bit of an opportunity to help himself and grassed them up whilst he was in Walton. When it come to the Assizes they said they was out screwing a warehouse in Manchester and they was staying with a woman there, but she wouldn't wear it. Rose Heilbron was defending Devlin and when she went to the Court of Appeal she said she'd got evidence that another man was the real killer. Goddard wouldn't listen but there was an inquiry which come to nothing before they were topped. They was still maintaining their innocence.

Balmer's third big murder was the killing of an old junk dealer, 82-year-old George Hugh Walker, known as Daddy, in the middle of January 1953. He lived on the Warbreck Road out near Aintree. One time he'd been quite smart, well turned out and well thought of but when his wife, a dancing teacher called Madame Pepper – all dancing teachers had to be French or Italian even if they come from the next street to you – died he sort of let himself go. The place had twelve rooms and each of them was piled high with junk. The neighbours didn't have much to do with him but when his dog wouldn't stop howling one of them went over to see what was happening. They found his body, which had been hacked about.

This time it wasn't a gang or anything like that, just an unemployed labourer John Lawrence Todd, who went and hit Walker 32 times with an axe. The axe had been clumsily hidden in a chimney. Todd went to the police to explain why he might have been seen in the area but he was identified through a watch he'd nicked from the old man and then sold. He was topped in

May that year at Walton. There wasn't any doubt about it this time.

Some people could just be in the wrong place at the wrong time. Take that girl Jean Larkin. She ran a company selling window blinds, and her boyfriend Gary Pettitt made his money out of selling drugs. They left their flat in Aigburth in April 1993. It seems Pettitt had had a call to a meeting in a McDonald's in Markey Street, Chorley, some 25 miles away and Jean Larkin went with him. They couldn't have expected to be away long because they'd left the television on and her dog, Bruff, was in the flat with no food left out for it. Her company was called Calypso Blinds and someone saw her van with the name on the side in Markey Street, Chorley and later it was found at Manchester airport. But they never saw either of them again.

In June the coppers started digging in woods at Coppull, which is a bit outside Chorley. There was some jewellery and burned clothing. She was just unlucky to have been around when it all came on top for her boyfriend.

YORKSHIRE

LEEDS

In my day the Chaps didn't use guns, not when we went out on
blaggings that is. We might have done when we was facing up to
each other, but kill someone on a robbery and that was a topping
offence. You couldn't tell some people though. Take Walter
Sharpe and Gordon Lannen; they was just twenty and seventeen.
In they go to a jewellers, the Albion Watch Depot in Leeds, just
after the place has opened and hold up the owner. November
1949 it was. The old boy who owned the place, Abraham Levine,
wouldn't give them anything and he got hold of Lannen by the
collar. What he got for his troubles was a stream of blows with
the butt of one of the guns and then he was shot. After that the
kids just ran out into the street firing. It must have been like
something out of a western. No one could tell if they was just
letting the guns off in panic or if they was actually firing at the
people who was running after them. The old man died that night
but he'd been able to tell the coppers what the boys looked like,
and they were picked up a few days later in Southport.

Lannen wanted to put his hands up but the judge wouldn't let
him and made him plead not guilty. What had happened is they'd
broken into a gunsmith's and stolen the revolvers and gone and
robbed Levine. It turned out it was Sharpe's gun which went off.

It was one of them cases when the judge has a go at films,
which was what they did in them days. 'Wretched gangster films',
was what the judge called them. Now it's supposed to be
television which makes people go wrong. Sharpe was topped at
Armley, the Leeds prison at the end of March 1950, but because
Lannen was only seventeen he got detained at His Majesty's
Pleasure.

For myself I can't say the films ever influenced me. I know I
didn't get to see them three times a week like Sharpe said he did,
but if I was going to do something, it wasn't because I'd see Bogey
or Edward G. do it on the screen. It's one of those good excuses
judges like and so do those people who like to work out why

people commit crime. It's either because they was twins, or their dad was away or they didn't have a dad or they come from a deprived background. Look at my family. You can't make it work at all. We come from a settled family. We was poor but we never lacked food and clothes. It was a bad environment – people like to say it's environment as well – but that can't have counted. The other thing is genes. Do we have bad genes? Well, my parents didn't have criminal records. So what happens? The first three of us kids turn out fine; not a day's trouble between them. Then there's Eva. A bit of shoplifting when she was young and then only in trouble trying to help me out. Finally there's me. Never out of trouble from about ten to seventy. How can you explain it?

I never liked those local prisons, Armley, Winson Green, Strange-ways. They were the ones for medium-term prisoners. There was only the Moor and the Island and, up North, Wakefield for long-term men. There was also a wing at the Scrubs for long-term star prisoners but that started in the late forties or early fifties. If there was any reforms which benefited prisoners it always seemed that they were the last ones to give the privileges. When I think back to my time in the nick, if a screw retired in 1960 that meant he'd been trained by people who'd started in 1930 and in their turn they'd been trained by people who'd begun in 1900. It was no wonder things hadn't changed much. There was the same mentality. When I started in the nick you got a letter a month. Now you get a telephone card and can ring your people every day.

Armley was the last place they hanged a man and woman together. At least they didn't do it back-to-back like they did in Canada. John Gallagher and Emily Swann it was in 1903. They'd done in her husband. She'd been having it off with Gallagher and her husband gave her a beating. Gallagher took a poker to him and there's not much doubt she was egging him on. She must have been one of the smallest women ever topped in modern times. She was only four foot two. Apparently he was on the scaffold with the blinds on when she's brought out. 'Good morning, Johnny,' she says. 'Good morning, love,' he replies and that's it.

As I've said Armley was where my mate Jimmy Essex got done for murder the second time during the War. He had a fight with a bloke in the tailor's shop. The man was coming at him and Jimmy had the knife you used to cut cloth and he done him with it. He was lucky it got knocked down to manslaughter but he still got a ten. I slipped in and see him just before the murder when I was on the run from the Army. There was always the risk you'd be caught but it wasn't that much of one. Things were a bit lax and the worst that was likely was you'd get a knockback. Otherwise you moodied you were someone's cousin back on home leave and they was generally willing to let you in. I think I'm right in saying Jimmy was the first man done for murder in prison, certainly in modern times.

Our attention was more directed at the screws and there wasn't all the association and visiting other people's cells there is today. That kept us apart. Of course, we could make knives and things but there wasn't the opportunity there is today even if we'd wanted to. There was people off their trolleys but not to the same extent and it was like on the outside if we had a quarrel it was usually a straightener. If we did use weapons the idea was to give a stripe or two but not to kill people.

Now, there's been a big increase in killings in prison over the years; not least in people who've topped themselves. There was something over fifty of them in 1999 and I think it's gone up since then. Then there's the prisoners who get killed by others. There was that big case in March 2000 when Zahid Mubarek, a black kid in Feltham, was put in the same cell as a white racist, Robert Stewart, who hit him over the head with a table leg. He just beat Mubarek to death. He'd got a poster for the Ku Klux Klan on the wall and a month before one of the staff had warned how dangerous he was. Poor kid was only doing a few months and was due out pretty soon.

That Mubarek killing was bad enough but the next week a fellow Colin Bloomfield got done in Cardiff; just about disembowelled. He was doing six months for child neglect and he was put in a cell with a fellow called Jason Ricketts who'd done a seven for robbery. Ricketts had told people he was wanting to get back to a mental hospital. He said he was going to kill and eat someone and then ring the bell for the screws, and that's just about what he did. He took the fellow's eye out and his liver and had his spleen as well. It seems like he thought that was Bloomfield's heart. He'd managed to make a sort of scalpel out of a toothbrush handle and a razor blade. He said it all come about by taking LSD and solvents when he was young. I think he was one of the ones who got his wish and went back to the bin.

There was a right man in Broadmoor after I was there, Robert Mawdsley. He'd been sent there for stabbing an iron in June 1974 in Liverpool and he'd carried on the good work ever since. He went to Broadmoor for that and whilst he was there, in 1976 he tried to kill an inmate called Monk, and later he managed it with a fellow called Francis in February 1977. That was enough for them and he was sent to the nick. He got moved to Wakefield in March 1978. When he was there he and another fellow they regarded as dangerous, Douglas Wakefield, had a spare cell in between them with a telly in it and they sort of shared it to keep them away from the others. One day Mawdsley tells a fellow in the tailor's shop that a couple would have to go and he'll be back in Broadmoor within the week. He did what he said he would and put away a couple, William Roberts and Stanley Darwood. Then he goes and tries to stab a screw. He got lifed off and the judge said he was sorry for the screws in the nick having to cope with him. So far as I know he never got back to Broadmoor but he did get a telly programme made about him. He went in a control unit.

My view is that the people who went in control units could be described as control fodder. They weren't Chaps so to speak. I mean, if they had been serious surely then I'd have been one of the first through the doors. I don't think either Timmy Noonan or Martin Frape was ever in one either.

The scheme started in Wakefield back in the '70s and if you went in the control unit you was there for two periods before you come out. The first was ninety days, when you didn't get any association with other cons. You didn't have to work but your ninety days didn't start until you did. Then you got another ninety days with limited association. At the start there was just the concrete slab on the floor and they chucked a mattress in at night. There was very heavy fine mesh on the cell windows so the con couldn't see out properly. If you didn't work or got into trouble it was back to the beginning. There was one fellow tried to get the courts say it was cruel and unusual but they wasn't having any of it. They said far worse took place in America. It was packed in a few years ago but things have gone full circle and I'm told there's a very similar system just been started again in Wakefield, although people say now it's much better.

Headingly was where they dug the pitch up when England was playing Australia as a protest to try and get George Davis released. George was very intelligent over the Ilford robbery back in 1965 when some people did the London Electricity Board in Ley Street. When he was inside he kept himself to himself and there was never the chance for the authorities to slip a prisoner into him. That was really a case and a half.

He always maintained he'd been wrongly ID'd and there was a big campaign to have him released; eventually the Home Secretary let him out in May 1976, about the time there was a lot of trouble about the danger of convicting on ID evidence only. Unfortunately George let the side down a bit because the next year he's found in a ready-eye trying to do the Bank of Cyprus in the Seven Sisters Road, Holloway. The copper who nicked him asked what he was doing and he said the shopping, and the copper says 'Why are you doing it in a balaclava George?' He got an eleven but now I'm pleased to say he's been out of trouble for years. I had a drink with him the other day. I met him down Sheila Kelly's place, the W9 Wine Bar. It's a lovely drinker, a smashing place.

There used to be a way so's women who were pregnant didn't swing. Once they'd been found guilty they could tell the court they was in the club and what was called a Jury of Matrons was put together from women sitting in the court or even in the building who then had to listen to the woman's story and decide if she was telling the tale. Sometimes of course it was obvious she was going to have a kid, but other times it was more difficult. At first they did it all by themselves but later they had a doctor give them advice. It was centuries old and I think the last time there was one was in the 1930s, but a bit before that they had a case at Leeds Assizes. It was a girl called Louie Calvert and she was a right bag of tricks. She must have been the only brass to go around in a Sally Ann bonnet.

She'd been the housekeeper of a fellow called Arthur Calvert from Railway Place in Hunslet and she convinced him she was in the club and he'd have to marry her. That's what the poor fellow did and as the time went by there's no little Calvert in the cot. You'd think she might say she'd had a miss but no, what she does is decide to go out and find a baby. There wasn't the difficulty there is now. There was always plenty of girls who'd gone and soiled the family honour and wanted to get rid of little Willie one way or another. She shows Arthur a letter which she's written herself saying her sister's invited her over to stay with her in Dewsbury for the confinement. Off she goes and sends hubby a telegram saying she's arrived safe, and then it's back to Leeds to stay with a woman called Lily Waterhouse. Then she goes and adopts the baby of a young girl and three weeks later comes back with it to Arthur.

That was on a Sunday. Next day Arthur sees a suitcase he doesn't recognise and she tells him it's from her sister and it's full of baby clothes. It turns out it's full of Mrs Waterhouse's stuff. The police are only half a step behind and she's nicked a few days later. It turns out Mrs W. has been found with her head bashed in with a poker. Louie's filled the suitcase full of crockery and anything else which might have come in handy. She claimed she was in the club but the Jury of Matrons reckoned it was another come on and she got put away in June 1926 at Strangeways. There's a story that whilst she was in the condemned cell she confessed to doing in another husband, John Frobisher, who'd been found dead in a Leeds canal in the early 1920s.

Another girl who ended up in a parcel was the twenty-year-old Ethel Wraithmell. Her head was found by a man out walking the dog in a village called Scholes near Leeds in May 1939. There was another couple of parcels with bits of her nearby. I say she was called Ethel but she'd got a whole host of names she went by. She came from the Chapeltown area and she was mixed up in a fair amount of stuff – passing coins for a gang of counterfeiters was one. Then there was a story she was a grass but the coppers denied it. People who knew her said she'd been frightened for the past six months. Eventually, nearly a year later, a fellow's charged with her murder and he goes down for manslaughter.

That bit was a strange story. In the following April he just walked into the police station and gave himself up. The pros's version of the thing was that Ethel was a brass and he'd picked her up whilst his wife was away. She'd tried a bit of black on him and he'd strangled her. There was a bit of evidence that some man had been seen with her on a tram the night she died and they reckoned he was the man.

What he said was that he'd had her pointed out to him on the street and she'd just turned up on his doorstep uninvited one night and when he tried to get her out of the place he accidentally kills her. She was in a pretty poor way by all accounts. She was homeless and she'd got a brain tumour and TB as well. The doctor didn't think she was going to live long anyway. Once she'd snuffed it he didn't know what to do. He thought if he went to the coppers they'd say it was murder and he was right. So he kept the body in the front room all night and after he come home from work the next day he cut it up. He got twelve months, which you can't say was bad.

SHEFFIELD

I've spoken to many men who've done in their wives and girlfriends. As I say they just don't think they're going to get caught, but their brains must have dropped off whilst they was doing it. They seem to me to be saying 'Look what I done?' Very often they give their wife or girlfriend's clothes or jewellery to a new girl the next day. It goes back as far as Crippen and probably a lot further. Within a few weeks Ethel Le Neve was wearing Belle's jewellery which he said she'd left behind when she'd run off from him. Run off as far as the cellar most likely.

Then look at that bloke from Sheffield, Kenneth Peatfield his name is. They call him Concrete Ken in the nick. He's meant to be moping around the house because his girlfriend, Susan Craven has gone and left him and in fact he's out over in Oldham having dinner with his new girlfriend, a third the age of the old one as well. If that isn't enough they go and buy two wedding bands. He must have been out of his mind because he brings her back to the house and shows her the old girlfriend's body under a tarpaulin. If that isn't enough to put a girl off I don't know what is. Still you have to wonder what Susan saw in him. He'd done a ten in the 1980s for trying to hire a hitman to do his wife and daughter. From what I hear Ken still says it wasn't him.

They never found the body but they did find her head in a concrete block in his garage about six weeks later. He said he couldn't explain what it was doing there but he'd never seen it. He must have heard of the case of that lawyer Warren Lincoln in Chicago, back in the '20s. He was able to explain things when they found the heads of his wife and brother-in-law in flowerpots on his porch. He said he didn't know who the heads belonged to. He'd found them in his greenhouse and put them in concrete to preserve the evidence. Didn't do him much good either. It seems he just couldn't stand them rabbiting on together when he retired and he wanted a bit of peace and quiet.

Concrete Ken got a good beating when he went to Doncaster prison. That's not that usual. Generally people don't mind about wives getting topped. It's people who do kids in that have the worst time, and quite right too.

They seem to have had a thing about heads in Sheffield. A few years before Concrete Ken, Tony Antoniou, the boyfriend of that singer who wears an eye-patch, Gabrielle, did in his stepfather, Walter McCarthy. He took off the head as well and left the body in a lay-by at a place called Cutthroat Bridge on the Snake Pass. You've got to give him credit for something like that. He'd certainly got a sense of humour because he called his fish and chippy The Lazy Codling. Just before Christmas 1995 it was. He said it wasn't murder because McCarthy had abused him as a child but the jury wasn't wearing it.

Back in the nineteenth century the biggest of all the criminals countrywide came from Sheffield. He was just about a one-man crime wave. Charlie Peace come from Angel Court on the corner of Nursery Street and Lady's Bridge. His father had been a collier before becoming an animal trainer and Peace himself later trained parrots and pigeons. He did his leg in when he was in the mills at the age of fourteen and when he was released they said he was incurable. A bit of red hot steel had gone through the back of his left leg, a sort of reverse knee-capping. It didn't stop him being about the best screwer in the country. That wasn't his only trade.

He was a top-class pickpocket. His trick was to faint in the street and when people who'd picked him up got home they found they'd lost a tie-pin or a wallet. I know a number of faces who played the piano well enough, but he was the only villain I've heard of who played the violin. I'm not sure he wasn't good enough to play in the pit at music halls.

He was good enough to stay out of trouble until he was nineteen and then he got a month for screwing. After that it was onwards and upwards. He did the house of a local beak and his sister was caught trying to pawn the stuff. That was the standard way of getting rid of gear. It's more or less safe for the pawnbroker who's got a name and address even if it's a moody to show the police, and he's giving a price on the stuff which he knows he can resell. She was trying to pawn some boots and when the coppers searched Peace's mother's house there was a whole raft of stuff. This time he got four years.

He was like me – no remission. He'd tried to escape and he'd also tried to top himself, which was a criminal offence back then. Once he come out in about 1858 he was all over the country screwing, never staying longer than a few weeks in one place. He took up with a Hannah Ward and they was more or less together until the end. Then he was picked up in Manchester. Him and another man hid some jewellery in a sewer but when they come back for the gear it was a ready eye and he got a six with penal servitude.

Then he was in Chatham, where he organised a mutiny. For that they literally shipped him off to Gibraltar and it wasn't until 1864 he was out and back screwing. Manchester wasn't a lucky place for him either because he and the other fellow was drinking whisky instead of getting out with the gear and the servants come and did them. This time it was a seven.

If you see pictures of him he looks really ugly. This may be because he was twisting his face up so the police couldn't identify him in future but I don't think he pretended he was handsome. Not like Ruby Sparks who used to screw his face up on police pictures. Now he was handsome. Ugly or not it didn't stop Peace pulling the women. He was back in Sheffield living in Britannia Road, a couple of doors from Arthur and Katherine Dyson. He certainly took her out but whether they had it off I don't think anyone will know now. Anyway Dyson didn't like it, and they moved to Ecclesall Road and found to their horror Peace had followed them.

At the end of November he went and shot Dyson. The coroner's jury said it was wilful murder but by that time Peace was over in Hull. It was then he really start to work his way round England – Birmingham, Bath, Bristol, you name it. The railways was putting their act together and so travel was getting much easier. It was probably faster than it is today.

Nottingham was where he met Susan Bailey, and they began living together as Mr and Mrs John Thompson. He went back to Hull and of all things he rented rooms from a police sergeant who thought he was a commercial traveller. Poor old Hannah was left behind. She thought he was on the run. Finally he come down to Blackheath and sets up house with Susan and sends for Hannah who brought the kids with her. He starts going to church and plays the violin at concerts. For the rest of the time he's out screwing with his tools in a violin case; just the sort of thing the Mob in Chicago did with their tommy guns in the 1920s. He'd dyed his face walnut coloured and shaved off the front of his hair and he looks like a perfectly respectable old man by now.

It all come on top when he's tackled by the coppers in Blackheath in October 1878 as he's coming out of a screwing. He shot one of them but the man still held onto him. When he was nicked he said he was John Ward and that he was 60. No fingerprints to check in them days. A month later he got penal servitude for life. Unfortunately he asked a neighbour to come and see him and when the man does so and finds out that Ward is Thompson he goes to the coppers and then it really is on top. By the time the coppers get to Peace's house everyone's long gone, but Susan puts him and Hannah away for the £100 reward.

Then Mrs Dyson, who's now in America, says she will come back and give evidence about the shooting of her husband and when Peace is being taken up for the committal in Sheffield he throws himself out of the train. It doesn't do any good and he's picked up pretty quick.

He was never going to get out of it and it seems that in the condemned cell he turned to religion. He may have been halfway genuine because one thing he did do was admit that it was him and not a young Irishman, Aaron Habron, who'd shot and killed a copper in Manchester back in 1876. The kid, who had been heard making threats against the officer, had been sentenced to death but had been reprieved. He picked up £800 compensation for his two-and-a-half year stay in the warehouse. It seems like Peace had watched the case from the public gallery. It was Marwood who pulled the string on Peace.

He was still talked about to my day. Edgar Wallace wrote a novel about him and there was a melodrama when I was a kid where the retired executioner James Ellis, playing William Marwood, hanged the actor playing Peace on stage.

The first brothers to swing for the same offence were the Strattons back at the beginning of the last century. They're in the books for two records really. They were the first people to swing on fingerprint evidence.

Fingerprinting's been around hundreds of years in China and in India but it wasn't really until the end of the nineteenth century that it took off in Europe, and America was a bit later than that. The first person ever to be nicked on fingerprints here was a fellow who got done for a burglary in Dulwich. Jackson his name was. He got weighed off at the Old Bailey and got a seven back in 1902. That was one thing and the pros was triumphant. But the real thing was whether a jury would actually let someone swing just because a copper said that he'd made a test on a cup and it matched the man's dabs.

Then comes the big one. A husband and wife who run a small shop in Dulwich are done during a robbery in March 1905. The husband had been done on the ground floor and his wife in the bedroom. There was a cash box under the bed and it had got some dabs on it. By this time there was a sort of filing system at the Yard with convict's prints on them. There was about 80,000 of them and the prints didn't match any of those and they didn't match those of the old woman.

Really, when it comes to it, the fingerprints didn't catch the killers but they put them down. It was the usual sort of thing. People in the neighbourhood said the Stratton brothers were capable of it and one of them, Alfred, had a girl who come forward to say he'd dyed his shoes after the robbery and got rid of his coat. He'd been poncing off her and then given her a beating. There wasn't much else in the way of evidence – a bit of an ID by an old woman who saw two men running away – but it was fingerprints with that bit of support from the girlfriend.

It was a good case to test the fingerprints though because there wasn't going to be much sympathy for the pair doing in an elderly couple. The defence was unlucky. They had a man give evidence saying the fingerprints were unreliable and they didn't know he'd already written to the coppers to say he'd give evidence for them saying they were reliable. And so Alfred and Albert were the first brothers to swing. By the end each of them was saying the other done it. A bit later it was the Reubens brothers who went down together. No fingerprinting evidence here. They did a couple of sailors in the East End. Then there weren't any brothers for twenty years or so.

There was a series of gang wars in Sheffield in the 1920s and they got sorted out by the copper Sillitoe, who went on to sort out Glasgow and to be big in intelligence during the Second World War. The Fowlers, who were involved, were the last brothers to be hanged in England as far as I know.

One of the big men in the Sheffield gang wars was Sam Garvin, who was a great mate of Darby Sabini who I carried the bucket for when I was a kid. People think the Sabinis was just racecourse villains but there was a lot more to them than that. Before Sam, during the First World War in Sheffield there's been the Red Silk and White Silk gangs, who were really muggers and they wore scarves round their necks just like the Crips and Bloods today. It isn't anything new. In New York years earlier the Plug Ugly gang got its name for the sort of hat they wore, and the Dead Rabbits always had one on a pole when they went into action. There was plenty of small gangs around the country. Just two of them was the Silver Hammer gang in Hull, which ran for years working the docks, and the Nuts in Sunderland.

It was the early '20s, when there was so much trouble at racecourses round the country, that Sam Garvin and his brother, Bob, fought it out with George Mooney and his mob. Really it wasn't racecourses then, it was over the pitch and toss schools. They've never been really popular in London, not like they have been over the rest of the country, but there was big money to be made running a school and quite a good bit mugging the winning punters on their way home. The idea is you have to bet on which way a number of coins is going to fall, heads or tails. It's the same as that Australian game Two Up. They were usually held outside the town where there wasn't much danger of coppers breaking the game up and people turned up from places like Rotherham and Barnsley to play.[1]

Mooney got his men mainly from the West Bar and the Park gangs and things worked well for him for years until there was a cut in allowances for families if the men were found gaming. Mooney's men began to drift away and a lot of them went over to Sam who ran a ring at Sky Edge. The Park Brigade was also formed and soon got rid of Mooney, but he wasn't laying down. After that there was beatings and cuttings and more beatings and then there was shootings, with the coppers turning up one day to find Mooney sort of holed up in his place at West Bar under siege from the Park Brigade.

It seems that now he had a look at an alliance with Billy Kimber and those of his boys who were left from Birmingham, whilst Sam Garvin and the Park Brigade were looking for help from Darby. Then what does Mooney go and do? He gives an interview in the papers. You'd have thought he'd have had more sense but there's always villains who like the publicity. They think it makes them big. I can't think of more than a couple it's done good to. There was that Squizzy Taylor in Australia who got a lot of good publicity, and Billy Hill didn't do badly, but the sensible villain keeps his name way away from people. Mooney says there's no such thing as the Mooney Gang and it's the Park Brigade who are the villains breaking up his hold on Sky Edge. Worse, he goes and names names and, not surprisingly, the men don't like it. So they start fighting with him.

---

[1] Pitch and toss had as many variations as venues. It was also known as Nearest the Mottie and Nudgers, Hoying and Burling. Playing had been banned on Sundays in Victorian England. It was played on any waste ground with rings, on pit banks in Lanarkshire and on the beaches near Swansea. It survived in places as a regular sport until the 1950s. See C. Chinn *Better Betting with a Decent Feller*, pp. 95–103.

By Christmas 1923 Sam Garvin's Park Brigade was well on top. One by one Mooney's remaining men was pushing off. One went down to Birmingham and in fact for a time Mooney cleared off as well. Sam was a brighter spark altogether. Once, when he was on bail for attacking Mooney, he had a boxing tournament for the families of men killed in the Nunnery colliery disaster. He also started taking an interest in politics, breaking up Labour Party political meetings. He was doing well because his family was one of the first to move into the new Walkley estate, with a bathroom. Just think, it was nearly thirty years before I could ever get a place with one.

The fighting went on for a couple of years with all sorts of people springing up. Then, at the New Year of 1925, it looked like there might be a bit of a compromise with Garvin and Mooney sharing Sky Edge. Everyone seemed to be pleased; summonses had been withdrawn and there was going to be a 50–50 split. But they didn't call Sam 'Slippery' for nothing. When Mooney's men turned up with a fellow, Tom Armstrong from Birmingham who'd moved into Sheffield, they was told to push off.

Then a fellow George Newbould took over against Garvin. And shortly after it all come on top for the Fowler brothers. In April 1925 William Plommer, who'd been a sergeant in the First World War and was now on the dole and father of two kids, one only three weeks' old, was stabbed to death. What had happened was that there's been a fight near Plommer's home in which a Garvin gang member, Wilfred Fowler, had got a beating. It seems Plommer had only been looking on but that was enough. I suppose there's a moral. If you see a fight that's nothing to do with you get on your bike. Anyway, the next night Fowler and his friends had toured the area threatening to do for Plommer.

Plommer come out of his house to meet them and was attacked by a crowd. It seems there was about eight of them and he got hit over the head with a child's scooter and then stabbed with a bayonet. Fowler and his brother, Lawrence, don't seem to have made much of an effort to run away. A copper found them with a fellow, George Wills, sitting on the steps of a shop not far from Plommer's body.

In the end eleven men, including both the Fowlers, were charged with Plommer's murder. They said that Plommer had run a tossing ring under the railway arches at Norfolk Bridge and he'd been the one who'd gone for the Fowlers with a poker and razor. They couldn't make it stand though.

Both the Fowler brothers were convicted of murder. Sam Garvin, who'd been charged with aiding and abetting, got a not guilty and Wills got a ten for manslaughter. In those days if you was found guilty you could say something to the judge about how sorry you was after your brief had spoken for you, before he passed sentence. Remember, a lot of people didn't have briefs even in serious cases. It didn't do no good usually and it didn't for Lawrence who said he'd only hit Plommer one clip with a poker. Wilfred remained stumm.

An appeal was lodged but like so many that didn't do no good either. The Court of Appeal took the view that it wasn't the Fowlers' bad luck they'd gone down for murder, it was the rest of them had good luck. If everyone had swung it would have been better. Then there was a story flew round that Wilfred had confessed and got his brother out. The trouble was there'd been so much trouble that summer round the racetracks that there was going to be an example made of someone. The brothers got topped on consecutive days – Wilfred first – at Armley. Lawrence had asked to be executed with his brother but no one listened. It was another man, Alfred Bostock, who had battered his mistress to death and thrown her in the river at Rotherham, went on the scaffold with Wilfred.

Garvin and Mooney went on and racked up a few more convictions, but they was never long ones. A bitten ear and three broken ribs was only worth nine months. When you think what we got for the so-called Torture Trial. But what the authorities did was bring in Percy Sillitoe who was given a licence to stamp out the gangs, no questions asked, and that's what he did. He had the biggest and fittest men out on the streets – one of the coppers was said to be able to hold seven tennis balls in one hand – handing out their own sort of punishment. If anyone complained and took out a cross-summons for assault the beaks weren't listening.

By 1927 the coppers had won. There was a bit of violence from people like the Junior Park but both George Mooney and Sam Garvin became bookmakers. Sam called himself Captain Mee and worked the Northern courses and Mooney, who was calling himself George Barratt by then, did some betting on the dogs at Owlerton. George, who'd had a personal talking to by Sillitoe, never got no more convictions, but Sam, who hadn't, ran up a string before he died in the 1960s.

When I was young there was a lot about the Great Yellow Peril. Fu Manchu and the Chinese was going to take over this country and only Sexton Blake could save us. In real life there was that man the Brilliant Chang, from Limehouse, who was meant to have given drugs to a couple of actresses who died as a result. Chang got deported and there was a lot of stuff in the papers warning girls from going with Chinese blokes. They was full of girls being found drugged in Chinese restaurants and so on and ending up on the game. In a way it was just like it was with the Jamaicans and the Maltese in the 1950s and 1960s. Of course, just like today the Chinese villains didn't mix with the rest of us. They have their own wars and don't like getting involved with outsiders.

In 1922, the year before I was born, there was a murder in Sheffield which, in a way, a girl Lily Siddal solved. She used to work in a Chinese laundry owned by a fellow called Sing Lee in Crookes, doing the books and marking the tabs on the washing. One day he asked her to come in special and then when she got there he didn't turn up. There was another Chinese, Lee Doon, who worked there and he said the boss had gone back to China and now he was taking over. Lily become suspicious because Lee Sing hadn't taken his hat and suitcase when he left, and also because Lee Doon was wearing the man's trousers. Lily checked out to see if Sing Lee had gone over to Liverpool to see his relatives and got a blank, so she went to the police. The coppers turned up and in a trunk in the cellar was the body of Sing Lee. At first Lee Doon said he'd killed his boss in an accident but it turned out he'd bashed him on the head and then strangled him with a rope. They topped Lee Doon. Over the years in fact there was quite a number of Chinese executed.

HUDDERSFIELD

If you've got a gun in the place there's always a danger you'll use it, even though the trouble you're in is hopeless. It's what I say about murders being done on the spur of the moment. Take that Alfred Moore who was a screwer in Huddersfield in the early '50s. The coppers come round and want to question him and what does he do? Even though he's surrounded, he opens fire and kills a couple, Inspector Duncan Frazer and Constable Arthur Jagger. He got topped at the beginning of 1953. No question of a reprieve for him.

I often had a gun about. It's what saved me from a bad beating that Christmas Day a few years before when the Carters come round to give me a seeing to. I put it to the head of one of them and pulled the trigger. I was lucky. My mate, Jimmy Ford, had taken out the firing pin or something because my young boys was at an inquisitive stage and they might have done some harm to themselves if they'd found it and started playing around. As a rule though I didn't take one with me when I went out thieving. There's no doubt when the coppers chased me back down when we did a factory in Luton, that if I'd had the gun in the van I'd have shot at the coppers. Not to kill them but I might have done. As it turned out the gun was in the other car and I got nicked. But then the reason I had that day it was in case I ran into the Carters.

I never kept crooked gear at home. Well, maybe a suit which my sister or one of her friends had lifted for me, but there was never 26 radios stacked up in the back room. Once it's found in your house the chances of a not guilty have gone out the window. What's the good of going out and getting it and then putting it where you live especially if you're a known rascal? In my day if you was found with stolen gear in your home even if you was found not guilty the pros could bring it up at a second trial if you was done for receiving again within the year, so it was kept down the slaughter. Would I have used a gun if the police come searching my home? You can never tell. If they'd been a bit flash and come on strong then my temper might have snapped.

HULL

Hull was the home of the man who killed three women over the years and got away with murder every time. William Birkett did the first of his girlfriends back in 1915. That was when he killed his married girlfriend and did nine years for manslaughter. He wasn't out a year before he did another married girlfriend, and this time he did a ten. He was out a bit longer this time. It was 1939 that he killed another married woman. He strangled this one. He'd cut the throat of the first two. He said he was jealous because they was looking at other men. You'd think they'd have locked him up for ever but he was out in 1954 and when it come to it I don't think he did another so perhaps they was right. He died a couple of years later. He'd have been nearly seventy by then.

BRADFORD

I never spent much time in Bradford but when I was there it was a lucky place for me. The first time was when I got taken up under escort to join up in the War after I'd done my 15 months for a screwing. What was so odd was that they just left me standing about and, since I was in civvies, I just walked off. There I was in Bradford with more or less nothing in my pockets and a place I didn't know. I couldn't phone anyone. No one I knew had a phone. Eva was at my parents and they certainly didn't. Even if I had got through how was they going to come up and get me? I bumped into a couple of people I knew from Camden Town who'd come up with their wives to get away from the bombing and to see if there was a couple of touches. What luck. I'd have had to take my chance and do a screwing on my own, but they pointed me in the right direction and we did both the jobs they fancied. Then we all went down to Newmarket and I made my way back to London.

The second time was when I got taken back up there again and this time I chinned the medical officer and got sent to the North Riding Hospital. They kept me there a bit and then sent me home to my mother saying I was unfit for service. I got a disability allowance and all.

There was a funny case in Bradford a bit after the War. A priest just disappeared. July 1953 it was. He was Father Henrik Borynski, an exiled Pole who lodged in Little Horton Lane. Apparently he took a call, said, 'All right I go', collected his hat and coat and walked out. His landlady watched him go walking up the road and turning right past a hospital. After that he just

Left A sketch of Charlie Peace by Frank Lockwood (Topham)

Charles Peace, as he appeared sitting in the dock, when I defended him for murder in 1879. F.L.

Below Eddie Chapman, safecracker turned spy, looking through a newspaper (Topham)

Left Archibald Hall: the butler killer (Topham)

Right Peter Manuel on the closing day of his trial for 8 murders (Hulton Archive)

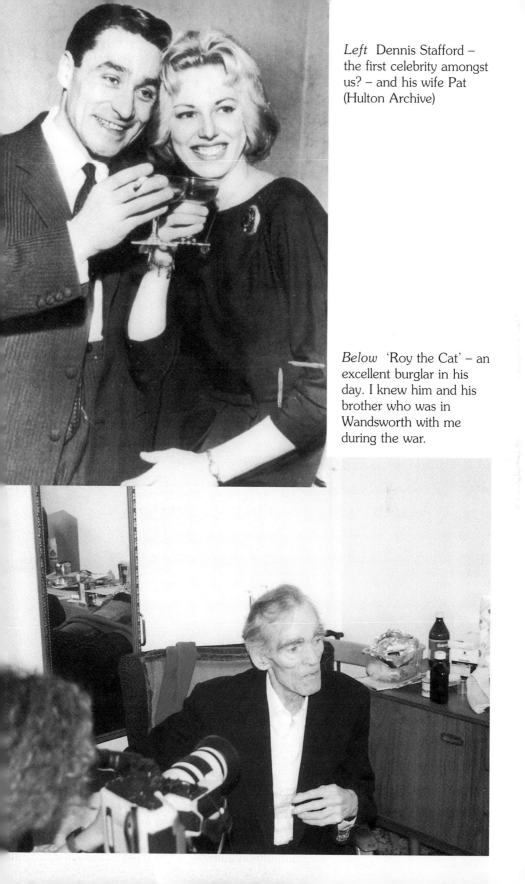

Left Dennis Stafford – the first celebrity amongst us? – and his wife Pat (Hulton Archive)

Below 'Roy the Cat' – an excellent burglar in his day. I knew him and his brother who was in Wandsworth with me during the war.

Top left Arthur Thompson's Glasgow – his 'ranch' . . .

Middle left . . . the Barrowlands dance hall . . .

Bottom left . . . and the Provenmill Inn, where his funeral was held.

Right Me, a little more comfortable now.

Right Me outside Lincoln Prison with a couple of well-wishers.

Left The forbidding
entrance to Dartmoor
Prison as I remember it
(Topham)

Right A prisoner on the
security wing at Durham
(Topham)

Above Barbed-wire encloses the exercise yard at Durham (Hulton: Keystone)

Right Drug detection dogs have their work cut out for them at Barlinnie Jail in Glasgow (Topham)

Left Inside the security wing at Parkhurst on the Isle of Wight (Topham)

Below Outside the security block at Parkhurst (Hulton Archive)

vanished. He took only ten shillings with him and left a few hundred quid in his bank account.

The landlady, Irena Beck, called the local police of course and the CID and MI5 was called in. The locals thought he'd been kidnapped and murdered by Communist agents. There was supposed to have been a lot of them in Bradford at the time and it was a real anti-Communist time. The Father had been denouncing them from the pulpit and people thought this might have got him into trouble.

There was another attack on a priest a bit after the Father disappeared. Someone left a message, 'Be silent, Priest' on the man who looked after the Lithuanians in town, in matchsticks on his table one night. But people reckoned that he was in a right nervous state and might have laid them out himself.

DEWSBURY

There've been some good escapes from prisons and there's been enough out of vans taking people to court or hospital, but there's not been too many out of police stations that I can recall. Mind you there was one fellow up in Sunderland when I was a teenager who did his best. He was up for disorderly conduct but when he was in his cell he managed to smash up two beds and then get out of handcuffs and a straitjacket before he set fire to the place. The coppers come and threw water on him. All he got was a month. I remember a few years ago there was a kid wanted for robbery walked out of Old Street in his stocking feet, got on the tube and went home, but he's almost got to be a one-off.

Generally people don't get out too easy. There's a lot of reasons. Firstly, people are a bit wary in the nick. It's not that they're frightened exactly but they're concentrating on their cases. There's always the chance they're not going to be charged so what's the point of escaping? Then when they are charged, it's too late. The second thing is the coppers haven't got too many people to look after at any one time so they can give people their attention. After all, in a police nick at any one time there's only likely to be two or three serious people. All right, half a dozen in the old days if everyone got rounded up after a blag, but they might not even know the others was in. The most important thing though is they aren't there long enough to do much about it. There's no chance to get organised. Anything has to be spur of the moment. The chances are the cells are underground, and if you managed to get out of the cell when you was being given food, the chances are that you couldn't get out of the cell block itself. In later years there'd be alarm bars on the walls of the cells which didn't help. Even if you did get out of the cell block you'd still got to get past the front desk. It wasn't worth giving it a spin really.

The best of the escapes from cells though was that Nikolaus Chrastny. In a way though he was different. He wasn't in the cells for just a day or so. He was in the same place for long enough to give him a chance.

What happened was that after that Bertie Smalls become a supergrass things changed. Supergrasses were kept in police nicks and they got all sorts of privileges. There was booze; they could have visits from their wives and girlfriends, and very often the coppers would take them out for a drink in the local boozer. Lots of opportunities to escape but there was none of them tried as far as I can recall. The reason for that is there was nowhere for them to go. They were safer in the nick. If they got out and went back to their manor then the chances are someone would have topped them before the day was out. They weren't all safe even in the nick. One of them, David Smith, topped himself and good riddance.

So Nikolaus Chrastny really was another one-off. Brilliant, he was; a very wealthy man and a great charmer – could get birds off of trees. He was nicked as a leading man in an international drugs syndicate back in June 1987 before these things was as popular as they are today. The customs found a whole lot of cocaine in Harley Street which isn't where you always find it. It was said to have been worth £14 million then, so you can work out what it was worth today. What he was also was a friend of Roy Garner, who'd been a top villain and a top grass at the same time.

At the time Chrastny was nicked, there was a whole lot of trouble going on at Scotland Yard with stories that some officers were involved in dealing drugs. Chrastny tells them he can help put one or two down and so, rather then let him stay down in London where there's always a possibility someone might get to him and explain the error of his ways in being a grass, he's shipped off to Yorkshire. It wasn't the last time this happened. A few years later it was thought that Garner was going to spill the beans and he got sent up to Attercliffe in Sheffield from the Long Sutton nick in great secrecy so there could be private interviews. That didn't do much good because the local paper had hold of it in no time.

First off Chrastny was sent to Rotherham, but they thought he was getting too friendly with some officers and it's over to Dewsbury. Anyway there he is in the nick in the area usually used for women prisoners. Soon, he'd got himself a television and stereo and his wife Charlotte's allowed in for dinner sometimes. Funnily enough she'd been a copper in Germany before she met him, and it's only natural they'd want to talk in German isn't it? Not too many of the local coppers was fluent but that didn't matter since they wasn't joining in. People liked Mrs C. There wasn't always a search and, it turned out later, even when she was found with £500 on her she was allowed to give it to her husband. It must have been reasonably comfortable. Apart from the telly and the stereo he was allowed to have beer and cigars, and jars of chutney, and 41 books including *The Hound of the Baskervilles*. And two files, which it was said his wife brought in hidden in the spine.

Poor devil, he's there on his own and its only right he should have something to do when they're not asking him questions and his wife's not around, so he's given stuff to make models, stuff like plasticine, Blu-tak, paint and glue.

That's one of the problems with grasses, you've got to keep them sweet. In a way you need them more than they need you. There's always that bit of gold at the end of the rainbow that's going to make you the most famous copper in the world. If they clam up it's gone. So when Chrastny gets the stuff he puts it to good use. As well as the models he's spending his time sawing through the bars. No one heard the sawing because he'd got the TV and the stereo on. That's the trouble with leaving someone in one place for too long. If they're shifted around regular enough they can saw as much as they like. It all goes to waste.

Anyway the day before he's being taken back to court in London he's managed to get through the bars. His cell didn't have a plug in it of course, and the cable for his telly ran from the medical room opposite, so that couldn't be locked. And that didn't have any bars on the windows, so he's up and running, across the prison yard, and he's never seen again; not here anyway. Of course there was an inquiry and what come out was there was a car waiting for him. It wasn't until the next morning that anyone looked for him. He was always given a lie-in, because it was 11.30 by that time. He left a note saying goodbye and they did hear from him again because he rang and said he was sorry for the inconvenience he'd caused. What was so amazing was that he was already on the run from the coppers in West Germany over an armed robbery. He'd had his face changed by plastic surgery several times. You'd have thought they might have taken more care of him.

Someone's got to suffer for things like that and they did his wife for helping him escape. She got a not guilty but she got a seven over the cocaine. After that there was all sorts of guidelines about how to keep hold of informers. No booze, no sex, officers in uniform on guard, that sort of thing. Anyway it didn't matter to Chrastny. There was some story he was in Costa Rica.

EDDIE CHAPMAN

I never tried my hand as a safebreaker. I didn't even want to try. That was a specialist's job. As a thief you had to know your limitations. In my day it was a question of stuffing jelly into the lock and standing back. It wasn't that difficult and what with the War the manufacturers took a long time to bring out new models. Even so, you always knew one or two who had died as well. It was no good unless you had training in some type of explosives. It was more or less handed down. That's where I was at a disadvantage with no one in the family interested in things like safes. I suppose I could have gone to that top man Jock Robinson, Jock the Fitter, who was with the mother of Paddy O'Nione – Paddy Onions – for years, and asked him to show me but I never did. Most of the really good safeblowers were Scots. It came from handling explosives in the mines.

Eddie Chapman was an exception but there again he came from the North East. I liked Eddie. He was class. I met him through Hilly and Albert. What a feat he'd done. All through the War he was game. He was a true working-class patriot. He come from somewhere near Sunderland, and it wasn't until he was well in his twenties that he started safecracking. He'd already got a life saving medal and he'd been in the Guards, the Coldstream I think he used to say. I think he did a bit of time in the Glasshouse as well. He'd fallen in love with a brass and when he left her she rang up the coppers to say he was a deserter. After that it was a spell in Lewes, where he teamed up with a really good blower and that's where he learned the trade. Some people say it was Jimmy Hunt but I'm not so sure it wasn't Freddie Ford, who went on to own a lot of spielers and had the scheme where brasses took suitcases into the hotels Fred had so it couldn't be said he was knowingly running a brothel.

Whichever it was they split up and in 1939 Eddie's found screwing a safe in Edinburgh with some other blokes. He got himself out on bail, and the others out when he did a screwer to raise their bail, and it's over to Jersey where he's arrested again.

One of the blokes who'd been nicked with him in Edinburgh sends a postcard to his girlfriend and it's traced. The girl had a brother who was a cozzer. That copper Greeno come over from England along with Fabian to nick him, but Eddie says he's blown a safe and so the Jersey court give him two years for openers before he's to go back to the mainland. By now the War's coming and the Germans occupied the Channel Islands.

The Huns made him an offer to go over to Britain and carry out sabotage and Eddie thought if he could get back home then he could join up again. They give him the codename Fritzchen and in December 1942 they dropped him by parachute near Ely. What he was meant to be doing was blowing up the De Havilland place near Hatfield where we was building the Mosquito fighting bomber. He was told he was going to get £15,000 if it went off all right and then he'd be sent off to America to do some work there. I think he said they'd give him a grand expenses up front, which was big money in them days.

The moment he lands he gets on the blower to the local nick but he can't get the coppers there to understand what he's going on about. Eventually he does manage to get to see someone who knows what the SP is, and he's retrained by us and given the name Zig Zag. What he does next is go back with an MI5 officer and pretends to blow up De Havillands. The whole thing was set up by the magician Jasper Maskelyne, who used to have a Christmas show in the Scala Theatre, just near where Alec de Antiquis got killed when he tried to stop a getaway and my friend was topped over it.

Anyway Maskelyne puts on this illusion that the factory's gone up the spout and it's all over the papers. The Huns are well pleased and they tell Eddie to get himself back to Germany where there's wine and women waiting for him and after that it'll be off to the States. What he really wants to do is have a go at killing Hitler but our authorities wouldn't wear it. I don't know why not. So Eddie's put on a boat to Lisbon which is neutral but full of Nazis. He's given a piece of coal and told to go and put it in the coalhole of the ship he's on. The idea is that it was going to blow the ship up when it goes in the boiler but Eddie's handed it over to the captain. The Huns don't suspect anything and he's a bit of a hero with them and they give him the Iron Cross just before he's sent back to England. Same thing happens; he lands, rings up the local police and they tell him he's drunk and should go to bed. The MI5 put him up in Knightsbridge but that was a bit too near to Soho for Eddie and he was forever meeting his pals, so he got dropped out. But he'd more than done his bit.

After the War Eddie wrote his memoirs; they got published in France, so he was done under the Official Secrets Act. He got fined £50, something like that. Eventually they came out over here and they've done very well. There was also that film about him with Christopher Plummer, called *Triple Cross*. By then though, Eddie was well in with Billy and the rest of us. He was a good man to have around. He wasn't a drinker like some of the younger men. But you'd see him in Ginny's in Archer Street from time to time. Until Aggie Hill opened the New Cabinet, that and Bobby's were the places to be. Well, before Tommy McCarthy opened the Log Cabin.

It was after I was put away for slashing Jack Spot that Billy decided to have him and a few others go to Africa. If I hadn't been away I'd have been with them. I've written about it before but they was going to kidnap some Sultan or other in Madagascar. They never got near. People started quarrelling on the boat and then they got into a fight in Tangier and were thrown out of there. I think the boat went up in flames as well.[1]

In a way Eddie was mixing with a different circle by then. He'd grown away from our life. He'd moved out of Soho and into Knightsbridge and Chelsea. Over the years Eddie put a good bit of money away because he had a sort of health club, funnily enough not far from Hatfield, and he spent a lot of his time trying to get people interested in police corruption but he never really managed it. He knew what was going on with coppers but no one wanted to know. He was in that television programme, *The Underworld*, with me in 1993, and a bit after that he went to the Canaries. I had a drink with him just before he left. He died a few years back. He really was one of the best.

---

[1] *Mad Frank and Friends.*

NEWCASTLE

Fortunately I don't like holidays so I've never been tempted to buy a timeshare. Many people have and some have done well out of them, but my advice would be not to go near most of them. They've often caused a lot of trouble and there's been a lot of problems, particularly down in Tenerife in that resort of Los Cristanos. A lot of big money's been made and lost over timeshares there and a number of big people from the North East had interests. There's also been a lot of stories about bad fights and beatings, and of girls being hung out of the windows by their feet as warnings from rival salesmen and, from what I know, they're more than half right.

That girl, Jackie Ambler, from near Doncaster got 27 years in Tenerife back in 1998. The pros out there said she'd got hold of a couple of men who'd agreed to do in Michael O'Hara, her boyfriend who was a partner in a bar she had in Los Cristanos. In 1995 he'd been beaten over the head with a beer barrel and then had a cloth stuffed down his throat at Stevie's Bar, which was the one he owned with Jackie. The story the pros had was that she offered £54,000 to a fellow, Gary Holmes, and another, Stanley Stewart, to do him in. Now, £54,000 seems a lot to me. You could have probably found a hundred people who'd have done it for a tenth of the price and they wouldn't even have wanted a business class ticket on the plane. Jackie always said she'd nothing to do with it but the trouble was the men had gone and confessed, a bit after they got arrested. That's the difficulty, once you say something, or put it down on paper more particularly, you're in trouble saying how you was made to do it.

When the trial came about, Gary Holmes changed his story and said that he'd killed O'Hara over a drug debt and he'd made things up against Jackie and Stanley Stewart because he thought she'd lollied him over drug dealing. He said that Stanley had just tried to break up the fight. In his statement Stewart had said he'd gone along with things because he was scared of Holmes and the men he worked for. The trouble in their case was they'd not just made the statement to the police; they'd done it before an examining magistrate. The men got 29 years apiece.

There have been some good people up in the North East over the years. In my day a lot of them was doing time for blowing peters. That was their strong coup. They'd worked in the mines and they knew what they was doing. Sometimes they was recruited to help out on a job but generally they kept to themselves. I know Newcastle isn't as far away as Glasgow but in them days it seemed like it was. Eddie and me had a couple of machines up there but it was really a bit far for us to go. We was doing so well in Manchester and Leeds we hadn't expanded further. If Mr Smith's hadn't happened we might have started there but it's history now.

More recently Viv Graham was one of the biggest but it's never been satisfactorily worked out whose side he was on. Like so many towns, Newcastle's had its bouncer wars. There was one back in 1988. People wanted to get their drugs into clubs and the bouncers are often there to make sure only the favoured friends can sell in them. It was reckoned to be a place to make a reputation, an easier place than, say, Manchester or Liverpool. There was big trouble again in 1993 with a lot of shootings and a couple of leading lights disappeared. Things have continued on and off since then even though they've got bouncers licensed now like they have in so many places all over the country.

Viv Graham come from the Winlaton area. The places there were clannish and tough small towns, ruled by such good men as Denny Haig. Graham's father was himself a hardman and Viv did a lot of boxing and bodybuilding. He become a doorman and a protector for many of the winebars and clubs in Newcastle and Gateshead. The police reckoned he was pulling in the region of six figures a year and a lot of it went to support his gambling habit. His right-hand man was Robert Armstrong and he'd been friendly with members of both the Tams and Sayers families. I knew Viv from being in Durham with him. He was quite a big guy physically, well liked and respected. I never saw a lot of him because I was in chokey so much of the time but what I saw I liked. In chokey there I'd be in a cage, but I could talk through the wire to the guy in the next one. So I kept up with the news.

Maybe the real Newcastle trouble of the time started in August 1988. That was when Robert Bell was dining in Santino's Restaurant in the Cloth Market with Viv when two men burst in. One of them cut the telephone lines and the pros said the other man went to the table where Bell was sitting and pointed a shotgun at him. Of course there was a ruckus and Viv Graham took the gun off him and smashed it against the wall and told them not to be so stupid. It was after that Bell got stabbed in the heart, but he survived. Graham took on the pair and give one of them a beating. They only found the man Viv had done over and later he got a not guilty for stabbing Bell.

A bit after that, but before the trial, Viv and Rob Armstrong had been shot at when they was outside the Manhattan nightclub in the city, in April 1989. Someone shot out the rear window of their Bluebird Nissan and around 60 pellets was fired into Rob. Viv wasn't hit. There's one version that Viv saw himself as some controlling influence on the clubs, a sort of roving Guardian Angel who went around town late at night stopping trouble, and maybe that's right, but that wasn't the way everybody else saw it. What it was of course was protection one way or another and there was stories a team from Leeds was trying to put things together in the town. Like I say, things on Tyneside weren't as difficult as they were over on Merseyside.

It was all go. A couple of months later a doorman, Mark Stephenson, had his ear bitten off at Idols, a club over in Whitley Bay, and then that good boxer Howard Mills, who was now working as a doorman at Hanrahan's Bar, was shot in the leg which he had to have off.

The next year Viv got three years for wounding Stuart Watson, the doorman of Hobo. You can never really tell what's what and who's who. At the end of the Watson trial the doorman said he was sorry for what had happened and went on to say the coppers had been using him as bait to get Graham and the others. There'd been an undercover bogey posing as a customer when the incident had taken place who had been under orders not to intervene. The briefs for the defence asked whether once he saw a man had got some sort of spike he shouldn't have broke his cover, but he said he was under orders not to.

Along with Viv were members of some of the families. Alan Tams picked up two-and-a-half years and so did Stephen Sayers. David Lancaster and Rob Armstrong also went down as well. It was one of those cases when the police guarded the court. Some of them had been up in court only a few weeks earlier when John Henry Sayers and Stephen Sayers was charged with a variety of things including conspiracy to handle stolen vending machines. Alan Tams was charged with a series of assaults. When it come to it he admitted biting a copper on the arm – he threatened to bite off the man's nose if he come any closer – and he had a bit added to his thirty months. The copper had tried to stop a sort of free-for-all when eggs, flour and ketchup was being thrown at each other. Alan was seen walking from a shop with a tray of eggs whilst the others continued fighting. One of the stories is that it was after he went down for the Watson case Viv went on his own and he fell out with some members of the families.

Viv got the unofficial credit for doing Gazza's knee in September 1991 in Walkers in Newcastle. The coppers could never find witnesses and Gazza, to his credit, said he wanted the whole thing dropped. The troubles had led to a registration scheme for nightclub doormen. It was started in May 1992 by the Northumbria police and it was the first of its kind in the country. Anyone who wanted a licence had to get all their doormen vetted. It's all over the country now but it hasn't got rid of dealing.

It was New Year's Eve 1993 Viv was killed by three shots from a .357 Magnum handgun as he walked to his car in the Wallsend district. It looks like his attackers had been shadowing him for most of the evening. He'd been drinking most the time at a couple of pubs. He crawled thirty yards before collapsing outside a newsagent's shop.

Just about the only unchallenged thing about the killing of Viv is that he's dead. How it happened and who ordered it depends on whether he was a friend. There was all sorts of stories why he'd been topped. One of them was that he was negotiating with the black dealers in Leeds – he was seen in the Hilton there in the summer of 1993 – and there had been attempts by a Yorkshire team to muscle in on the North Eastern trade. Some people have it that he'd upset some of the big North East families and there's a story that goes back to the timeshare business in Tenerife. Then there's people that say that the killers came from suppliers in Liverpool or London, or that the men were Italians brought up from London on contract to do the business. It's really a question of take your pick. If people had been brought up from London it wouldn't have been the first time, but there's plenty of homegrown talent up in the North East.

The timeshare story is related to the death of his arch-rival Andy Winder, who died in Tenerife in 1993. Winder was in charge of the touts for a big firm in the timeshare business in Los Cristanos. Winder'd already got control of the touting in a couple of the other islands, Lanzarote and Gran Canaria, and he wanted control of South Tenerife as well.

The story is there was a bare-knuckle fight between Viv and Winder who needed a lot of work done on his face to make him look respectable again. What he did then was put out a sort of insurance or revenge with a £30,000 contract on Viv, only to be executed after his own death. In fact he got done in late September 1993 which makes the timing about right. You don't do the contract the very next day. You've got to look at things carefully. This time Winder had tried to stab a fellow Teessider who was over in Tenerife and, when some others intervened, he stabbed them as well. That was when someone shot him.

There was all sorts of stories flying around about the contracts out on Viv's life. One man meant to have had an offer was Lee Duffy, from Eston near Middlesborough. He'd already got a slice of the protection in Cleveland and he'd been offered a good slice of Newcastle by one of the families if he could get rid of Viv. Not that he didn't have enemies himself. There'd been three goes or more on him. He'd been shot in the knee and in the foot different times. It seems he'd tried to meet Viv Graham on a number of occasions but Viv hadn't turned up before Duffy got stabbed to death in a fight with David Allison in Middlesborough. Duffy had him on the floor banging his head but Allison managed to stab him and I'm pleased to say he got a not guilty. David, poor man, didn't have much luck in his life. He come home one day and found the girl he'd been living with for years had topped herself.

Then there was the question of whether Graham was really in the rackets. A lot of people thought he was well out of the way and they included some licensees. At the time of his death he was talking with designer drug suppliers in Holland.

The story is that the coppers reckoned Andrew Winder was involved in importing drugs through Teeside and Hartlepool and they linked him with a seemingly straight man who they fancied for laundering the proceeds of major crime, along with the businessman's enforcer. I'm not going to name the hardman, just call him Frank – after me that is.

Frank's employer had gone abroad by now and Frank was working in the construction industry so was able to travel the country legitimate, looking after the man's interests. That was when he was approached by a young man and asked how to deal with Viv. Frank reckoned the best thing was to make an example out of Viv as a warning to other villains, particularly the West End families. The idea was he should be kneecapped and so people could see him being wheeled about for the rest of his life. A car was stolen from Birtley, which is between Newcastle and Durham, and a kid was supplied with a .44 short barrel Magnum which had come from Ulster.

If it was to be just a kneecapping it didn't work out. If you're going to do that sort of thing it's like putting a bullet in the nut. It's got to be done at short range. What went wrong is that Viv just sort of dominated the man and the shot come from too far away. The idea if you're doing it for keeps is you follow up with a second shot to make sure. The story is that the fellow who actually shot Viv went into the nick abroad for credit card thefts and robberies.

I've known Joe Stafford – his real name was Siegenberg – and his son, Dennis, most of my life. Hilly was going to do Dennis Stafford once, but his father rang up and said 'Please don't touch him' and Hilly left him alone. Joe Stafford was a publican and bookmaker. He'd buy a bit of crooked gear here and there and laid a few bets and of course he was a straightener. If you wanted someone to talk to the coppers then Joe was one of the men to get into them for you. Joe could always be relied on to go and talk to someone he knew. Of course he wasn't doing it for nothing.

It's amazing that the really big murder on Tyneside took place as long as 35 years ago now. It's never really been cleared up as to who did it and why and who was behind it, but one of the men involved was Dennis Stafford. He'd already had a bit of a career up there before then.

Dennis was a good-looking boy, a bit flashy when he was younger but that was when we all had brilliantine or Brylcream on our hair. He made his name as a high class con-man and burglar and he was a good escaper as well. He picked up a seven at the Inner London Sessions for breaking and entering and having a firearm back in July 1956 but he didn't stay in long. Four months later on a wet and windy day he escaped over the wall at the Scrubs, along with Tony Hawkes who was another high class con-man. He was doing a six-year sentence for false pretences over a textile fraud. Over the years he'd been a foreign attaché, a cavalry officer, a city businessman and I think he'd even been a foreign butler at one time.

They had help, of course, because they was up in Newcastle within three weeks and by then they was flush enough to set up another long firm in the clothing trade. Dennis was Hutton and Tony was Whelby. They got out just before the creditors and the coppers arrived. They got Tony quick enough in a hotel off the Bayswater Road but there wasn't much sign of Dennis, which wasn't surprising since he was in Trinidad. He'd changed his name again and this time he was Wally Birch which was the name of the close mate of Joe Wilkins. Dennis's real problem was that women was always after him or the other way around and he'd ditched the girl he had up in Newcastle and he'd got a new fiancée. The trouble was the coppers knew who she was and was watching her and so when she sent him a telegram saying she was coming out, so was the police.

Old Dennis was a rascal. Whilst he was in the nick in Port of Spain he wrote his exclusive for the *News of the World* saying how sorry he was he'd let everybody down including his dad, Joe, which was a bit rich really. Now he was going to go straight. Joe played his bit saying it was the War which had led the boy astray and if he'd had a bit of dad's right hand he'd have been a lot better. If Joe'd said that today, the kid would have been removed into care and he'd probably be doing a few weeks himself.

Once he was back Dennis picked up another eighteen months. He was sent down to Dartmoor but he didn't stay long there. He tried to get out twice and failed and it was third time lucky. Just after New Year 1959 he got out with William Day, who was a house and garage breaker and was also doing a seven. They reckoned Dennis was abroad within a few days.

It was a bit of bad luck for Bill though. Unfortunately he didn't get clear. It was driving rain and thick fog as well. That's a good time for an escape, of course. If you've never been on the Moor you don't know how it can blanket things down and you can have rain and fog at the same time. That's when the condensation starts in the cells, everything's damp. Bill was found drowned in a reservoir. It seems like he blundered into the water and Dennis had thrown him a lifebelt but hadn't raised the alarm.

In fact Dennis never got abroad this time. He stuck around in this country and a bit over six weeks later he got picked up in Leicester Square and it was back to solitary for him. I was in Dartmoor by then; on stage which is the special wing, where you got privileges after you'd done four years. Some people didn't think Dennis'd done enough for Bill and there was a bit of bad feeling, but in them situations it's every man for himself. You've got to take your own chance and if you go on an escape you know it. Dennis was allowed out of solitary by the Governor to tell Joe that there wasn't any trouble over Bill. He said that he had not just thrown him a lifebelt but he'd gone in the water after him and grabbed him but had lost hold in the dark.

Then what happens? 'Happy' Sambridge, the man I took a leg off for grassing me down at Brighton Races, makes a statement that he'd planted the gun in Dennis's car. He said he'd been approached by a detective who had the needle to Stafford and wanted him nicked. Sambridge says he'd been given a gun by the copper and he left it on the shelf under the dashboard. He'd got a fiver for this, which shows what an evil bastard he was. Doing something like that for a fiver. Still, I suppose you don't know what hold the copper had on him. It goes all the way up to the Home Office and Joe Stafford says this proves his boy's got too long a sentence for the screwing but, of course, nothing happens.

Dennis is out in March 1961 and it's one of those bright dawns. He's a bit of a celeb really which goes to show that all this lionising of the likes of us didn't just happen in the last ten years. He got a job with a car and a four figure wage which wasn't bad considering you could buy two houses for that in Tottenham and probably four in Newcastle in those days. People was saying how he'd settled down and he'd learned his lesson. But rascals like Dennis and me don't learn our lessons until we've lost the legs to run away. Three months later he's found with a Browning and this time he's called Fielding, so it's back in the nick.

Then when he's out in 1965 he makes what's going to be his most expensive mistake ever. He goes back to Newcastle and starts working for Vince Landa. He was another who'd changed his name. He'd been Vincente Luvaglio, who was the big man with the machines up there and who's also running cabarets. One of the other fellows who was working for Landa was Angus Sibbett.

Sibbett was a big man; had a beard in the days when they wasn't as fashionable. He'd been around. He'd worked with people in London and he'd run a Chinese restaurant of all things. I think he did a twelve-month stretch for receiving before he went up to the North East and teamed up with Vince Landa who'd got the Social Club Services Ltd. It was a bit like Atlantic Machines – put the one-arm bandits in clubs, took the money out and split it with the club owners. Like I've said, there was good money for everyone provided you could make sure the staff wasn't skimming.

Landa'd been a copper in the RAF before he came up to the North East and started putting together the machines and things. He really made it – country house, a villa in Majorca. He'd got a Roller and goodness knows how many other cars. His younger brother Michael worked for him and all.

Sibbett got done at the beginning of January 1967. Some miners was passing on their way to work about five in the morning and there was a Mark X Jaguar parked near a bridge at South Hetton and Angus was dead in it. And so it all started to go wrong for Dennis and Michael. He was the one who'd been driving the Jaguar recently.

Someone had bubbled Dennis about his LF all those years before and they done the same over again. Now ten years later someone told the coppers there was a damaged E-type Jaguar in a garage in Sunderland.

It seems like the whole Luvaglio family and Dennis and his girlfriend had been over to Majorca and everyone had flown back up to Newcastle after the New Year. Everyone that is except Vincent who had stayed in London and then pushed off back to Majorca. It seems he'd given permission for Dennis to use the E type.

It wasn't what you'd call a strong case against them. There's no doubt the E type had been in some sort of a smash with the car Sibbett was found in and they'd been planning to meet Sibbett that night. They said he hadn't turned up at the Bird Cage Club and whilst they was waiting Dennis went outside to get some cigarettes he'd left in the car and that's when he saw it was damaged. He told the club doorman what he'd seen. There was some tyre marks in the snow which looked like someone had driven into the motor and then pushed off.

It was one of those cases where the pros said that even with alibis, and both of them had good ones – one of them was that good singer, Selena Jones – the men could have got out of the club, killed Angus, dumped his body and been back inside three-quarters of an hour. And of course it was like one of those detective stories and the time of Angus's death. Did the cold that night make any difference? Anyway, they said, why should they kill Angus who was their friend? The judge didn't do them no favours, saying that friends could be like Judas or Brutus. The pros never said why they thought he'd been done.

The jury was out three hours before returning a guilty verdict. No one was very happy, least of all Dennis and Michael, of course. The Court of Appeal knocked them back and even when that dodgy Home Secretary Reginald Maudling sent it back for a re-hearing of the appeal that didn't do any good. Of course Maudling was well mixed up with the North East. Michael's parents stuck by him and they got hold of that London brief, David Napley, who always reckoned Michael was innocent.

Joe Stafford did what he could as well. If you read Nipper Read's book you can see he was offering to turn the Krays in if Read could do anything about his boy's conviction. He even tried to see the then Prime Minister, Harold Wilson. It's funny how things go circling round. Just like 'Happy' Sambridge who said he'd been paid to plant the gun which did for Dennis all those years back, in 1967, a North East face, George Shotton, come forwards and said he'd been offered five grand to do Sibbett. He'd been in the Bird Cage when he'd been approached and he thought the man was Italian. George was a car dealer now but he'd got a string of form and the authorities wasn't going to listen to him if they didn't need to. Another geezer come forward and said the same thing but he thought the fellow who put the offer up might have been a bubble.

There was something of a campaign for them and it went back to the courts but the House of Lords give them their final knockback in the October. Both men were paroled in 1979 and that was when Dennis did neither of them a favour. Well, he might have got himself out of a mess short term but it didn't help long term. He went and told a fellow from the papers that he'd done Sibbett. He was said to have got ten grand for the confession.[1] He'd done it whilst Michael was in bed. That really messed things up. He was wanted for a few credit card frauds and was on his toes again. Poor old Michael. He'd done well for himself in the nick and he'd got an Open University degree. Since he come out he's been working with disabled kids.

Dennis tried to get out of the trouble he'd caused by telling another paper he'd only given the interview for the money and it was all cobblers, but then he went and said something about how he was trying to expose the judicial system. The next I heard of him was when I came out from the twenty and someone told me he was in the nick in South Africa over another fraud out there.

The killing did for just about everyone involved. Vince Landa's empire went bust and it turned out that Sibbett had had his forks in the till. He'd been screwing the firm out of around £1,600 a week, which was serious money then and it's not even bad now. Landa had pushed off back to Majorca once more and sort of moved around the Mediterranean for a few years before he showed up in Malta in 1977. He got brought back here and got fined for frauds on working men's clubs which had happened in the Sibbett days. The judge give him credit for the time he'd been in the nick abroad waiting to be brought back which is more than

---

[1] *News of the World*, 7 September 1980.

my David got when he got done over drugs a few years ago. The last I heard of Landa was that he was in Florida but that can be wrong.

A bit later Dennis got pulled in for breaking the conditions of his licence. Something to do with a bit of fraud, non-violent anyway. He went back to the courts to get them to say the Home Secretary was wrong but he got blanked off over it. I heard Dennis was out and about a year ago but I haven't seen him. Then I heard he was trying to get his conviction looked at by the Criminal Review Board. It was about that time that I heard the story that the killing had been done by a London firm and was nothing to do with either Dennis or Michael. I knew the names put up and from what I know it was possible but where I come from you hear stories like this every week.

Over the years there's been some other big murders up in the North East and one of them was one of the early railway murders. Of course, the first murder on the railway was big news. It was back in 1864 when that fellow Franz Muller – they named a hat after him – killed a fellow called Thomas Briggs during a robbery whilst the train was going between Bow and Hackney Wick. He only got away with the man's gold watch and he left his own hat behind, taking his victim's. There was a lot of publicity and a man came forward to say he recognised it. After that it was a bit of a chase with Muller trying to get to America. The coppers went on a faster boat, just like Dew did when he was chasing Crippen and that was that so far as Muller was concerned.

After that come a number of killings. There was Percy Lefroy. He did a fellow called Isaac Gold who was a coin dealer from Brighton, in the early 1880s. He shot him as the train went into the Merstham Tunnel in Kent. Lefroy's story was a load of flannel. He said he'd been knocked out by three men who'd shot Gold. He never could explain how he came to have Gold's coins. They topped him quick enough. Then come a woman who was found dead when the train arrived at Waterloo. Another fellow got done near Wimbledon and the last before the one up near Newcastle was a real mystery. A girl called Sophie Money was killed. Funny, that was also down near Merstham. They could never work out what she was doing on the train in the first place let alone who did her. You'd have to bet on a secret boyfriend though.

Nearly fifty years after the first murder came the case of John Dickman. March 1910 it was. It was a wages robbery and Dickman was said to have done John Nisbett who'd collected about £370 to pay the miners at the colliery he worked at. People said they saw Dickman getting on the train with a man and Mrs Nisbett had seen her husband on the train with a man when she come to give him a wave at the station. She knew Dickman but she never picked him out as the man with her husband. When the train gets to Alnmouth, a porter looks in and there's blood under the seat and Nisbett's been shot five times with two different guns. Remember in those days there wasn't open carriages like there is now. You sat four or five aside facing each other.

The bag, without the money, is found down a mine shaft near Morpeth where Dickman got off. The police never found the guns that was used but they could prove Dickman had one and they could prove he'd got gambling problems. What it amounted to was that Dickman admitted he been on the train and when he was nicked and the house searched there was a pair of bloodstained trousers and £17 in gold sovereigns. He said the blood had come from a nosebleed and, of course, in them days there wasn't the testing there is now. He said the coins was part of his commission from a bookmaker but if that's right it was a lot.

The ticket collector said that when he handed in his ticket at Morpeth, Dickman had kept his other hand out of sight and what he meant was that he was trying to hide the bag. No one ever managed to get over the fact that there'd been two guns used which makes it seem like it was a double handed robbery. In fact it came out later that Dickman sometimes wrapped smaller bullets in paper and that made up for the difference in the bullets.

There's no doubt when the murder went off he owed a few hundred to money lenders. There really wasn't anything but circumstantial evidence but everyone was against him at the start of the trial. By the end, when he was sentenced to swing, people had turned around, saying there wasn't really enough evidence to top him. Five of the jurors asked for a reprieve. The day before he was due, there was handbills all over London but by then it was too late. There was about 1,500 outside the nick to watch the flag go up.

Funnily enough his name was mentioned over a case in Kent in August 1908. There'd been a big unsolved murder down there near Ightham when a woman, Caroline Luard, was found shot dead in a summerhouse. Someone had pulled the rings off of her fingers. There was a bit of evidence Dickman had forged a cheque which she'd sent him in reply to an ad asking for financial help but that was about all. Her husband topped himself soon after – threw himself under a train. It came out later that all the judges who heard Dickman's appeal knew Luard and that case and so did Winston Churchill, who was the Home Secretary and turned down the reprieve.

It was about twenty years later came one of the really big unsolved murders. It was a girl called Evelyn Foster back in 1931. She ran a taxi service with her father and one night in early January a bus driver came across their cab in a place called Wolf's Nick on the road to Otterburn. Their new Hudson was on fire and the girl was laying nearby badly burned. They got her back home and she'd got a funny story saying she'd picked up a fare who wanted to go on to Ponteland where he could pick up the bus to Newcastle. A few miles before they got to Ponteland he tells her to turn back and, when she does so, he throws fluid over her and sets fire to her. Then he puts the car in gear and it runs off the road with her in it. The girl's last words is when she tells her mother she's been murdered. She's also told her she's been assaulted. She said he'd got a bowler hat on and he was a heavy smoker and had a Tyneside accent.

It was a funny old case as I say. It turned out from tests that the car had been carefully driven off the road and then set on fire, not the other way around. There wasn't any evidence she'd been raped either. The inquest comes back with wilful murder but the police said they were convinced the man didn't exist. They thought she'd topped herself and there was a story it was for the insurance, but it's a hard way to collect. You'd have thought she didn't need to set fire to herself if she was going along those lines, but when you're dealing with petrol and the like it's easy enough for the wind to blow back a flame.

Just like when Neville Cream was being topped and he called out 'I'm Jack . . .' and started people thinking he was Jack the Ripper, so a fellow called Ernest Brown started a story that he might have been the man who did for Evelyn. He was a groom who'd shot his employer, a Frederick Morton, and had tried to get rid of the body in a burning garage. Brown had been having it off with Morton's wife. It just shows you shouldn't have it off with the servants. Brown cut the telephone wires whilst Morton was away and terrorised the woman and the maid by shooting outside the house. There's a big explosion about 3.30 the next morning and the garage is on fire. When it cools down enough for people to get near, there's Morton's two cars burned to bits and Morton himself is shot in the chest. The story goes that just as Brown was about to swing he said something like 'Otterburn'. It may have been 'ought to burn' for all anyone knew because they didn't stop and ask him what he meant. But the thing stuck. I don't think there was any evidence against him at all except, as a groom in them days, he wore a bowler hat and he'd been going around the North East going to agricultural shows.

There was a sort of early Craig and Bentley case back in 1940 when a PC Sheill got killed. There's no doubt who was involved and one of the men was Ostler, the son of a copper from Leeds. Him and another kid Appelby was out screwing the local Co-op at Coxhoe, Co. Durham at the end of February 1940 when Sheill saw them. Sometimes it seems that the Co-op was the only place that was screwed back then but, if it was, it was because every place had one and often it was the only shop for miles. Sheill blew his whistle for help and then chased them into Westley Place, where he was shot. The kids got away and he was taken to the local hospital where he said he was finished.

The local justices' clerk was called to take what they called a dying declaration from him. The dying declaration was quite often used in those days when people had respect for religion. Normally if someone said something against you it had to be in your presence before the beak would allow it to be given. It stands to reason. Otherwise it was called hearsay and wouldn't be allowed in. This dying declaration was an exception. People was thought to be so fearful of dying and God that they wouldn't lie about what happened. This time the copper said he'd cornered them and one had pulled a revolver and the other had said, 'Let him have it. He's all alone'; almost the exact words that did for Bentley.

One of the reasons I got an acquittal in that murder trial after Dickie Hart got killed at Mr Smith's was I was alone in the dock. I didn't have to worry about what other briefs was going to say to the court or what the other defendants was going to say. Not that it come to my giving evidence, but I didn't have to worry about what I said harming anyone else either.

The real worry is if you've got too many defendants and they start running what's called a cut-throat defence, putting the blame on someone else in the dock. Very often they cut everyone's throat and their own. That's why the pros likes to have as many in the dock as possible all together. That's what happened this time. Ostler ran an alibi but what happens is Appelby says he was present when Ostler had shot the copper. And he went and gave evidence to that effect. Appelby denied saying 'Let him have it. He is all alone.' What he'd really said was, 'Let's give him a clout.' The judge wasn't having none of it. He reckoned they was both in it and if Appelby hadn't called out then Ostler might not have shot Sheill. They both swung of course, just like Bentley.

If I had a pound for every time I've heard the story about how the Krays tried to take over Manchester or Leeds or Newcastle or wherever, and the local villains banded together and gave them a beating, or the police put them on the train back to London, I'd not need to write these books. The story's just not true. For a start they always went by car. The stories have become part of those urban legends you read about, like the fellow who goes to bed with a girl and next morning he finds she's gone but she's left a message, 'Welcome to the World of AIDS' in lipstick on his mirror. That would have made him miss his breakfast. There's no doubt the Twins did go up to Newcastle. They took Joe Louis up with them and they met with the top people just as when they came down they've the same hospitality given them, but Ronnie and Reggie wasn't interested in taking things over.

By the middle of the 1980s there were rumours that some of the big families who'd been at war with each other for years was going to come into an alliance. I was away at the time so it was only what I heard as I was being moved about, but if they ever did it come to nothing. They're still at war today from what I hear.

It was just around when I came out for the last time in 1989 that a fellow, Nigel Robinson, stabbed his girlfriend. Up in Billingham it was, near where my friend who I was with in Borstal all them years ago, came from. It turns out at his trial that Robinson's done a previous girlfriend when he was seventeen. He'd only been out six months when he did the second. Sometime you do wonder if the authorities know what they're doing.

It was up in the North East that ramraiding really took hold some years back – stealing big heavy cars like Rovers and Jaguars and driving them through shop windows so's you can get at the televisions and things. They used to have paving stones in the cars as well so they could chuck them at the police if they was being chased.

There was one blagging a bit ago where the people sealed off a whole town, just like the Wild West. Back in August 1993 it was when a gang took over Rothbury, Berwick on Tweed. What happened was that five men in ski-masks turned up in the village, cut the telephone wires and threatened the residents with crowbars.

Then they took over the main street with a stolen council van and told the residents who were looking out of their windows to go back to bed and stay there. After that they then forced their way into the post office and got away with £15,000 in cash and stuff. For the amount of bird that would have been handed out if they'd been caught it wasn't even worth while. Work it out. Assuming they get even money for the stamps they took, which isn't likely because there're going to have to give a discount unless they want to be sending letters for the rest of their lives, the top clearance is £15,000. Divide that between five and it's three grand each. What are they going to get? Fifteen minimum and that makes it about £200 a year unless they get parole when it makes it £300. I know people don't think like that. We think we're never going to get caught and if we do we won't be convicted, but that's taking a chance for silly money. They got away with it but I still think I'm right for that sort of dough. Funnily enough the year before the village store there had been ramraided.

There's still plenty of trouble up in the North East and it's just the same as everywhere else – drugs. You look at the linens. Drug dealers shot in gardens, another shot in the back at Kirkheaton Showground; it goes on and on. They had a big undercover operation in Blythe in the middle of the 1990s. There'd been something like seventeen drug-related deaths in and around the town and they had a copper, who'd grown up in the Gorbals and knew the Cumbie gang up there, come down and live as an addict. It gave him what people now call street cred. His moody was that he wanted to buy drugs to re-sell in Scotland. He was set up in a flat with an intercom system, a camera hidden in the kitchen cooker and a cupboard with a false bottom in which to hide the drugs. He'd a false passport, bank cards and a car with video equipment in the dashboard. And, of course, he went to meetings wired up. He did well because it ended up with about twenty convictions of dealers. It took it's toll on him though. He'd worked undercover in different cities for three years and he ended up going out of the police for ill-health. He's really a lesson to people. Don't trust anyone you haven't known since your childhood or who has someone vouching for them from the day they was born. It did for poor Charlie Kray and plenty of others, and it'll do for you.

DURHAM

When I'm signing books I often have a laugh with the younger girls. I say 'I knew your father' and they giggle and say 'Did you?' That's when I say I was in Borstal with him. They always look surprised and then I say 'Course I wasn't, I'm only joking.' Anyway James Morton, when he's with me, says it's insulting to them and at my age I ought to say I was with their grandfathers. It turns out he's right. We was in Hammicks in Walthamstow the other Saturday doing *Mad Frank's London* and this young girl comes up for a book to be signed. So I go through the routine and she interrupts and says 'No, it was my Granddad.' So of course I ask his name and she tells me. I say 'From up Northumberland way?' and she says 'Yes, from Workington.' I remember him well. Big man he was physically; in Portland with me, for fighting rather than thieving. I remember he had a good straightener with another kid. I can't have thought of him for fifty years. Just think of the coincidence.

By the time topping was coming to an end Albert Pierrepont, the one I attacked in Wandsworth, reckoned it was ten seconds from the moment he got in the cell to the time the trap opened. It wasn't always like that. When Sir Gilbert Middleton, who was leading a sort of brigands' band, kidnapped the Bishop of Durham on the Great North Road nine miles from Darlington back in 1317, Edward II, who was the king then, devised the punishment himself.

The poor sod had his feet tied beneath a horse and dragged a couple of miles through London to the gallows where they hanged him. They cut him down and beheaded him, tore his heart out and burned it. Then they chopped his body in four and sent one bit to Newcastle, and one to York. The other quarters went to Bristol and Dover. I don't know how they chose them last two.

I missed the riot in Durham Special Wing by about a month. February 1968 it was. Eddie and Charlie Richardson were there but I'd chinned a guard. After the seeing to I got I was put in the hospital and then I was moved to Leicester. That was another time I was asked if I wanted to go back into Broadmoor. It was the same after the Parkhurst riot; Dr Cooper, the doctor who did so much to help us, asked me again.

I wouldn't have been sent to Broadmoor by the courts and so they couldn't have thrown away the key. I had enough people behind me who would have kicked up trouble if necessary. By then you could get the press to take a bit of interest. Jimmy Brindle could have said, 'Nothing wrong with my brother-in-law'. Particularly after the Parkhurst riot which was a bit, but not that much, later, people were beginning to take some sort of interest in prisons.

I can't say I wasn't tempted to go back to Broadmoor. In fact I badly wanted to go. It would have made things much easier for me but Doreen really didn't want me there for Francis' sake. It was bad enough for him at school having me in the nick. Having me in the nut house would have made things that much worse for him. Doreen meant well, don't get me wrong, but that was her big mistake. If I'd gone to Broadmoor from Leicester there wouldn't have been no Parkhurst riot. Not with me in it anyway. No extra five years. I knew how to behave in Broadmoor and it would have been easy bird.

I liked life in the security wing although you was hemmed in. There'd be usually about eight or nine of you but at Durham there was probably about eighteen. We were all high grade trouble makers or escapers. You wouldn't have had someone like Brady. No sex cases at all, just us career criminals. Many prisoners were fighting to get in. It wasn't where you wanted to be if you was applying for parole, however. The mere fact you'd been in one could severely put you back. On the other hand it upped your status for a start.

The parole thing never worried me. I never asked because I knew I'd always get a knockback. If I thought I'd have had a fair chance I'd have gone for it but I never did. I never got any home leave in all them years either. Discipline in the security wings wasn't so fierce. There was more screws than prisoners. You didn't have to work and you did your own cooking. You could get so much a week out of your cash and you could buy food. It was the easiest bit of bird I did but the screws didn't like it. It was killing them seeing you get privileges and so there was always some screw looking to cause trouble, and it wasn't that long before I was down the chokey. I think it was their aim to close down the Security Wings and that's what happened eventually.

Charlie and Eddie and the others did wonders in that Durham riot though. It was all over another set of petty restrictions to make life difficult. The whole wing was taken over by the inmates and they managed to get into the E wing office, looked through their records and rang up the *Daily Mirror*. The records wasn't that accurate. One said that John McVicar was a friend of Charlie and Eddie and I don't think they'd ever even met.

In the end the cons more or less got what they wanted. A man from the Home Office came up to discuss things and it wasn't until then the barricades come down. Even the Home Secretary, James Callaghan, come up to Durham to see what was going on. There was no taking them outside to the courts. You could get the equivalent of three years anyway so it wasn't worth the aggro to the authorities of giving the cons a chance to be heard. It was only after Parkhurst that they took us out and did me for incitement to murder and a few GBHs. Then when it all came out about the conditions there and how we got a beating after the riot I don't think the authorities ever prosecuted anyone for disturbance again on the outside, certainly not for years. They'd learned their lesson how to keep things buttoned up.

As I say I was in the chokey at Leicester. At first you did chokey on your own wing and so I got all the news but as I became more violent I got taken down the punishment cells beneath the security wing. Even there I could shout out the window and I could get things which the fellows would attach to a bit of string and lower down for me. I had small hands so I could reach through the window and collect it. I was even caught with some tea a couple of times by screws who were patrolling with their dogs whilst I was meant to be on bread and water. But they sort of smiled as if to say 'if that's all he's up to let him do it'. So I won even then.

News travels fast in prison. The grapevine's the thing. Prisoners are always being transferred back and forwards and there's visits from the outside to a brother or a cousin and you can have relatives in more than one nick at a time so there's a constant flow of info going backwards and forwards. Then there'd be cons who was in the officers' mess. A lot of them would be grasses but if you got a stand up man then you'd get a lot of good information about what these screws was thinking of doing. There'd be other cons who worked in offices and were good at reading things upside down. They'd relay it out to a guy in the bathhouse and he'd pass it on. It sounds very melodramatic but it was very effective. As the years went by the screws got wise and they started feeding the grasses false information.

It was from Durham that John McVicar made his great escape, along with Wally Probyn who was so well thought of until he went down for interfering with kids and lost all respect. The third member was my friend Joey Martin, who did a six for shooting a bird over in Tottenham and wasn't out barely six months before he was lifed off over a blagging at a dairy in Wood Green when the milkman got shot.

No disrespect to John but he was a better escaper than he was a thief. He got something in double figures in a raid with Billy Gentry who got put away later by the first woman grass. But as an escaper John was just about in a class of his own, although his son Russell wasn't that bad either. Even when he'd been in Borstal John had been over the wall and it was 1966 when he got away from Winchester. He was part of a group of cons who was going to give evidence in the trial of a fellow in Parkhurst charged with stabbing. In those days they didn't have a proper courthouse on the island and so they brought everyone over to Winchester and took them on a coach to the court in the middle of the town, just by the cathedral, which I suppose makes it a city really. Anyway the fight in the nick was a get-up and the whole thing was a well thought out long-term escape plan. Funnily enough the fellow who's charged with the stabbing gets a guilty and five years for it.

On the way back to the nick at the end of the trial there's thirteen cons on the coach and nine of them are like John and known to be escape risks. There's seven screws and the cons are handcuffed, three to screws and ten in pairs. Whoever did the search of them before they got on the coach missed three sets of keys and the ten soon unlocked themselves. The authorities must have got word that something was on top but they reckoned it was going to be at the ferry terminal at Portsmouth and they'd got the heavy mob there ready. When it came to it the coach never got to Portsmouth. They was going through a little village, Bishops Waltham, when the cons got hold of the screws and grabs the driver. The coach comes to a halt and they're off on their toes. Some good men got away that day.

Mind you the authorities weren't that foolish. There'd been a police car behind the coach and even though the men had gone in different directions it didn't do them no good. The place was full of dogs and roadblocks within minutes. They got hold of an RAF helicopter and seven was pulled in by the next morning. John was one of two who got clean away. He stayed out about four months when he got nicked on a botched security van job. Like I say, he was a better escaper than he was a thief.

What was lucky for John was that when he was in Durham he'd run into Wally Probyn who, give him credit, was a great escaper as well. They discovered that there was a ventilation shaft under the wing floor. Probyn was very good with his hands and he started digging whilst John distracted the screws by dropping his weights. He was always a big fitness man. Probyn had lifted the equipment from the prison workshop when he pretended the cage he had for his hamster had broken and he needed wire and tools to fix it up.

Joey only turned up the day before they was due to be off. He'd been having a bit of trouble in Leicester and they fancied him as an escaper so they took him up to Durham. They went at the end of October 1968. I know Charlie had wanted to go as well and he was very upset. They got through the hole they'd dug in the shower, into the air-shaft and through a gate and climbed out onto a plastic roof. The trouble was they made a din and half the prison knew they was off before they'd got fifty feet. Poor Joey got grabbed pretty quick but Probyn and John kept going over the roofs and then they separated. Probyn went through a trapdoor and was cornered. He didn't get out until 1974.

John did a lot better. He dropped into the garden of a terraced house and then unfortunately fell over on some waste land and sprained his wrist. He also realised he'd lost a shoe and the screws had the dogs out by now. He swam twenty yards across the River Wear and hid on the other side, listening to the dogs and the crews barking at each other. Then he does this tremendous thing. He decides he's going to swim out of the city. There wasn't any other way but it was midwinter. He's dead fit mind and in he goes. Even he couldn't stand the cold though and he had to get out, so he stayed hidden for three nights in the freezing weather until he managed to get a reverse call through to his wife Shirley and she sent two men up in a car to get him. They did the right thing. Wouldn't take a penny for it. They never even knew him before and they was looking at a five for helping him if they was nicked. That's goodness for you.

It may be that I'm old fashioned but I've never fancied having my greens after another man's had his. But there's plenty who don't mind. There was a couple up in Jarrow, where that famous march started. Robert Upton and Charles Gribben were the men and they shared their housekeeper, a Mrs Burdon. Monday to Wednesday was Gribben's turn and then it was Upton who was getting it for the rest of the week. She moved beds so at least they didn't all have the same sheets. I think they was all three well on the booze. It worked perfectly well for a long time until in the middle of December 1914 Mrs Burdon told them she was fed up with being a buttered bun and was going to go off to live with a third man, Jack Bloy. They was leaving the district because I bet the neighbours was pointing their fingers from behind the curtains.

Gribben didn't mind so much but Upton wouldn't wear it and said if he couldn't have the woman then no one else was going to either. They calmed him down but just before Christmas he went out with his son Joe and with Gribben. During the night he took a razor to his mate and then turned it on himself. The police was called and he said he wanted to die but they wouldn't let him. They had to patch him up for the hangman who topped him about three months later.

Talking of buttered buns there was another case like that a few years later, a woman called Charlotte Bryant, down in Nether Compton in Dorset in 1936. Black Bess she was called and from the pictures of her she was quite a good-looking woman, about six years younger than her husband, Frederick. She was a gypsy from Ireland and she'd met him when he'd been there with the Black and Tans. She used to bring men home and sleep with them in the same bed as Frederick. I don't know if he got his turn or not. She was doing it for money and she was a good little blackmailer as well. She conned some man into paying £25 for an abortion, which was big money in those days, and then brings out a child and tries to get a few shillings a week off of him. Fred must have been in on things. He was warned about living off immoral earnings but he said that £4 a week was better than thirty shillings.

Then she goes and falls for another gypsy, Leonard Parsons, and has a kid by him. It's now she decides the husband's got to go so she can keep a hold on Parsons and get him away from another woman whose also got a few of his kids. So she poisons Fred. She give him arsenic over quite a long period. She was bound to be found out and it all come on top. The doctor wouldn't issue a death certificate and there was an inquest. Then the coppers got hold of a friend of hers and played her off. The woman was nicked and let out when she'd made a statement. Casswell defended Charlotte and he thought she was unlucky to go down. Her hair turned white whilst she was in the condemned cell and she was only 33. She learned to read and write there and made a will in which she left everything she had to be divided between her kids. All she had was less than six shillings. Parsons doesn't seem to have missed her. He was out drinking with his mates when she got topped. Over the years the story is he used to complain that whenever he tried to sell a horse people mentioned the case and it hadn't been good for his business.

Funnily there was a woman who went clinically blind when she was on remand. She was Yvonne Sleightholme and she was done for killing Jayne Smith at a farm at Salton near Malton in Yorkshire. She'd been in love with Jayne's husband and she thought he was going to marry her, but he changed his mind and married Jayne instead. Yvonne said it had been hitmen who'd done Jayne but the jury went against her. Back in 1991 it was. She never got her sight back. Even after Yvonne had done the ten years which the judge said was the tariff, she was still inside. She wouldn't admit her guilt and she was in the trap like so many others who won't do what the authorities want. Until they admit their guilt they aren't likely to get out on licence.

Mind you there's been plenty of people sold their wives over the years, particularly when divorce was so difficult to get. They'd take them down the market and auction them. Then there was a burglar sold his wife to a mate in about 1912 but then he went and shopped him so that wasn't much of a success, and in the 1920s there was a story that a woman had been sold up in South Shields along with the fixtures and fittings when a fellow sold his house. She denied it but she had a kid by the second bloke later.

There was a story about a woman, Nancy Dodds, a bit before my time; she came from Hamersley near Bishop Auckland. Married twice, buried twice and both husbands was hanged was the saying. It worked out that her first husband had committed suicide, hanging himself, and the next one, Matthew, who'd only got one leg and who'd been a miner, killed her in 1908. They'd only been married three years. She'd made a bit of money by then and at first was going to leave him £40 but either he talked her round or she changed her mind, because she told him she'd left him the lot. She only lasted a month after that. At first they thought she'd suffocated when she'd accidentally set fire to herself but there was talk in the village and an exhumation was ordered. That's the buried twice bit. When they did the examination it turned out she'd been strangled. He always maintained he was innocent and the last thing he wrote to his brother was that, 'It seems very hard that I have to suffer when I am quite innocent'. In fact he was the first person ever to go before the Court of Criminal Appeal but they set the trend with him. That was the second hanging.

He was the third person to swing in Durham that year. The first fellow, William Lowman, cut his girlfriend's throat, but they had a double hanging after a robbery at the local Co-op at Windy Nook. There'd been a lot of night time screwing the previous year and so some security guards was brought in. In the November they caught Joe Noble getting through the back door. One of the guards give him a terrible beating and the other, John Patterson, said to lay off him. Noble managed to get a gun and shot Patterson for his troubles. He got away but they found some of the property at his blacksmith's yard. They had a good line in talk that year. He's supposed to have said to the judge, 'You may break my neck but you won't break my heart'. They swung Lowman and Noble together.

There was a killing just like that Craig and Bentley case up in Gateshead years later in 1990. All those years arguing whether Bentley should have been hanged when he was in custody at the moment Christopher Craig shot the copper and it all happened again. This time the kid who got lifed off was only fifteen. People had been drinking and there'd been some trouble up on the Cloverhill estate and this Philip English and Paul Weddle, who was ten years older, became involved in a fight with a copper who'd come to sort things out. The story for the pros was that Philip struck the copper, Sergeant Bill Forth, with a fence post. He ran away and got tackled by other coppers and was in handcuffs a hundred yards away from where the Sergeant and Paul Weddle was having it out. It's then Weddle went and stabbed the copper in the heart. What the pros said was that it was a joint enterprise and that even though the kid had run away and was in custody he hadn't done or said nothing to stop his mate still taking part. I suppose he should have shouted out, 'I don't want nothing more to do with this' or 'Stop it Paul', but seeing he was a hundred yards away it's a bit difficult to know what good that would have done. Philip went down on a ten to two majority and both him and Paul, who got a unanimous, was lifed off; well because he was so young, Philip was detained during Her Majesty's pleasure, which is just another way of putting it. It took three years before the House of Lords let him out.

Over the years there's been a good clear-up rate of murders in Durham. It may have changed a bit now with drug dealers but, I think I'm right in saying, back in the early 1990s the murder of Ann Heron was the only one they'd never cleared up. She'd been done in her garden sunbathing in the village of Middleton St George near Darlington. Whoever had done it cut her throat with a weapon like a Stanley knife and part of her bikini had been removed.

Her husband found her when he came back from work and he put up a five grand reward. The coppers conducted literally thousands of interviews but they never found anyone. Then in 1994 there was a series of anonymous letters written to the police and the editor of the *Northern Echo* which began, 'Hello, editor, It's me, Ann Heron's killer!' It was signed The Killer. I'm not sure the person didn't send some to Mr Heron as well. They thought there might be a lead from that but it may have been a hoax. When it come to it there was still no charges.

GLASGOW

The Glasgow gangleaders in the '20s and '30s were funny people. A bit of protection not to break the shopkeeper's window was about the biggest thing they did, but their fights were something else. Of course half the trouble was it was Catholics and Protestants. The Glasgow boys didn't take no prisoners; choppers, knives, razors, bayonets and most of them well, they was just kids. Percy Sillitoe, who'd cleaned up Sheffield, eventually brought a lot of it to a halt in the '30s. He never shut it down fully though. By the 1960s, just before I went away for my twenty, there was fighting gangs all over the place. A lot of people had been moved out of the old Gorbals, which was on the south side of the river as you come in on the train, over to Easterhouse and they fought all over the place. In his day though, Sillitoe just had the biggest, roughest coppers organised into what they called batter squads to go in and beat the daylights out of them. He did it subtly in a way. The coppers would arrive and watch the gangs do each other and then go and nick the winners who was half exhausted and give them a beating as well. It's the same today with bouncers in clubs. You don't break up a fight straightaway. You wait till they've weakened themselves and then you do the winner. You don't do yourself so much damage that way.

Like I say they were a funny lot. There was one Glasgow gangleader would only dance with boys because he thought that people would call him a cissie – Jessie was the word they used – if he was seen on the floor with a girl. The dance halls up there were where it went off a lot of the time. They'd have their girls take in the weapons for them and the police didn't dare search because of the screams they'd make. It caused trouble if the coppers tried to search them because there weren't all that number of women police around then. One of the last to hang was James Smith who stabbed a fellow Martin Malone in the Hibernian Hall on 16 November 1951. That was at Barlinnie, of course. Big L they call it.

They used to call the place they did the topping in Barlinnie, The Hanging Shed. There was only ten of them hanged there altogether. Afterwards the bodies were wrapped in hessian and then put in lime in unconsecrated ground along the outside wall of D Hall. I never saw it but there used to be a row of plaques with the men's names on but I heard even that got taken down.

Before that there'd been other nicks where you could get topped. If you went out to the docks area at Greenock about twenty miles away, there had been the old Nelson Street prison. The last person to hang there was way back in 1891 when a fellow, Frederick Storey, who was a circus manager, killed a girl who worked there when she wouldn't come across for him. He'd stabbed her in Argyle Street. After that they pulled the nick down.

You don't get brothers topped too often. If there'd been the death penalty then of course the Twins would have gone, but as far as I know there was only the Stratton brothers and then the Reubens around the 1900s. Both of them robberies in London. There were the Fowler brothers in Sheffield like I've said elsewhere, and the Rowlands brothers were set to swing in Cardiff, only one of them went mad. But in 1950 there was nearly a pair of brothers hanged in the Shed. If one of them hadn't done the decent thing they'd both have swung. This time it was the Harris brothers, Paul and Claude, and they went round to Neptune Street in Govan. They were with a man called Drennan and they were going to sort out someone who'd beaten up his sister. Her kids had had to get out of a window otherwise they'd have got a piece of it too. The fight seems to have spread out into the yard and, just like with Paddy Carraher, it was a man called Martin Dunleavy who was just there who copped it – got a broken bottle in his neck. Good man, when the coppers questioned him he said he knew who it was and he'd deal with it himself. Then he started bleeding again and that was it. The charge of murder against Drennan was dropped but both the brothers got a guilty and although the jury recommended mercy the Scottish Office wasn't having it.

The likes of us never knows what exactly goes on behind the scenes but when there was the death penalty there was definitely all sorts of comings and goings. When Ruth Ellis was due to swing, the day before she was going to be topped her solicitor got some info which might have helped her and they tannoyed a

Home Office official who was at Ascot Races to sort it out. It seems like this time the Scottish Office would have worn a confession from one of the brothers and reprieved the other, but at first the brothers weren't having it and so they thought both could swing.

They were both in the same death cell and then when they got the news there was no reprieve, Claude says to Paul that he could have saved him if he'd told the truth. That's when Paul sent for the priest and got him to help write a confession. Claude thought it would be too late but they held his topping back a week and then gave him life imprisonment. He did eight but he didn't last long on the outside. He died of drink.

They say that Paul took it very well. The papers had it in for him though. One of them said there should be no sympathy for him and 'Let other back-land bravos be warned. The mood in Glasgow is to meet toughness with toughness.' Nice.

As I've said before there hasn't been too many people acquitted of murder in this country that goes and gets done again for it. There was my pal Jimmy Essex of course. He got chucked twice of the murder but got put away for manslaughter both times. First was over a fight at a coffee stall near the Elephant and the second time was over a fight in the clothing shop at Armley. Another was Patrick Carraher who wasn't so lucky the second time. He got done both times in Glasgow. He was a hardman in the days when people in Glasgow was really hard. I know we didn't have much in the way of luxury in Waterloo when I grew up there but you wouldn't even say the word luxury in the Gorbals district then. No one would understand what you was talking about.

The first time he was done was August 1938 when he stabbed a soldier, James Shaw, who got involved in a dispute between Carry, as he was known, and a pimp called James Drurie. Carry wanted the girl and she didn't want to go with him. The soldier tried to intervene and his jugular vein got slashed.

Carry just got one of those Scottish verdicts of culpable homicide, which is what we'd call manslaughter, and three years' penal servitude that time. Then again he was lucky because Glasgow juries of them days weren't keen on people being topped and they'd do what they could not to bring in a murder verdict.

That and he had a brilliant brief by all accounts. When he come out it didn't half help his reputation on the streets. After that he was known as Killer and he liked that.

He never learned though that knives could be dangerous, not only to the people that got cut but the people who used them as well. He was back in the nick for a slashing in 1943. He got another three years for that. Then the second murder charge was in November 1945 with his brother-in-law. They were a good pair of street fighters but Dan was on his own when he ran into some brothers called Bonnar. He got away and went and found Carry and they went looking for the brothers. What they did though was pick the wrong man completely. It was another soldier, John Gordon. Carraher stabbed him in the neck thinking he was one of the brothers. This time he wasn't so lucky and he got sentenced to death. With his form there was no question of a reprieve and they topped him at Barlinnie in April 1946. My friend Paddy Meehan told me Carraher fought all the way to the gallows.

By then juries in Glasgow had got over trying not to send people to the gallows. John Lyon had been topped in the February that year, also at Barlinnie. He was the first person they topped in Glasgow for eighteen years. He'd stabbed a kid with a bayonet in one of their gang fights. The topping before him had been back in 1928 of a fellow called James McKay, who cut his mother to pieces and put bits of her in the coal bunker at their home and other bits on the banks of the Clyde. You might think he'd have been found insane but you'd be wrong. He was topped at the old Duke Street prison. The other that year was the last person to have swung at the prison and that was George Reynolds who killed one of his workmates. He thought the man was after his job and he did him with a shovel after they'd been out drinking.

Another one of the top men was Danny Cronin who was a big man in the 1930s and 1940s, and then a rival put glass in his booze. Well, that's the story. The police didn't do anything about it so he may have died of natural causes. It was no big deal. This would be in the late '40s. I met him a couple of times when I went to Glasgow to do some work for Arthur Thompson. You hear of the glass trick quite often. I've tried it myself but it's never worked.

Once was in Manchester when I was doing it as a contract. The man must have had a cast iron stomach; never so much as a murmur.

If I went on a contract like that it would be for a good friend. I'd be doing it out of friendship really although, of course, there'd be a few quid in it. You wouldn't do it for any Tom, Dick or Harry. Only if they're a friend of yours and even then you'd be dubious. If it came back to them they could collapse and shop you.

It was the same with cutting someone. If you did it for Arthur Thompson or Manuel Morris well, then it was for a friend and there'd be no question of a fee or even exes. But if Arthur had, say, a businessman who wanted someone done, well then that was different and the fee could be £500 which was a lot of dough then. Remember you could buy a small house for that money in London in the 1950s. You could probably buy a whole row in some parts of Glasgow.

You might have to go up there twice; once to have a look at him and then for the job. Arthur or Morris would make sure they were well away when it went off. You'd do it out in the open and you'd want a motor standing by if you could. In a bar or a club there'd be witnesses, and not all of them would be crooked people. You're not up there to knock on a door and go to prison. Provided you took care it was almost literally impossible to get caught. There was none of the stuff you get in films either. No 'This is from Michael Corleone'. If you were topping them, well that's one thing, but if it was just a cut, then you don't want to open your mouth. They'd know full well who it was from anyway and if they didn't, that was a bit more trouble for them to worry about. Later Morris or Arthur would let it be known. It would be rubbed in. As for the mug going to the coppers, there was not much chance of that; 100–1 on he'd be a hooky man himself.

We had a good relationship with Scotland, funnily much more than with Wales or even Manchester or Leeds. It worked both ways. There'd be people to be hidden, like Andy Anderson when he got out from Wandsworth by mistake with Ronnie Biggs. There'd been a plan to spring Biggsie and Andy and another geezer took advantage. When the rope was lowered for Biggsie, Andy takes the opportunity and he's up and off. They didn't know what to do with him when he lands in the lorry so they give him a few quid. He knows where I am from when he was in the nick with me and so he makes his way across London. Like I've said, he just turned up blind at Atlantic Machines which I had off Tottenham Court Road with Eddie Richardson. I got him to my mother's and then rang up Arthur and he agreed to have him up in Glasgow straight away. No payment, no questions. That was friendship. I drove up with him myself.

There'd be jobs to be done as well. If I went up for one for Arthur Thompson I'd stay in his flat in the Gorbals on the sofa in the front room. It would be a couple of times a year. A lot of the stuff we wanted the Scots for was safeblowing.

As I've said the biggest man in my day was Arthur Thompson. He took over from Manuel Morris when Manny was getting out. Manny taught him just about everything he knew about city life. Arthur really came good when he beat up a hardman, Alec Earch, who reckoned he was top of the pile at the end of the 1940s. Earch never recovered from the humiliation and he fell further and further away and ended up a meths drinker. Arthur went on from strength to strength. A big, hard man but respectful with it. He didn't take advantage of people.

I've written a lot about Arthur over the years, but it's been sad to see how the empire he built has just faded away. Firstly, there was his son the Fat Boy, who was killed and then there was his boy Billy, who fancied he could take over, started sampling what he was selling and become a heroin addict. By the end he was begging a few quid off of people and two men done him really bad one night in 2000. He'd tried to blag three quid off them and they wasn't having it. They just kicked him and trod on his skull. It seems like for the fun of it. I read that the doctors said they'd crushed it like it was an eggshell. He lived but apparently he can only follow really simple instructions. The people who did it got an eight and a five.

Funnily a namesake of mine got topped in Glasgow; Alfred James Fraser, same spelling but he was no relation that I know of. He was an Australian deserter from the First World War. He was working with an Irishman, James Rollins, rolling people with a girl as the decoy. It was the old, old story. She picked up a fellow Henry Senior and said they should go for a walk in Queen's Park. Once she'd got him in there they knocked him down, give him a beating and stole his money and some of his clothes. Then they hopped it to Ireland. They were found in Belfast the next week and the girl gave evidence against them. She went and said that she'd left them giving him a seeing to and had said they shouldn't be too hard on him. They put in a plea of culpable homicide, which would have meant they wouldn't have been topped if it had gone right, but the jury wouldn't wear it and they both swung.

Once you was a deserter it was like being on the run from prison, you'd nearly always got to thieve to keep yourself alive. It wasn't quite the same thing with Percy Barrett and George Cardwell. They'd deserted but they'd managed to work at a colliery and they was staying with Cardwell's sister. They was only nineteen and 22. They'd been out three months or so and things was working out quite well. Then what do they do? They change back into their uniforms and do an elderly widow, Rhoda Walker, who's got a jeweller's shop in Pontefract. They give her a very bad beating and she dies the next day. So it's down to London, where they stayed with Barrett's girlfriend. When the coppers eventually come round there's a lot of rings found from the blagging. They blamed each other at the trial and they was hanged together in the December. Funnily Cardwell had been a good soldier and that was how they come to him. He'd been wounded five times, gassed and put up for medals. He'd got six 'wound' stripes sewed on his uniform and that was what was noticed by a fellow who saw them hanging around Mrs Walker's shop.

Another good man in Glasgow was Sammy McKay – they called him Dandy. He'd be a couple of years younger than me if he's still alive. He had some bad luck. Once he got nicked after a robbery and whilst the coppers were questioning him he took out a fountain pen. The coppers had him unscrew it and inside was the cloakroom ticket for where he'd put the gear.

He was a big man in the nightclubs and he was a good gambler as well. There was one in Paisley he liked, the Cuba I think it was called. Manuel Morris owned it. Then he was the manager of the

Gordon Bridge Club which Morris also had. That was a bit like the Mayfair Bridge Club in Mount Street where Scotch Jack Buggy was done. Bridge was about the only game not played in either of them. He got out of Barlinnie in 1959 and went off to the States where he blew the better part of forty grand he'd made in a blagging in the Clydesdale Bank in Shettleston Road. He'd managed to get himself in the prison hospital and did a bit of sawing and was out over the wall. He had help, of course, and there was a car waiting for him. His wife and kids were at Butlins at the time and they left. Asked to, I expect, but they got their dough back. There was all sorts of stories flying about, how he'd had plastic surgery and how he was smuggling himself back on a liner. Usually most of them is rubbish but not in his case.

He did go down to London and have a nose job. It cost him £61 and £25 for the hospital bed, which is a bit less than nowadays. You wouldn't get much more than a bandage and a few aspirin for that today. Then he went to the States and stayed on the East Coast. He come back to London in the November and drove up to Glasgow, picked up his wife and kids and came down south again. That's where he made his mistake. If you think you're going to stay away for ever, like Ronnie Biggs, you've got to be ruthless about losing touch with your family. The wife and kids is going to be the weak link; the way they can get to you. Then it was over to Ireland where he rented a house in Dublin and then bought one in Killiney. They picked him up in the June. Like so many he opened the door in his pyjamas and that was it.

They'd had the trial of the others the previous year and Alex Gray got a ten. Sammy's brother John got three years for re-set, which is what we call receiving or dishonest handling, and a kid who'd worked in the bank and had arranged to let out the keys got a three. Alex had had the keys cut by a man in Manchester. The boy from the bank gave evidence against Sammy. It was ten as well for Sammy, including a couple for escaping. The judge said he shouldn't think escaping was part of the game. Sammy had that crooked brief Jimmy Latta as his solicitor. Latta was big in Glasgow in them days. He defended an awful lot of people but he liked mixing with the likes of us too much; called the villains up there his boys. He went down in a big way himself. He's dead now. The week Sammy went down was when that Victor Terry pushed off to Glasgow after shooting the bank clerk down in Worthing.

Whilst Sammy was back in Barlinnie doing his bird someone tried to push gelignite through the ventilator of his cell but there was an explosion on the outside. After that he must have made his peace with the others and he was left alone. He'd given evidence against that Peter Manuel the previous year. Of course with a dog like that the usual rules about grassing don't apply.

Peter Manuel was about five years younger than me and he'd been in trouble since about the same age as when I started, but by the time he was fifteen he'd got a con for indecent assault, and by the time he was twenty he'd got eight years for rape. For that he went up to Peterhead. Before then he'd done a bit of work in London but he wasn't regarded as reliable. Couldn't shut his trap. He got out in 1953 and started going out with a bus conductress. But he couldn't stop himself. He says he's bought her a decent engagement ring and he tweedles it, giving her a fake. Then she gets a note saying his real father had been topped in America and that he had spied in Russia for the British Secret Service and, sensible girl, she calls it off. She must have looked back a thousand times and thought what a decision she made. Some people seem to think he sent her the note himself. The day he was due to marry he defends himself against another indecency and gets an acquittal.

In December 1957 there's a whole lot of killings. It starts off in Carrick Drive in the suburb of Mount Vernon which is a nice area. Just after Christmas, a young girl, Isabelle Cooke, doesn't turn up to go to a dance with a bloke. The parents started looking for her just after midnight and by next morning there's a full search. They found a cosmetic pouch under a railway bridge but it wasn't for a fortnight that they found her buried in a field on a farm.

There was another killing on New Year's day when the Smart family – Peter and Doris and their eleven-year-old son Michael – were done in their home at Uddingston. Their bodies weren't found for nearly a week. They were the last victims, but another couple, John McMunn and his wife, was lucky to escape. Mind you it shows what you can do if you think quick enough.

McMunn had woken and found a man at the bedroom door and he'd pretended he'd had a gun, which got rid of the fellow.

Manuel got picked up a bit before 7 a.m. a week after that. He'd been kipping on a chair in his parents' place in Birkenshaw. If the coppers came in those days it was usually a bit before seven. You was still half asleep and there wasn't always the chance to get hold of a brief. They could take you to any nick they fancied. 'All right, Mrs Fraser, we're taking Frank to Paddington. He'll be there in half an hour', and they could have you half way across the country. Your wife would have the brief ring up Paddington and he'd get the reply, 'No, he's not here. Never heard of him. We haven't got a DI Smith here.' And of course they was right. I remember Terry Dewsnap, who was related to my mate Joe Wilkins, saying how he'd been swagged up to Stoke or somewhere like that when he'd been nicked over a robbery in Dunstable. Things have changed now.

One reason they picked Manuel up was because he wasn't sensible. There'd just been a change of colour on some Scots' banknotes and he was flashing some around. Peter Smart had picked up a load from the bank just before he was killed and it wasn't Brain of Scotland at least to have a look at Manuel. Then again they'd fancied him for a lot of things including the killing of a young girl the year before, but he'd put in an alibi which held. The coppers had also got a mate of his to give them the SP on what he was up to.

They lifted Manuel's father for receiving some of the stuff which had been nicked from another house in Mount Vernon just before Christmas. Then people picked Manuel out on an ID as the man who'd been paying for drinks with the new notes. He went and said he'd been given them by Dandy McKay and that's how he come into the case. Dandy wasn't pleased at all and he told the coppers how Manuel had had a Beretta.

Give Manuel a bit of credit. He tried to row his parents out of it and he wrote the senior copper a couple of letters starting to say what he'd done. But the coppers was crafty, they must have sensed he couldn't wait to tell them everything – just like he couldn't stop blabbing when he was down South – and they said no. All they had to do was wait a bit and he spilled his guts. During the evening he showed the police where he buried Isabelle Cooke's body and then he showed them where he'd put the iron he'd battered another girl, Anne Knielands, with. That was the one he'd put up an alibi for. Nowadays DNA would have done him for that much earlier. Meanwhile he's written a long confession. Of course he tries to get round that at the trial, saying he only did it to get his Dad released.

When it came to it he went down for a whole raft of killings. Apart from Isabelle Cooke and the Smarts there was the Watt family who'd been found by the daily help in September 1956. Now I know I've said look for the husband but this was a case where the coppers did just that and they was wrong. They had him locked up in Barlinnie for the better part of three months before they offered no evidence. Then, worse for the poor man, Manuel lodges an impeachment against him. In Scots law if you say someone else did the crime it's sort of like an alibi. You have to name the name and give particulars. So poor Watt has to go through the torment again.

Manuel always liked defending himself. There's often an edge in that. You get a bit of leeway from the judge when your brief wouldn't. You can try and get in bits which are technically inadmissible and then say sorry you didn't know. The judge is always a bit afraid of you. He's got in the back of his mind that if he comes on too strong the jury's going to say, 'Poor Mr Fraser, the judge didn't give him a chance', and they'll bring in a not guilty. Alfie Hinds was good at it and Manuel had done it when he got the eight for rape; half-way through this trial he sacks his brief and takes over himself. When it came to it nothing was going to help him; he got a guilty on seven murders but not on the one of Anne Knielands. He got topped at Barlinnie in the July. I was in Rochester with Manuel's brother, who we all called John. He was a good man but I never saw him again.

What was interesting was what come out after he'd been topped. Apparently he'd done a taxi driver from Newcastle, cut his throat and a couple of women in Glasgow. He also said he'd done the brass 'Red' Helen Carlin in Pimlico, a couple of years earlier.

* * *

It's not often you get a father and son who've both gone down for separate murders but Robert Mone and his son, who was called that as well, both did in their day. I suppose this time the son was more famous and his father tried to live up to him. It was a bit confusing because it was the father who was known as Sonny. Robert jnr started things off when he took a whole needlework class hostage at St John's Secondary High School, Dundee for a couple of hours in November 1968. A nurse who knew him tried to persuade him to give himself up but that didn't do any good and he attacked a couple of the girls and killed the teacher before the police dogs was let loose on him. He wasn't fit to plead and he got sent to the Carstairs State Mental Institute. He met up with another fellow, Thomas McCullough, in the place and they began to plan an escape. McCullough had had an argument with a chef over some sandwiches and had gone home, made a tape recording about what he was going to do, and then gone back and shot at the man and his wife.

It's wonderful what you can do if you really try. McCullough made a whole lot of weapons including a sword in the prison workshop, along with a ladder. They also got hold of a map of the area, a torch and £25 as well as some moody ID.

They got out at the end of November 1976 when they killed a nurse and a patient and got the nurse's keys. That's when they picked up a large fire axe and it was out over the wall. They was gone half an hour before anyone noticed they was missing They was now wearing nurses' caps and they flagged down a driver saying there's been an accident. It's almost unbelievable the coincidence, but just as the man got out of his car up comes a police van. McCullough cuts the throat of one of the officers and starts on the other. The driver of the other car gets away and goes to the hospital to tell what's happened; at first people don't believe him. It was heavy snow and Mone and McCullough got off with the police car and then crashed it about ten miles down the road. The blue light was flashing and when a couple of men stopped to help they was attacked as well. They drove off in the men's van and got to a farmhouse where they took an Austin Maxi. But the farmer's young daughter managed to phone the coppers whilst the pair was arguing with her father.

After that they made a dash for England with the police after them, and they got as far as the M6 where they crashed again. This time four young people got out of their car to help but just as the pair was about to do another hi-jack, the police turned up and recaptured them. They both picked up life imprisonment this time. McCullough said it was mostly his fault but no one was taking another chance with either of them. It's interesting that they was insane when they broke out, but by the time they was caught and had killed three people three hours later they was sane. It's as if you get a shot in the mental hospital and if you blow it that's it, sane or not it's off to prison. Just like Straffen. It seems like they don't want people in psychiatric hospitals who are a bit tasty. They say they've got a personality disorder and are untreatable.

Anyway next it was dad's turn. He kept saying there was nothing better he wanted than to be inside with his boy and he did three women in Dundee in 1979. When it come to it though he said he'd been in the house with them but he'd not done them. He'd had a five back in the 1960s. Then whilst he was in the Aberdeen nick he went and insulted a fellow, Anthony Currie, known as Cyclops and he was killed in January 1983. Cyclops got eight years for what the Scots call justifiable homicide. The Mones was a bit of a violent family because Robert Mone jnr's sister, Rose, did three years for attacking a fifteen-year-old girl with a bottle and knife. She said she'd just been standing up for her dad.

As far as I know Robert Mone jnr and McCullough are still in their nicks and they don't look likely to be coming out. McCullough got put away in a special cell where he's got a couple of rooms, really, and three warders with him night and day. He makes a lot of toys for local kids' charities and I heard recently he's getting a bit of association with other prisoners. Robert Mone's been in the prison normal.

One of the big teams up in Glasgow was the one known as Norval's Criminal Syndicate run by Walter Norval. He was the king of the armed robbers up there at the time until he was put away by his henchman, Phillip Henry. In November 1977 the North Court was set alight just before Norval's trial commenced. No one could say exactly who'd done it. His daughter was charged but I'm glad to say the case against her was chucked. His son-in-law picked up a five for threatening a witness and Henry, who was meant to be in solitary for his safety, had boiling water tipped on him. John McDuff, who was then 22, received 21 years. Joe Polding had eighteen. When it came to it Norval only got a fourteen. I suppose that was because he wasn't involved in as many robberies even though he was reckoned to be the Daddy. It wasn't bad when you consider the bird that had got handed out to the Workers' Party of Scotland a few years before. Maybe they was regarded as more of a threat because they was a sort of political organisation.

Walter went down in the November of 1977, six months after his stepfather Joe 'The Pole' Kotarba was stabbed to death in the April at his home in Maryhill, by one of the brasses he ran. He'd been beating her and Joe Beltrami got her acquitted.

When I'm giving talks, people say they think I shouldn't be making money out of crime. What I say is that people remember me and Charlie and Eddie and the Twins but there's plenty of others like coppers who've done dreadful things and their names are never mentioned. Take that Glasgow copper James Robertson, for example. What a wicked thing he done.

July 1950 it was when they found the body of a woman laying on Prospecthill Road in the Mount Florida district. It looked like a car had driven over her, the body had become trapped and then the driver had reversed again. It turned out it was a girl called Catherine McCluskey. What happened was a woman who was looking after her kids come forward to say she hadn't collected them. Catherine had told her that the father of one of them was this copper from the Glasgow Southern Division.

It was the usual story – a copper goes off the rails, but people turn a blind eye and try to cover up for him out of loyalty. It seems like he'd been a non-drinking, non-smoking family man who was up for promotion. Then he'd fallen off the wagon and he hadn't been turning up on his beat in the Gorbals. Not that I'd blame him for that. He'd also been seen driving a large black Austin car. He could never have afforded it but he said he'd borrowed it from a friend.

When they checked it out he hadn't been on his beat the night Catherine was done. When he said he didn't know her he was put on an ID and was picked out by her friend. By the time he got to court there was not only the murder but breaking into a car showroom and stealing a radio and registration books, and stealing a car another time. What he'd done to her was to batter her with his truncheon and then driven the car, which had false plates, over her to make it look like an accident. I don't understand it. Here he is a copper. Why does he think a doctor can't tell between a blow with a truncheon and being knocked down by a car?

It was quite a long trial for those days. He went in the box and said he did know the girl. He'd met her when he was called to a disturbance. He said he'd found the car. He thought it was abandoned and he'd begun to use it. I don't know who he thought he'd convince. You don't find too many large smart cars abandoned nowadays, and you certainly didn't not long after the War.

As for doing the girl, it had all been a terrible accident. He'd been down to meet her and they'd gone for a drive. She'd asked him to take her to see a friend some fourteen miles away. He said he was still on duty and couldn't and told her to get out of the car when she began to cry. Then he says he changed his mind. He slowly reversed about a hundred yards and that's when he heard a sort of jarring, and when he got out to look he'd run over the girl. He tried to get her free and when he couldn't, he'd panicked, reversing the car and then driving forward. After a few minutes he succeeded and he pushed off. He wasn't the copper who'd been paying money to her for the child and he hadn't hit her with a truncheon.

Of course no one believed him for five minutes. Well, certainly not for an hour because the jury was back in that time with a majority verdict of murder. You can do that in Scotland. Fifteen on the jury and it could be eight to seven one way or the other. Of course there was always that non-proven which saved a lot of people. Robertson lodged an appeal, which rightly got blanked, and people say it was only in the last few days before he was topped at Barlinnie a bit before Christmas 1960 that he realised what was coming to him.

*   *   *

A couple of my friends went down over a raid in Glasgow. Just before Christmas 1973 it was. A team went up from London and a guard at what was British Rail's St Rollex Works was killed. Robert Marley put it together and the team included Siddy Draper, who later got out of Leicester in a helicopter, and Steve Doran whose brother, Ian, picked up 25 in that Scottish Workers' Party case. The job seemed fairly simply but Jim Kennedy, the security guard, had a go and was shot. They didn't half get some bird – 183 years between them.

One of the team was Billy Murray, whose dad had been with me at school. He was the last of them to get nicked. Down in Brighton it was, funnily enough. He was staying in a boarding house when the police burst in about five one morning. Someone had grassed him. He did get to the stage in his bird where he got out on leave but then he didn't come back and they nicked him again. He's still in the warehouse as far as I know.

The other, Alan Brown, was also a friend of the Twins. By March 1999 Alan had got himself in the situation where he was working outside the prison. He'd had a bad time in his early years. In 1985 he'd taken some staff hostage, he'd been involved in a riot and he'd tried to escape twice. When Marilyn and me went up for Arthur Thompson's funeral we went over and saw Alan. Now in 1999 he was on day release at a church-run Undercroft Café in George Street in Edinburgh. He'd just had another knockback on his application for release on licence and he'd been told he would not be eligible to appear before the Board for another review for four years. He was due to return to the prison at 3.30 but he just disappeared from the café around lunchtime. I don't think anyone thought too much about it until he didn't show. I hoped he'd gone abroad but it turned out he hadn't. As I've said, he was found in Brighton with a load of drugs, so the coppers said.

Of course not all robberies which went wrong was professional jobs. Take that Charles Templeman Brown. A bit before Christmas 1945 he decides he's going to do a single-handed raid at the Pollockshields East station in the evening. There were three staff on duty and he shot all three of them – William Wright, Anne Withers and a fifteen-year-old kid, Robert Gough. The kid and the woman didn't survive but Wright was able to give an ID of Brown.

You'd think that in a case like that the authorities would be keen to put up a reward, get the grasses nibbling so to speak, but when it was said it was coming from the police fund the Lord Advocate said no it wasn't and the Secretary of State said it had to come from the council. In the end a newspaper put up a grand. That was good money back then. Still, no one come forward for about ten months, then in the October the police makes a move on Brown's mother's place.

He was in regular work, very respectable, and the next day he goes up to a copper and asks him to telephone the Glasgow police and tells him he did the Pollockshields job. He went and handed in a gun, a Luger it was, and another thirteen bullets he had. Whilst he was waiting for the coppers he wrote a note to a friend saying he hoped that the man wouldn't think too badly of him and how he'd tried to top himself anyway. When the coppers questioned him he said he'd only fired because the kid had tried to dive for the gun. In fact the boy had been trying to shield the woman.

Of course there was no defence to the killing. The only thing left was to show he was mental but he got found guilty. It's funny how things turn out. When that Victor Terry told the trick cyclists that he was being controlled by Legs Diamond they wouldn't listen, but Brown does a whole lot better. He probably was a bit simple. He wore spotted bow ties as a tribute to Frank Sinatra, he said, and a white whipcord jacket of which he was so proud he wore it to collect his wages. The doctors said he was 'addicted to swing music' which, in them days, was a sure sign he was off his trolley; he got a reprieve and he only served about a ten. Then he was released and went back to work as a travelling salesman. Just under three years later he's killed when his car hit a wall near Dunblane. That's where the massacre was a few years ago. Some nutter goes into a school and starts shooting the kids. It was after that handguns got banned. Tribute to the kids, the politicians said. Of course it didn't do any good at all. I was reading in the papers that there's more handguns around now than there was before the ban. The going price in London was £200.

Back when I was working it wasn't that easy to get a gun. There's guns and guns, however. It depended on what sort you wanted. Of course shotguns were no trouble. After all, they were more or less legal and you could do a bit of work on them yourselves. As for a revolver, that was more difficult. The trouble was you had to be very careful where you got them and who you got them off. The man might not be able to keep his box of tricks shut one hundred per cent. Then there was no telling who'd used them first and I've always liked a clean knife and fork. If you weren't going to use it yourself, only wave it about, well that might not be too bad unless you were caught with it. Then the police might start checking up to see if it had been fired before. The price would depend on how quick you wanted it. It was always best not to buy but get it from someone you trusted and on condition that if, when it came to it, you didn't use it you'd return it and if you had to then you'd get rid of it and pay him. You could get a good clean gun in 24 hours.

The big dance hall in Glasgow was Barrowlands, named after a part of the city and just off Gallowgate North, east of the city centre. I think it's big still but back in the '50s and '60s, you could hardly get in at the weekends. Pick up place it was. It wasn't my sort of place at all. It was a place the women took their wedding rings off and what you thought was Miss Right turned out to be Mrs Wrong. Same applied to the men. That was where that serial killer they called Bible John did three girls. That was a big case back in 1969. He used to hang around the dance floor, pick up women and then, when he went off with them after the dance, strangle them. The first one had been in the February and no one thought too much about it, not as a serial killer that is. Then the next one come in the August and the last in the November. All of the women were raped and they was all on at the time it happened. There was a bit of ID because Jeannie Williams, the sister of the last of the girls, Helen Puttock, went in a taxi with this Bible John and Helen when he was spouting off the scriptures. She was dropped off and he continued with her sister. He was quoting the Bible and called Barrowlands a den of iniquity, which is how he got his name. She told the coppers that he had sandy hair and he was well spoken. They had more than ninety ID parades but nothing came of it. The murder at the end of the year was the last but the case kept coming up over the years. They had

Jeannie up on an ID parade within three days of the death of her sister but she never picked out John McInnis who they fancied for the jobs.

Anyway, like I said, the killings stopped and McInnis topped himself in April 1980. What the police had done was keep a semen stain off of Helen Puttock's tights and when DNA come in they decided to exhume McInnis and check it out. The coppers said they was pretty sure but five months later they said it wasn't a match. Apart from anything else the fellow had bitten Helen Puttock and the bite showed he had a deformed tooth, and McInnis didn't. The last I heard there was a fellow written in saying he thought it was his cousin who was still alive and living in England. But that was a couple of years ago and I don't think anything's come of it.

I never really knew James Griffiths. I met him in the nick after he got that four for robbery back in 1963 but he'd walked out of Parkhurst before I got there. He was, I think I'm right in saying, the only man ever to get off the Island. If there was others they were very rare. It wasn't as if people hadn't tried, and with three nicks on the Island, Camp Hill, Albany and Parkhurst, it wasn't as if there wasn't plenty of punters, but it was like Alcatraz in San Francisco Bay, the currents was such that you couldn't swim or row away. Also it was easy for the authorities once they knew someone was loose to shut down the exits. After all there was only the ferry and from time to time a hover back in those days. So it had to be pretty organised. Someone had to have a boat lined up or a plane and they didn't come all that easy. You could stay out on the Island and people would put food and clothes out for you, just the same as they did on the Moor, but really if you couldn't get off it was only a matter of time.

James just walked away from an outside work party in December 1965. He had a few coins on him and he got on a bus to Ryde where the ferry goes and got a ticket for a £1 note. The man in the booking office never even looked up. At Portsmouth he sees there's a lot of coppers so he gets a cab to the Town station instead of getting on the train at the harbour, and he shares a compartment with a prison officer and his wife. Apparently he got some funny looks from the man because he was still wearing overalls, but the screw said nothing. He made his way up to

Scunthorpe where he was put up by a fellow, Wally Gow, and he started courting Wally's sister. Of course he had to continue screwing to make a living and the story was that once when he was hiding out waiting to do the owner of a scrapyard, he sees a figure and gives it a bashing with some wood he's got. It turns out it's just a kid come for his bike and he makes the boy hand over all he's got on him.

It couldn't last of course, and in March 1966 he got another four and was sent back to Parkhurst, which is where he met Paddy Meehan. In July 1969 there was one of Scotland's biggest cases, certainly of the time, although I suppose the Ice Cream Wars case has been bigger since. An old girl was the victim of a tie-up at her place near Racecourse Road, Ayr. Her husband was hit with an iron bar and stabbed. One of the men knelt on her chest and she later died in hospital. Her husband said he'd heard the men call each other Pat and Jim. That was enough for the coppers to start a lookout for Paddy Meehan and Jimmy Griffiths. They'd been in the area and a couple of young girls ID'd them as being given a lift by them. Meehan told the coppers where they could find Jimmy and they went looking.

Jimmy had always said he'd never be taken alive again and he wasn't. He sort of went on a rampage. The coppers come with a warrant to his place in Hollywood Crescent and when the door was opened there was Jimmy firing at them. One of the coppers was shot and by the time the rest of them got out the way he was firing at more or less anything that moved. All in all he shot five coppers in the space of a few minutes. Then there's silence and it's clear he's somehow got out the back. He got in a car and crashed at the Round Toll, so he goes into the Round Toll Bar at Possill Road tells them he'll shoot if someone moves, and puts a couple of bullets in the ceiling. Then some man goes to put down his glass of beer and Jim shoots him and all. It's funny how some people act in circumstances. The barman just goes to Jimmy and pushes him out the place. Jim fired a few shots at him after that but he missed and he made his way back to Kay Street, where he holes up and fires at another couple of people. That's where the coppers caught up with him. One of them opens the letter box and there's Jim pointing a gun at him, so the bogey fires and kills him. The whole thing lasted an hour-and-a-half. Possill is where tourists go and buy clothing nowadays.

There was a bit of a stink even after he died. A TV producer wanted to do a reconstruction of the case. It's all the rage now but it wasn't then. The man found himself hauled up in front of the Sheriff when he had actors firing blanks and bashing a window in Hollywood Crescent, and someone in camouflage rush into the Round Toll. Fined £50 I think he was. The authorities said he was breaching public order.

It wasn't the first time someone had shot it out with the coppers in Glasgow and I'm sure it wasn't the last. One a few years earlier had been a bit of a funny case altogether. There was this kid, Edwin Finlay, who nicked around £900 from the British Linen Bank where he worked. He was only eighteen and it didn't seem a problem to arrest him. A couple of coppers saw him in Hyndland Road early one morning where he'd gone round in the hope of seeing a girl he knew. When they approached him he just opened fire. He killed John Macleod and wounded another and then he turned the gun on himself. What was amazing was the kid had got three guns on him including a Walther and a Derringer. He'd also got a wrist bandolier as well as a body one. It seems he'd been over to Ireland the previous week and he'd smuggled them back in. Back in September 1952 that was.

As for Paddy, the Griffiths shoot out didn't do him no good at all. You can see how public opinion wasn't going to be on his side. First, an old lady's been killed and second it looks like from what Jim's done they got the right man.

Paddy went down on a majority verdict but there was soon rumours that a couple of different hardmen, Ian Waddell and Tank McGuinness, were the real blaggers. There was all sorts of appeals and petitions for Paddy. McGuinness kept visiting Joe Beltrami, the top lawyer, and dropping hints, but he never come outright and say anything concrete, and anyway a lawyer can't betray a client's secrets without permission. Just like a priest.

In March 1976 McGuinness was done over close to the Celtic football ground down Parkhead way in the East End and he never recovered consciousness before he died a couple of weeks later. Not that he'd have said who did it. Although it was never proved it was put about that Tank had been killed over his involvement in the murder. Then it turned out Waddell's alibi was false and he'd been pushing a good bit of dough about after the blagging. So what happens? Paddy gets pardoned two months after McGuinness is killed and Waddell's put on trial for the Ross murder. That didn't do any good. Just like Manuel he put in a special defence saying 'It wasn't me. It was Meehan and Griffiths.' Jury was only out an hour before they give him a not guilty.

It was all change. A few years later Waddell's murdered in Blackthorn Street in Springburn in the north of the city by his mate, Andy Gentle, who was lifed off. Then there's an inquiry into the Ross case and it comes up with the theory that all four, Paddy and Jim, Tank and Waddell, was involved. If you want a lawyer on your side, that Beltrami was a man to have. He worked and worked for Paddy and eventually he got him over fifty grand compensation, but Paddy wasn't that grateful. He slagged Beltrami off for not trying hard enough and wrote another book himself which he'd peddle at the railway station saying it was an MI5 conspiracy. Eventually it all died down and he died in Swansea a few years back. He'd got throat cancer.

That's a thing with people who get a long stretch of bird. Eventually they convince themselves it was all their brief's fault. Either the man didn't try hard enough or he actually sold him to the pros. It's never their own fault. It stands to reason. You sit in the peter day in and night out and you go over things in your mind. It's like being in a car accident. You readjust things. Even if you come out of a side turning and bang into a car on the main road, well he was going too fast and he should have seen you. Of course, sometimes it does happen and the brief has gone bent on you. The next thing is they'll turn on the man who found the brief for them. He's in league as well. In fairness, I've never thought that about any of the cases I've had. Briefs have always done what they can for me, but there's plenty about who reckon they should never have gone down.

Sometimes you get an unsolved murder which you think should be easy to solve and the coppers just can't do it. There was one up in Inverness back in 1976 when a woman, Renee Macrae, and her little boy Andrew just disappeared. Mid-November that year she was going away with her boyfriend, William Macdowell, who was the kid's father and that was the last she was seen of. In fact he'd worked for the company her old man owned. She'd been driving a BMW and it was found about ten miles away in a lay-by on the A9 near Dalmagarry. It was big stuff. They had Canberra bombers with heat-seeking devices flying over the place and of course there was divers and frogmen, but they never found the bodies. Macdowell agreed he'd arranged to meet her but he'd had a touch of seconds and never turned up. Later, he went on to say he'd no intention of leaving his wife. A few years later Macdowell picked up thirty months for fraud. And that was about it.

When I was young I use to read those Peter Cheyney detective books. They cost about 1/6d. He was a right old fascist, supported Mosley, but they was good stories. They was always about men in dinner jackets eating chicken sandwiches and drinking scotch and soda in clubs in the West End after the War, and women in silk dresses who were accused of doing their husbands in for the insurance. The detective was called Slim Callaghan, I think, and he always sorted it out so's it was the brother-in-law. I saw one again the other day on a stall in a market; £2 it was, so someone made a profit. It reminded me there was a case up on Deeside a few years back when a woman did her husband in and claimed the estate. That was another thing in those books, under English law you couldn't benefit from the estate if you murdered someone and that was always a reason to frame the girl.

Anyway, back in 1994 this lady, Daphne Pertwee, just walked out of the living room leaving her friends, shot her husband and then their three-month-old son point blank, and I mean point blank, something less than a foot, and then she come back saying what she'd done and that she'd got bad depression. I should think she had. She got popped in a mental hospital once she'd admitted the topping. The little boy had survived his father for a few seconds and so he inherited. Once he was dead it should have gone to the husband's family. What she said was that under Scottish law the judge should make an exception and let her have a share at least, but before it come to a hearing it was all settled out of court. It never happened like that in the books.

WALES AND THE BORDER COUNTRY

I never did a lot of heavy work in Wales. I did a fair bit of work for that Welsh family who stood by me all the years I was in the nick but overall it was really just as I went away that things were getting started. What had happened was there were new trunk roads and motorways and you could get about a lot faster; remember there was no speed restrictions on motorways then. Go as fast as you could. In a way that was what made crime national; that and putting people from different areas in prisons. Of course that led to trouble for us. You didn't know the people and while you got on well with them in the nick you couldn't necessarily get anyone to vouch for them if they come up with a bit of work after you was both out. So you took a chance and a lot of people come a tumble finding out they was wrong 'uns, or lacked bottle or technique.

It's always hard when you get a Dear John in the nick – you know the kind of thing 'Dear John, I have met this man and I am having his baby . . .' Some people just can't take getting a Dear John. I've seen really mentally strong men just broken up by them and turned into shambling wrecks. They're devastated. They change from being very level people getting on with their bird to a mixture of everything – disruptive, depressed, violent. Pride comes into it of course and, particularly in the old days, it was the feeling of frustration. You couldn't do anything about things on the outside. People say prison's got easy but it's the being locked up that does it. There's a story – I don't know how true it is – of the con who yells at the judge 'You stupid cunt' just after he gets five years. The judge has him back and says 'Listen. When I leave here about four o'clock I'm going to drive home in my new car and I'll probably have tea with my wife and sit by the swimming pool. Then around six o'clock I'll have a glass of wine and then we'll have dinner, something like salmon and salad and some strawberries. Then I may have a cigar and perhaps a brandy. You are going to go from here in a van which stinks and is hot and you'll be sweating by the time you get to the prison. There you're going to be searched with people looking up your backside. Then you'll get clothes that don't fit you and you'll be put in a cell with two others and in the morning you'll have to go and empty your chamber pot and you'll do this for five years. Now, who do you think is the stupid cunt?' And whether it's true or not, in a way he's right.

There was no such thing as compassionate leave or even a letter, let alone a telephone call which would have helped people keep in touch. Remember, you could send out a letter but if one come in from a person you hadn't written to, it was put in your property and when you was released you'd get a bundle of letters in your hand. So if a friend wrote saying there was a bit of trouble at home there was maybe no way of you knowing. Letters could just go missing. 'Proof of posting is not proof of delivery, Fraser', and so every letter Doreen sent for twenty years was recorded.

There really wasn't any welfare before 1948. There was the bag of yeast (priest) might come round. He did when my grandmother died in 1947 but there wasn't any possibility of my going to the funeral. Things did change for the better after April 1949 when the Criminal Justice Act come into force.

Back in the '40s and earlier the Chaplain was really the only outside influence – but there again, if a priest or a vicar come round back then, the screws would often say, 'Don't go near Fraser, he's in a bad mood' whether I was or I wasn't and they'd listen to them. Don't forget very often the C of E Chaplain had a house next to the governor. One or two did raise the question of beatings of prisoners but they was very much in the minority.

I never went to the chapel of a Sunday though there was plenty who did it to get out of their cells. When you first went into prison at reception it was 'Religion?' and if you said 'No religion', they'd hammer on at you. You had to have some sort of religion put down and atheism didn't count. You had to go through it a bit at first. There'd be some bread and water for having no religion but eventually you won through. It wasn't my style, even to get out of my cell for an hour.

You could hear them of a Sunday. The screws would come round unlocking people and the cons would be ringing their bell and banging on the door in case they was missed. 'All right, we ain't forgot you.' There was no talking in chapel. There's stories about how people sang questions and answers to the lines of hymns but I doubt it really. It may have happened, I can't say because I wasn't there, but the number of prisoners nicked for talking in chapel, I wish I had a £1 note for every one. I'd have a nice few quid. Really you had to be daft to go. You could always end up sitting next to a mug, 'Got any 'bacco? Got tinder?' because there wasn't matches in them days. You had a sort of flint. Both of you would be nicked even if you never replied. And there was plenty of people nicked just to make up numbers just like in the workshop.

The chance of a Dear John never worried me. Me and Kathleen had more or less finished before I went in for the Bedford job when I was nicked on the way back, but then Eva heard she'd been larking about and she told me to forget her and she marked her card and all. That was one of the best bits of luck I had. I've never seen her from that day to this.

The last time I saw my three boys as kids, the eldest ones that is, was when I went off to do that job in Bedford. Then it wasn't until the 1960s, when I'd finished the seven over Spot, that I saw Frank again. He'd have been nineteen then and already a good thief at the heavy work and all. I think he got three years and I went to see him in Maidstone. He'd been working with sons of the guys I worked with.

When I went to Broadmoor from Durham during that stretch I told them that Kathleen and me was finished. In them days it was different. If they thought you was married or had a girlfriend and there was bad feeling, that could hold you back on your release. Since you was mad they didn't want you going round topping your ex the moment you was out and them getting the blame. Anyway, I was sensible. First chance I had I explained things and Eva and my mother went and saw the doctors.

It was a good job we all did. I was well in my sentence and I hadn't heard from Kathleen when, blow me, she turns up with the three boys at Broadmoor out of the blue. Never says she's coming. Then one afternoon she's just there. I turned down seeing her straight away and I've never seen her from that day to this. I did hear of her a few years back when she wrote in some paper about me, but I haven't clapped eyes on her. She's six years older than me so that'll put her in her mid '80s now. Over the years when I was away Eva kept in touch with the boys.

As for Doreen, she was a one-off. Twenty years she trailed round prisons with Eva. Visits were terrible with me being brought up from the punishment, aggressive screws, not allowed to touch. People may say why didn't I tell her not to come and to go and find someone else but I wouldn't have insulted her by even mentioning it. That was the amazing thing about her, her loyalty, even though she didn't come from a criminal family.

Often it's the ones who've been violent to the girls in the first place who react the worst when they're told it's all over. Take that Phillip Manning. His marriage broke up in the early 1990s and he did his ex, Margaret, then. He picked up four-and-a-half years for attempted murder. He did just two and got parole. Then, when he comes out he tries to get her back but things have moved on. So, Christmas 1994 he lays in wait for her. She comes home just after midnight with her new bloke to her house in Abertillery and he shoots both of them. He got her in the jaw and she died straight away. The new bloke lived but he had to have a plate in his skull. Then Phillip goes off to London where they find him in a pub. He's got a nail bomb strapped around him. He got lifed off of course. It'll be a long time before they let him out. That's what the judge said anyway.

There've been some good murders in Wales over the years. By that I mean ones which never got solved for one reason or another. One of the problems for the coppers is that they call in Scotland Yard and the local people don't take to them. Clannish. The copper who was meant to be the great detective of his time, Reginald Spooner, come a cropper with two of them, and he did his level best to have one fellow swing and all.

The first was when Ernest Melville, who was a known top of the roof, was found by some children near the Full Moon pub on waste ground near Croft Street in the Swansea dock in January 1949. Someone had done him around the head. In fairness it wasn't a promising case. Even round the docks people weren't that tolerant of irons. It might be all right on board when it was rum, bum and concertina, but on shore it was wine, women and song.

Melville wasn't a big man, came from a family of six and he'd always been regarded as a bit iffy. That evening he'd been importuning men and he'd tried to touch up at least one bloke. Then he'd been seen with two seamen and it looks like he must have pushed his luck once too often for someone had squeezed his balls and then throttled him. After that he'd been knocked about. The police checked the men on the ships which had recently docked but when they did no good there, they called in the Yard and Spooner.

The locals weren't going to tell him anything. They might have helped the Welsh police but they were certainly not going to assist people they reckoned were intruders. Spooner stuck it out but he got nowhere. He wasn't the only one. It seems no one else had cleared up a murder on the docks either.

Even if he had they could probably have got away with what was called the Portsmouth Defence in them days. If a top of the roof come up to you, you give him a good beating and took his watch. Then when you was prossed you said it was because of his outrageous behaviour. It wouldn't work now but it did often enough then. The Swansea Defence it would be in Wales.

The other Spooner case down there was in January 1953 when an old girl, Elizabeth Thomas, who was a retired schoolmistress, got done. A man who was passing heard screams and went for the local law. She'd been beaten and stabbed and although she lived to the next day she never regained consciousness. If they was after money they didn't get it because there was £200 under her mattress. You could buy a cottage in Wales for that money in them days, possibly two.

They could never find the knife, and it was one of those cases where the whole village was out looking and went and trod all over the place so the coppers didn't have much to go on.

The man they fancied was a 46-year-old odd-job man, George Roberts, who lived in the village. He had everything going for him. He was illiterate and he was Mutt and Jeff as well. The only way he could talk, as it were, was by sign language and he couldn't do much of that. That was when they called in Spooner. So far as he could work out Roberts had been seen by another of Elizabeth Thomas's neighbours, a Miss Lewis. At about 4.30 p.m. Roberts had called round to show her a pair of gloves he had bought and an hour later he had been seen by the local grocer standing on the pavement near his shop. Other people said they saw Roberts near Miss Thomas's cottage up to a quarter to six. They said he was wearing a mackintosh and cap at the time.

With the help of his uncle, Roberts made a statement that he had come home about 4.45 p.m. and then later that he had come home at 5.30 p.m. The next day, with a deaf and dumb interpreter he made a statement that at about 4.15 he had seen Miss Thomas on her doorstep and had waved to her. He said he had not been out after 5 p.m. It shows how they did things in them days. He stayed in the station for the next four days. The coppers' version of events was that he was told he could go home but just stayed there. Just like anyone would. You'd have thought they'd have got his uncle to take him home.

Next Spooner got hold of him, without an interpreter, and by the time he'd finished he reckoned Roberts had killed the old girl and thrown the knife into the sea. After that they brought in another couple of interpreters and it seems like Roberts confessed again. That was what the pros said anyway. The brief he had said he didn't think anyone could make Roberts understand anything but the simplest of things. So off he was slung to the Assizes.

The first thing was, was he fit to plead? Because if he wasn't it was off to the asylum and he wouldn't have got out of there in a hurry. The jury was told no one had heard him speak for 29 years and they found he was mute by visitation of God. So then the case got transferred to a new jury in Cardiff. But he was lucky he had that judge Devlin who threw out the confession, which was a big thing to do in them days. Normally if the coppers said the man had said something, he had. After that the pros chucked its hand in. Roberts drew two pictures after his not guilty. One was of a spade and the other of a man in a boat. The interpreter said it meant he was going fishing and then going back to work, but I suppose Spooner could have said it meant he was going to bury her at sea.

In fact, all the time it's looked as though Roberts didn't do it. Before they got Roberts to confess they thought a witness had heard the old girl call out something like Harry and as for Roberts's confession, all he may have been doing is trying to tell what he saw. He may just as easily have been recounting in his own way what he saw the actual killer do. Later there was a story that she'd been done by another local man, Ronald Harries, who was topped at Swansea jail in April 1954 for killing his aunt and uncle.

When you're dead you get the blame for everything. You can't sue people so they can say what they like. Take my friend Jimmy Moody who got out of Brixton and just vanished for years. Once he was dead he was blamed for just about anything which had happened up and down the country that hadn't been cleared up. A sort of one-man crime spree with nothing like evidence to back it up. He was even said to have done in a middle-aged couple, Peter and Gwenda Dixon, who vanished whilst they was out walking in Wales in the summer of 1959. The man's credit cards got used a few days after they was last heard of, and their bodies were found on a cliff top a bit after that. There was all sorts of stories and since Jimmy had escaped with an IRA man it was put about they might have stumbled on an IRA cache of arms and Jim had done them in on behalf of the Republicans. Or it could have been Father Christmas. When he finally turned up was when he was shot in the Royal Oak down the East End. No one was ever found for that. A lot of us knew it was coming on top for Jim but there was nothing we could do about it. I made sure I was well out of the way. I was staying with Jack Trickett at that nice hotel he has in Stockport but no one ever questioned me when it came to it.

There's a case in Wales which is meant to have been a legal precedent, but it wasn't really. It was the idea that you had to have a body before someone could be found guilty of murder. The idea went way back to the 1660s when a fellow disappeared and a man confessed, saying him and his mother and brother had done it. Since she was meant to be the local witch there wasn't a lot of support for her when she said it wasn't right. Anyway they strung them all up and as they did in them days, they left the bodies in sort of cages as a warning to others. That was when the missing man turned up. Anyway after that the rule was clear. No body, no murder.

As things happen though the rule gets watered down and there's an idea that if the body disappeared at sea, well, that's different. That case was when the steward pushed a woman he'd been having it off with through the porthole. But there had to be a body if there was a case on land. That's how it was thought to be when a couple of Poles started farming in Wales after the war and one of them, Stanislaw Sykut, was last seen alive a bit before Christmas 1953 when he took a cob to be shod by the local blacksmith at Cefn Hendre near Llandilo. He'd been the working partner of a fellow called Michail Onufreczyk, who'd been a major in the Polish army, and now they farmed something like 120 acres in the valley.

Onufreczyk didn't get on well with people and Sykut was his third partner in four years. Eventually Sykut had complained to the police about bullying and had a solicitor draw up a notice to dissolve the partnership. The idea was that if Onufreczyk didn't buy him out, then the farm would be put up for auction. New Year's Eve, when the local police officer paid a routine visit to the farm, he was told Sykut had gone to London for a fortnight. The police did things like that then, come round to check people was all right. Sykut still hadn't come back a few weeks later and this time Onufreczyk said that around 8 p.m. one evening a bit before the holiday, three Polish men had come to the farm in a car and, after Sykut had sold his share for a down payment of £450 with the balance in May, he had driven off with them. Onufreczyk produced the receipt, apparently witnessed by a man called Jablonski. He'd borrowed the money from a Polish lady in Holloway, North London, a Mrs Pokora, but she said it was a moody.

Sykut never collected his mail and he never drew off of his post office account and the police did start making serious enquiries. Onufreczyk said his partner must have gone to rejoin his wife behind the Iron Curtain. When the police began a search of the farmhouse they discovered something like 2,000 tiny blood specks on the walls and ceilings and a tiny bit of bone. There was also a large bloodstain on the Welsh dresser. They couldn't find Sykut though. I should think the pigs had had him for an early Christmas dinner.

They still went ahead against Onufreczyk and it was reckoned the first conviction in modern times of murder on land in which there was no body. There was an appeal, of course, and it come up in front of Goddard, who set out the rules for making sure there couldn't be any other explanation.

When it come to it though Onufreczyk was reprieved. It seems like the Home Secretary was afraid that if he had allowed the topping to go ahead there might be someone from behind the Iron Curtain who would come forward and claim to be Sykut. There was always that joke that at the end of the trial, the brief would say, 'I call my final witness; step forward Mr Sykut.'

Onufreczyk didn't speak much English, but he was a good chess player and he taught a lot of people in the nick. He was allowed out in 1965 and went to the Polish community in Bradford. That's where he was killed the next year in a car accident.

In fact it wasn't the first no body case in England in modern times. Before the war a fellow called Thomas Davidson had been done in 1934 over his eight-year-old kid. He'd made a number of confessions that he'd drowned the boy in a canal and then dumped him on a blazing refuse tip in Yiewsley in Middlesex. He went down and the Court of Appeal said 'Quite Right', but he got a reprieve as well.

There was some tragic cases though. Take that Somali seaman Mahmood Mattan. He was hanged at Cardiff prison in the September of 1952 for the murder in March of a Jewish shop owner, Lily Volpert. She'd got an outfitters in Bute Street in the Tiger Bay district. Mattan was really unlucky. The killing took place not long after there had been anti-black rioting in the area. He'd got a Welsh wife, Laura, and she'd been targeted by the neighbours, calling her stuff like a black man's whore.

There wasn't much against him, and it was based on a bit of circumstantial evidence. The coppers had also got a grass who came forward when there was a sniff of a £200 reward. She said she had seen Mattan with a roll of money shortly after the killing in which £100 was nicked. The other key witness claimed that Mattan had been seen coming out of Miss Volpert's shop around the time of the murder. This witness, who'd got form for violence himself, said a number of other black men were near the shop at the time. Mattan called an alibi that he was with his wife a mile away from the shop at the time. It didn't do him no good at all.

What was so evil is that there'd been a witness all the time. She'd seen a black man with a moustache go into Miss Volpert's shop at the time of the murder. There hadn't been an ID parade but a straight confrontation with Mattan, which is usually a good way of getting an ID. She had said that he was not the man she had seen. The pros didn't think that was going to help their case and they never told the defence. Although they was meant to it didn't always happen. It was the first case the Criminal Review Commission sent back to the Court of Appeal and it was a stone certainty. Not that it did poor Mattan any good. It must have been a bit of comfort to the family but I couldn't ever forgive if I'd been them.

Another terrible case was that of the boy, Harold Jones, who was said to have done a little girl in February 1921. She'd come into the shop where he worked and he'd taken her to a shed down the road and killed her. Well, that's what the pros said. The jury wouldn't have it and gave him a not guilty. The boy returns to a triumph in Abertillery where he lived. It was like a boxer winning the world title. There was a charabanc with flowers all over it and he gave a speech to the crowd from the balcony of the local hotel.

A few months later he does another little girl. This time he cut her throat. It was all up and he confessed he'd done the first as well. The judge said that if there hadn't been such a fuss made of him after the first case he might not have done it again but I think that's rubbish. He'd got it in him from the start.

There's not too many solicitors get done for murder, nor barristers neither. In fact if one of them hadn't been acquitted for doing his wife just after the First World War I don't suppose the second brief would have even tried. He comes in my second class of murderers, those that think they'll never be caught. Funnily both of them took place a few miles from one another. The first one to go was Mabel Greenwood whose husband Harold worked in Kidwelly, Herefordshire. She died in June 1919 and the pros said Greenwood had poisoned her. He seems to have done everything he should; called the doctor when she said she'd got pains and he sent for a district nurse. The doctor was in and out their place all night but she didn't last.

Greenwood wasn't popular. People can be very clannish in Border country, particularly back then and he wasn't a local. He wasn't making money out of the law but she came from the Bowaters, the paper family, and he stood to pick up a bundle when she died. Then there was stories he was a ladies' man and the doctor's sister had been seen on his knee in a railway carriage. People soon added it up and made five or even six. Then what does he do? He goes and remarries, only four months later. Not the doctor's sister but a girl, Gladys Jones, who's nearly twenty years younger than him. That's it then. They dig up Mrs Greenwood and it's not the gooseberry pie which did for her but a whole load of arsenic, so it's off to the Assizes where he has Marshall Hall defend him.

The pros said it wasn't the gooseberry pie he'd put the arsenic in but weedkiller was in the bottle of burgundy they'd drunk. What saved him was their daughter Irene said she'd drunk some of the burgundy and it hadn't made her ill.

Even so Greenwood was ruined. He was another they made a waxwork out of and he got £150 damages for it. His practice was finished and he applied to be clerk of the local council and got a knock back. He ended up reporting the trial of the second brief, Herbert Armstrong, for a magazine. Maybe Greenwood's getting chucked had nothing to do with Armstrong. He must have been mad because he almost certainly had a go at another local solicitor, Oswald Martin. He had him round for tea and give him a buttered scone saying, 'Excuse fingers' and the poor man near enough died. He wasn't the only one. It turned out that, before he come to Hay, Armstrong had been a brief in Plymouth and one of the men there had been taken ill after going for tea with him. Then there was another fellow in Hay was taken bad after having eaten a chocolate which had been sent to Martin.

Armstrong had a practice in Hay in Brecknock and he was the clerk of local justices as well. People rather liked him because his wife, Katherine, was a nagger and he never did anything but smile. In June 1920 he got her to make a will in his favour and next month he got her committed to the local bin. She was back in January 1921 but she didn't last a month. He ran the defence she'd committed suicide but the pros said it was him. Armstrong agreed he'd got arsenic in his pocket when he was nicked but it was for killing off dandelions. Still the local bookies fancied him for a not guilty, but they was wrong and he was topped at Gloucester. After the trial, one of the jury gives an interview to a paper about what went on and the court was real fierce about it. There's some people who think that Darling, who was the judge, went in too strong and there's a brief who's recently written a book showing how Armstrong was really innocent. All my eye and Oswald Martin.

Just one last thing. When I was in Shrewsbury after the War they was still using gas to light the cells. There was a bit of thick glass in the wall and behind it was the gas light so you couldn't get to it. The screws would come round and turn the gas off individually. You had to do your mailbags of an evening in the cell of course, eight stitches to the inch and punishment if you only did six or seven stitches. There wasn't much in the way of rehabilitation for your eyesight in them days.

There's always been a saying, 'It was the butler who done it', and over the years there's been a few of them that has.

When I was a kid there was Charles Houghton. He'd been the butler to the Woodhouses, a couple of middle-aged spinsters who lived in Burghill Court near Hereford. He'd been there twenty years or more but as the years went on he started lifting his elbow instead of the serving trays and they reckoned he had to go. In September 1929 the older one, Elinor, give him 24 hours notice and two months wages to go along with it. That was her mistake; she should have had someone come and put him out straightaway. He turns up at family prayers the next morning and then, whilst she's in the kitchen talking about lunch with the cook, he comes in with a gun and shoots her. A couple of minutes later he does the younger sister May. Then he goes upstairs and tries to cut his throat. There was some story that he had fits but it wasn't enough to save him. You can't have the servants behaving like that and not make an example of them. It's bad for discipline. They topped him a bit before Christmas.

I suppose the most famous of the butler killers was that Archibald Hall and, in a way, I suppose he was a bit unlucky at the beginning. He'd been taken around the place to good hotels and stuff as a youth by an older woman. A toy boy they'd call it today. Then she dropped him and he started embezzling. They put him away as mentally unstable during the War, but once he was out he got sent to the nick for a string of stuff, theft, a bit more embezzlement, that sort of thing. Then he got himself a job as a butler to a couple up in Scotland in Stirlingshire. That was all right for a good while but he just can't stop dreaming of the good life he had with this woman. One day, whilst the couple are on holiday, there's an invite to a royal garden party in Edinburgh in the post, which he's taken to opening. He rents himself out a morning suit, borrows the Bentley and he's off. The trouble is he goes back and robs the fellow who gave him the monkey suit. The coppers are called and of course they tell the employers. Give them credit they say he can stay but there's local gossip and this is when he starts his real career.

He does a series of jobs and ends up with thirty years PD. His father dies and he's let out for the funeral without an escort and he's back on time. Next it's proper parole after seven and he's back to being a butler, nicking the guests' jewels and changing the diamonds for glass which he's had cut by his friends. I think he even worked for the millionnaire Charles Clore for a few days. In fact Charlie Clore didn't have too much luck with his butlers because he employed an old screwsman, Roy Fontaine, at one time. He ended up in Parkhurst as well. Anyway once he's got the sack from Clore, Hall's really into jewellery theft and he winds up with a ten in Blundeston. He got out of there with another couple of cons and he took up with an Irish girl. He was out for about two years before he was nicked and got a five on top of the ten. They let him out after he'd done seven and he took up with

243

another Irish woman, Mary Coggle. He was at a few more jobs and he went back inside in 1973 for another four years.

When he comes out in 1977 he gets another job as a butler to a Lady Hudson up in Waterbeck in Dumfriesshire. He really seems to have settled down, but what he does is have one of his old mates David Wright come up and do a few jobs around the place. That's when Wright nicked some jewellery and silver. Hall managed to get a ring back from Wright's girlfriend but soon after that Wright comes in at night and shoots the bedhead where Hall's sleeping. Hall gets him to quieten down and promises to turn the place over with him. Next day he takes Wright out rabbit shooting and Wright's the rabbit. He buried the body near a stream and covered it with rocks. It's quiet after that but then in the autumn the coppers tell Lady H. that her butler's got form and she gives him the shove.

It's back to London and he gets a job with an ex MP, Walter Scott-Ellis, and his wife in Richmond Court, Sloane Street. It doesn't take him long to work out that they're really rich and here's the chance for one last job and retirement. Well, that's what he said. I'm not sure any of us retire until our nerve or our legs give out. Mind you he was in his fifties by then. Then, who does he bump into but Mary Coggle, who's got a new man Michael Kitto who's just done a pub at the Oval. The idea is that Kitto should screw the place and Hall would stay on and do a bigger fraud.

They thought that Mrs Scott-Ellis was in a nursing home and her husband was a solid sleeper so they start to screw her room but there's the old girl. Hall must have panicked and they shoved a pillow over her face. A few seconds later they realise she's dead. The old man wakes up and they tell him Mrs Scott-Ellis has had a nightmare. He's fairly ga-ga and now they have Mary Coggle in to impersonate the old girl and give him sleeping pills.

That night they drove him up to Scotland with the old boy still thinking Mary Coggle was his wife and the real one in the boot and spent the night in Cumberland. They buried the old girl in Perthshire and took him to Glen Afric where they tried to strangle him. Eventually they hit him over the head with a spade and buried him and all. The idea was to get hold of the couple's bank accounts, but then it was a case of thieves falling out. Mary wanted the old girl's mink coat but they wouldn't give it her. She was the next to go. She got hit with a poker and her head put in a plastic bag. Her body got chucked in a stream, on the Glasgow–Carlisle Road. Then the pair came back down South and sold off the Scott-Ellis' possessions.

The trouble was that Hall's brother Donald, who he didn't like, came over. He started asking about how they had so much money and they gets a bit worried. Still they all went up to Cumberland together where Hall had rented another cottage. This time it's Donald who goes. What he does is say he knows how to tie people up with six inches of string and he'll let them practice on him. Well, that's too good to miss. He's there with his thumbs tied behind his back and they chloroform him and drown him in the bath. The trouble is that the ground's frozen and they can't bury him, so they book into a local hotel and start charging their booze to their rooms. The governor thinks they might be trying to stiff him of the bill and he gets the local police to run a check on them. That's when it goes all on top. The police find they've rung the plates on their Ford Granada and it's down the nick. Hall gets out through a window but he's only out a few hours on his way to Dunbar. By the time they get him back to the nick the coppers have opened the boot and that's it. He got lifed off and Kitto got a fifteen. Hall's just a few years younger than me if he's still alive. I haven't heard he's dead.

DUBLIN

Dublin always had an appeal for a good thief. Once you were successful and back across the Irish Sea that was really end of story. Once you'd made it the Irish police had to be in touch with the Yard, and they might come round and touch you for a few quid and call it a day. The Dublin police more or less had to give up. It was the same if you did a job in the sticks; if the local police left it to the Yard to investigate then it come to nothing for them. That's why they had to come down themselves if they wanted anything to happen. Even then they was supposed to go and check in with the local coppers before they could move. Very often they didn't because someone at the local nick would have got out the word out double time.

The other thing with Dublin was that provided you was able to get across the border into Northern Ireland you was safe there as well. In my day there wasn't all that amount of co-operation.

I remember Jackie O'Connell, small curly-haired fellow, doing a job over there. I never knew him well because he didn't do a lot of bird. Lucky Jackie you could call him, until someone blew his leg off and then he didn't half suffer. I did know his cousin Frank well though. He was with me a lot. He picked up a fifteen in around 1966 so we was often together. Anyway Jackie and two others and a girl blows a betting shop in Dublin and the other men and the girl got lifted by the Gardai. Jackie, like Billy Hill did years earlier, just walks away. In them days you had to put up cash for bail over there and like a good 'un that's what Jackie did. Got the girl out and then the men one after another. It was big stuff I believe. Five or ten grand each when five or ten grand meant something. Anyway, there's an adjournment and, of course, they have to go over for it so that costs; then there's another adjournment and then another. Finally one of the fellows dies and the other picks up a long stretch over here and the police don't think it's worth having him back, so they offer no evidence against the girl and Jackie sends his brief over to collect all his money. It was the shop's money really.

As for Billy Hill, he just walked out of a jewellers and away whilst poor old Bimbo Smith walked out into the arms of the coppers. They've screwed the place and then they find they're surrounded. Billy manages to brazen it out but poor Bimbo got a twelve I think. He was a good man. He was the type who could have been to Haileybury. He was a good all-rounder. You could have him act the crooked copper who stumbles on something and will take a bit of money off the mug to let him go. He came from around Chelsea way and he was a cut above the rest of us. In the end he just faded away. It must have been just before Mr Smith's club I saw him for the last time.

In recent years there's been a big campaign against the drug dealers in Ireland. It's not all that long ago – 1996, I think – that a crowd beat Joseph Dwyer to death with baseball bats in the Dolphin's Barn area. They reckoned he'd been flogging drugs and he'd done a four over it. The people chased him and another man, and gave them a beating near the ice rink they have there, not far from the Guinness brewery. After that it was another bashing at Basin Lane and he went and died.

It was one of the ploys that they used against Ronnie and Reggie when they sent Nipper Read over to Dublin. He'd just been brought to the Murder Squad and the high-ups reckoned when the Twins heard about it, which they was bound to do within about five minutes, they'd know he was on to them again. So they sent Read over to Dublin to do a case there as a sort of camouflage. The coppers thought a British officer had gone and killed a brass over there and Read had to take him back from England and then later go back for the case. She'd been strangled and left on the beach at Sandycove Point. When it came to it the man got a not guilty but it looked to Ronnie and Reggie that Read was not on their backs. It was at Shannon Airport that the hit man who Ronnie and Reggie had in mind to do Read and had brought over from America was nicked and turned back.

I was watching a television programme the other night and it made me think about that big case they had in Dublin after the War. An abortion went wrong and the woman was done for murder. The programme was about those girls who got knocked up in villages in Ireland either by their boyfriends or often enough their brothers and fathers, and got put in sort of asylums. There was one in Co. Cork but there was others. They didn't even have to be in the club. If the family thought the girl was a bit lively in she went, and it seems like many of them didn't come out until the family signed them out and they weren't too quick to do that. The nuns were pretty severe by all accounts. No question of sparing the rod and spoiling the child. Their wickedness got beat out of them. The places were called Magdalene Asylums and the girls was known as Maggies, nothing to do with the matrons in our Borstals. You'd think maybe that happened in the nineteenth century or at the beginning of the twentieth, but it looks like it continued right up to the 1960s and maybe later. No wonder girls with a bit of money come to Dublin to get an abortion or get rid of the kid to an adopter. There wasn't proper adoption in Ireland till well after the War and so there was a good trade in baby farming. Of course some girls came over to England for the abortion but it was still illegal here, and that cost even more money. There's a big movement now to try and get some money for the girls who was treated so unfairly over the years.

The woman who got done for murder had made a good living out of everything for years. Her name was Marie Ann Cadden and she was known as Mamie. I think she was originally American and she was a good-looking blonde by all accounts. When she was younger she drove around Dublin in a red sports car, which wasn't that usual for women. From the start she was an abortionist working out of a place on Rathmines Road but she also had a line in disposing of unwanted kids. For a fee of £50, which was big money when you think the average weekly wage for a girl then was well under four quid, she'd agree to place the kid for adoption. What she did was take the poor thing into another local authority's area and dump it. When the kid was found then that authority had to take care of it, so it was pure profit, except for the petrol, and she'd have already taken a good few quid from the girl over the birth. She got twelve months when she was seen dumping a kid in Rosetown, in Co. Meath. She said she'd just been out for a drive with her boyfriend but she wouldn't give his name. She also got struck off the Roll of Midwives; not that that stopped her. She just carried on doing abortions. Of course she wasn't the only one. There was a doctor in Merrion Square, who was a bit more upmarket by all accounts.

Mamie Cadden was done a second time in 1945. She'd moved to Upper Pembroke Street by now and she did a roaring trade there. It was the usual story, one of the jobs went wrong and the girl ended up in hospital where they got the story out of her. This time it was five years, which was quite strong but then the authorities there haven't ever been keen on abortionists. Even less than over here.

When she came out she dyed her hair and she was probably going a bit off her head. She started a quarrel with the Revenue over tax and then she threatened to shoot her landlord when he wanted the rent. If you're going to be in the sort of business she was you want to keep your head down, not make yourself known all over the place. It all come on top in June 1951 when a girl who used to dance at the Olympia got herself in the club and went to see 'Nurse'. She ended up bleeding to death on the street, but for once Cadden kept her trap shut and there wasn't enough evidence to pin her down. Of course, by now the coppers were just waiting for her. Had to wait a bit because it wasn't until April 1956 another girl's found dead near St Stephens Green by a milkman. He goes and gets help from the Hume Street Hospital and once the Gardai started searching the place they found Mamie Cadden had a flat nearby. She was reckoning to be an adviser on hair loss and constipation. This time she couldn't keep her trap shut. When they found a couple of specula and asked her what they was for she said it was to save you using your hands to have an Auntie Ciss on a cold morning.

It was funny, the girl she's done was Helen O'Reilly, whose husband was a sort of minor Lord Haw Haw, making broadcasts in favour of the Germans, but that didn't cut any ice with the jury. Mamie's brief didn't dare call her, but he made a six-hour speech for her. It didn't do her no good. She must have been seriously going off her trolley because when the judge asked if she'd anything to say before he passed the death sentence she said she was going to report him to the President of the United States. Of course she got a reprieve and it was off to the Dundrum Central Criminal Lunatic Asylum. She only lasted a year there before she died.

* * *

You don't get too many cases nolle prossed; that's where the Attorney General says he's not going to go on with the case. Even if the judge don't agree he can't do anything about it. It's what happened in the case of a fellow called Michael Pratley on a murder charge in Northern Ireland. In March 1924 he went on a wages snatch at a factory in Belfast and one of the employees, Nelson Leech, had a go. He was shot in the back. By this time the local peelers, which is what they call them in Northern Ireland, was on their way and Pratley tried to shoot one of them but his pistol jammed. When he come up for trial he said it was one of the others who shot the fellow, but there was a lot to say he was the one and he was topped.

How the nolly came about was that he'd been charged with another murder from 1922 but once they'd convicted him over Leech they didn't bother a second time. They just brought him up in the dock and took him down again. They went on against the other fellow, a James Woods who was an officer in the Irish Free State Army though. The claim was they'd shot a William Waddell who was an MP in the new Ulster Parliament. One of the men involved in the shooting of Waddell had a limp and so did Pratley. That and the fact he was in the Irish Free State Army had been enough to put him in the frame. Woods got a not guilty but he got interned afterwards.

Over the years I've been in the nick with a lot of IRA men, and good men they've been as well. As a rule they've kept their politics to themselves and got along with the other prisoners. I never saw them get stick from the others; from the screws yes. They've been careful though, making sure which cons they could trust. The ones I was in Bristol with back in 1975 was really good men. I was losing a terrible amount of remission over trouble with the screws; 700 days it was. That's almost exactly two years. They wanted to give evidence for me in front of the Visiting Magistrates but I said no. It was bad enough for them as it was. They didn't need any more aggravation from being seen speaking up for me.

It was through the wire mesh in the punishment cells in Durham I first spoke to Eddie Butler who was in that siege in Balcombe Street. I asked him why have a siege when they must have known they was going to get taken and he told me it was to give other people time to get out. If they'd just been nicked then the alert wouldn't necessarily have gone round. As it was, with all the publicity this was a warning for the others. Good man. I was also in the nick with Billy Armstrong who was doing around 25. After we'd both come out he invited me to his wedding in Dublin, and I went over with Marilyn and her Mum and Dad because Tommy Wisbey was in the nick with him as well. Billy married a lovely girl who helped the families of IRA prisoners. After that we went up to Belfast where there was another do in a social club on the Falls Road. It was terrific. They had a band and Marilyn sung at both of them.

Later I went back and did about ten shows in Dublin at the Abbey Lane Theatre and a lot of the people I'd been in with came to see me. Whilst I was there I went on the Gay Byrne television show. I wasn't that keen. People was telling me he might have a right go at me and it would be hard to hold my own, but he was a smashing fellow, never took advantage of me. We had a drink together afterwards.

GOODBYE

London's changed so much, even in recent years. I was in Old Compton Street a month or so before last Christmas and it was packed, but it wasn't packed with the faces that you used to find there. We was in an Indian restaurant up the Charing Cross Road end and we had a table in the window looking out. There was cars parked all along and black guys were sitting doing their business with drugs. It was beyond belief. Two or three cars with black guys in them. People jumped in, bought and jumped out. There wasn't a copper in sight. If the police had come up there was no way the dealers could have driven away. It's like the police have give up. If I was wanted I think that's where I'd go in future. A wanted man could stay there all night and not see a copper.

If I had to say I regretted something in my life it would be that I never saw my boy, Francis, play football for Brighton. He was seven when I went away for the twenty years, and by the time I came out his career was over. I could see even at the age of seven he was shaping up. We'd play at the front of my house in Hove, him attacking the garage doors. I was always careful to play that way around so he didn't run into the road if the ball got past him. I made sure it never did.

He's got two boys now, just coming up to their teens. They'll never be in any trouble. Of course, they mix with their cousins; some's got form even at their ages, but there's no question of their corrupting them. My other sons never corrupted Francis and they were all into heavy work. The more I think about it, the only thing that makes people into criminals long term is if they want to be. When I think of all the research I've done on the ground over the years I reckon my guess is as good as anyone's.

It's always sad when people die in prison. Billy Blythe – he was another terrific guy – who was with me in the Jack Spot slashing, died just a few months into his sentence in Liverpool. His wife Dot was the sister of Harry Barham, the bookmaker. Harry was kidnapped in Red Lion Street, Holborn a few years back and his body was found on Hackney marshes. No one was ever nicked for it. Poor Billy, even before he went away he'd a duodenal ulcer. People didn't think nothing of them then – a bit of stomach ache that's all. He'd complained a bit and kept drinking milk. The guy who had a pub in Shoreditch took him to see someone in Harley Street and the fellow said Bill was all right, but he wasn't.

I was at Gartree at the time Freddy Sansom died. He was a lovely man, very popular. He gave evidence for us at the riot trial. He'd been playing football at Albany and just collapsed. We had a collection round the prison. People who had money in their property applied to send it to his widow and those that didn't made arrangements for people at home to send stuff. It was a tribute to Freddie but also it was to get up authority's nose. 'I'd like to have it sent out to Mrs Sansom.' 'Why do you want it sent out Fraser?' 'I just want it, sir.' And they couldn't do nothing. They'd dock you the cost of registering it but that was all.

Some people kept a lot of money in their property. It would either be money they'd had at the time they was nicked, or the family would send it in, or there'd be a bit from the wages. I never kept above £25 but there was some who'd have as much as two or three grand. Of course the governor would try and make them put it in a bank account where at least it could have a bit of interest, but some fellows thought it gave them a gee to have so much laying around doing nothing.

When I think the risks they've taken, it's surprising more wheelmen haven't been killed, but there again, many of them was so good they could have been racing drivers themselves. Look at Roy James and Danny Allpress, both of them had a go round Brands Hatch and places like that. Roy nearly made it to the big time before the Train. But as for the people that have been killed, there was Jack Rosa, who's meant to have said 'I wasn't driving', because he'd had his licence taken away from him, when the coppers came and found him laying by the roadside. Then there was 'Cadillac' Frank Copley, died in a smash during a chase over Tower Bridge. My friend Adgie Pitts was another. He was killed on the road down to Brighton. There was also another fellow – I can't remember his name now – he was a driver, got killed a few months after he got a not guilty on a bank robbery. The other fellow in the accident was to blame and the man's widow sued, claiming loss of his robbery earnings. That went down big, I can tell you.

I was really sad to see George Francis, the boxing trainer who got Frank Bruno a world title, had hanged himself last April. I'd known him years. He was a little bit younger than me and he was part of the Camden Town mob which ran around with Billy Hill. He'd been a bit wild in his youth but then every kid from a poor family in Camden Town was a bit wild. He wasn't that old in the War when he went to Bedfordshire, evacuated like so many, and he ran a black market in tinned corned beef. They had to send him back to London and that's when he become involved in boxing. He was a porter in Covent Garden and I knew him when he was with the amateurs at St Pancras. The last time I saw him was at Waterstone's in Finchley just before Christmas last year when I was doing a signing and he come in and had a chat and bought a book. People say bad things about boxing but it's taken many a kid off the streets and out of trouble. What George was good with was handling black fighters at a time when there wasn't many who would. He got Bunny Sterling a British title and also a European one back in the early '70s, and of course he trained John Conteh to his world title. He was a lovely man. He was the last person I'd have thought would have killed himself.

Funnily, the man he come in the shop with was Leslie McCarthy, from the Atlantic Machine days. I've kept in touch with him over the years and he's put my website together. When you think the average age of a website is around six weeks mine's been going nearer six years. What was really good is that the site was chosen by the *Guardian* as their website of the month for March 2002. I'm really pleased for Leslie. It gave him a great gee.

Because I've lasted so long there's many people, good men and women I've known, who've died. The Twins and their brother Charlie, of course. I went to the funeral of Charlie and Eddie Richardson's mother in April this year. She was a lovely woman. There was quite a few faces there I knew. Bobby Welsh from the Train was there. He's lost a leg and he was on sticks; I saw Jimmy Hussey the other day in my nephew's; we gave him a lift home. Tommy Wisbey, he's still about and I hear he's writing a book so good luck to him. But there's a lot from that job who aren't. There's Charlie Wilson, Roy James, Billy Boal, Lennie Field – all gone. Poor Ronnie Biggs is still inside and in a very poor way at the time I'm writing. Others like Roger Cordery have dropped away and Gordon Goody's in Spain. He's been there years. I heard Clifford Saxe went this Spring. He'd been in Spain ever since the Security Express job Johnny Knight did. They'd been trying to extradite him but he beat them in the end. His friend Ronnie Everett's been brought back and done over some drugs in Leeds. He's got an eight. He'd been in Spain for years as well.

Talking about bumping into people, the other day, just after I'd seen my editor, Humphrey Price, I'd been to the photo shop to get more copies of the picture of me with Reggie just before he died. I always give one to the people on my tour and, of course, I sign it. The shop's just by the Elephant. When I come out who gives me a pull but Dominic, George Carman's son. I didn't know him before then but he looks like his father. He'd seen me on the programme about his Dad and he was well pleased with what I've said.

Most of the men I worked with have passed away but I ran into one of them the other day. The man who actually nicked the World Cup back in 1966, not the one who was done for it. He and I had done a bit of thieving years back and he just comes up to me in the Walworth Road, threw his arms round me and said, 'Hello Frank'.

The nicking of the World Cup was a right coup. It was on view at an exhibition in Westminster Hall and my friend took the screws from the plates of the padlocked double doors, and the lock off the glass cabinet, and that was that. That World Cup was a good job. The trouble was just like nicking a famous painting, unless you've got someone who'll keep it in their cellar there's not a lot you can do with it except try and negotiate with the insurance. I don't know exactly what happened because I was in Wandsworth at the time but eventually the cup was dumped and a fellow out with his dog in Streatham found it. The dog got all the credit and it become a right hero. A year's supply from a dog food manufacturer and a medal from a dog's society. I think it even starred in a film. The story is it didn't last too long. It strangled itself on its lead chasing a rabbit, but I don't know if that's true.

The old quarrels have been patched up. I saw Billy Hayward from Mr Smith's a bit ago and we had a few drinks and quite often I've seen his brother, Harry. He's not been well. When you think what that evening cost me and the rest of us. Henry Bottoms who grassed me that night is dead and good riddance; shot at his front door. Nothing to do with me I'm sorry to say. On the other hand Jimmy Moody, that good man who helped me after the fight, has been gone over ten years now; shot down the East End.

It's funny, the Twins could have learned so much from us going down but they never did. There was never any need to spring Frank Mitchell as a weapon against me. I was locked up and going nowhere. They'd managed to get away with the Cornell shooting. They was the masters of London after we went away, but they never learned.

Marilyn is doing well now. She and I split up a couple of years ago but we still see each other. Apart from the flower stall in Covent Garden her family's got a souvenir stall at the top of Haymarket and she does a bit to help out there. That and she's gone back to college. She's studying interior decorating, so when she's got a bit of experience she can come over and do my place up.

I don't think of death. It could happen anytime. I accept it. I'm fit but I could get an illness and not have the strength to fight it off as I could have done when I was younger. Years ago I'd have dreaded death but not now. I've had a decent innings, a good innings for my lifestyle. I can't grumble.

BIBLIOGRAPHY

For those interested in the debate over the abolition of the death penalty, Fenton Bresler's *Reprieve* (Harrap) looks at how the decisions were made, both generally and in some individual cases, beginning with that of Florence Maybrick. Terence Morris and Louis Blom-Cooper provide an analysis of cases from 1959 to 1964 in which a reprieve was or was not granted in *A Calendar of Murder* (Michael Joseph). Elwyn Jones deals with the case of Peter Allen and Gwynne Jones in *The Last Two to Hang* (Macmillan).

As for the thieves and robbers, the legendary country house burglar George Smithson wrote *Raffles in Real Life* (Hutchinson) and his some-time partner, George Ingram, wrote *Hells Kitchen* (Herbert Jenkins). In the latter's book Smithson is referred to as The Other Bird. Ruby Sparks wrote *Burglar to the Nobility*.

Eddie Chapman wrote two books, *The Eddie Chapman Story* (Wingate) and its sequel, *Free Agent* (Wingate). Billy Hill writes about Chapman in *Boss of Britain's Underworld* (Naldrett Press). In Ted Greeno's *War on the Underworld* (John Long) Chapman is referred to as Mike S.

There are a number of books about Sir Edward Marshall Hall and his famous cases. Perhaps the best is by Edward Majoribanks, *The Life of Sir Edward Marshall Hall K.C.* (Victor Gollancz). It includes detailed accounts of the Holt-Breaks and Bennett cases. J. D. Casswell, who defended so many people accused of murder including Neville Heath, wrote his memoirs, *A Lance for Liberty* (George G. Harrap & Co). There are many judicial memoirs and biographies of judges, including *Lord Goddard* (Harrap) by Fenton Bresler.

After her release from prison Florence Maybrick wrote her memoirs, as did John Lee after his. Alfie Hinds wrote his version of the case with Herbert Sparkes in *Contempt of Court* (The Bodley Head). Herbert Sparkes' version of events is covered in *Iron Man* (John Long). There have been two books about Archibald Hall. Norman Lucas's *Monster Butler* and the second by Hall himself (Blake). Stephen Richards has written a trilogy of life and crime in the North East centred around the death of Viv Graham. The first of these is *Viv (Graham) Simply the Best* (Mirage Publishing). John Allen, the so-called Mad Parson, wrote about life in Broadmoor at the time of the Second World War and his escape, in *Inside Broadmoor* (W. H. Allen).

There are many books on the case of the Stratton brothers and the development of fingerprinting. One is James Morton's *Manhunt* (Ebury Press). J. P. Bean has the story of the pitch and toss wars which led to the execution of the Fowlers in his book *The Sheffield Gang Wars* (D & D Publications). His other book about North Country crime, *Crime in Sheffield* (Sheffield City Libraries), contains an account of the life of Charles Peace. There is a good deal about the Sabini brothers in James Morton's *East End Gangland* (Warner Books), and there is a fictionalised and entertaining, if not wholly accurate, account in Edward T. Hart's *Britain's Godfather* (True Crime Library). A W. Brian Simpson wrote a history of internment in Britain in the Second World War, *In the Highest Degree Odious* (Oxford). For those interested in the experiences of women who marry prisoners serving lengthy sentences, Angela Devlin has written *Cell Mates/Soul Mates* (Waterside Press).

There have been numerous books and accounts of the Wallace case arguing his guilt or innocence. The most recent contains new research which provides a possible motive. Similarly there have been dozens of accounts of the Gilchrist murder in Glasgow. Perhaps the definitive one is Richard Whittington Egan's *Oscar Slater*. Peter Manuel's story appears in Murder Casebook No. 26, *Glasgow's Multiple Killer*, and John Gray Wilson wrote *The Trial of Peter Manuel* (Secker and Warburg). Ludovic Kennedy examined the case for and against Patrick Meehan in *A Presumption of Innocence* (Gollancz) and Meehan himself wrote *Innocent Villain* (Pan). Meehan's lawyer, Joe Beltrami, wrote an account of his attempts to have his client released in *A Deadly Innocence* (Mainstream Publishing). Chester Lewis and Peter Hughman collaborated on *Most Unnatural* (Penguin), a study of the Stafford-Luvaglio case.

The Scottish Records Office has details of the confession of Paul Harris and the circumstances of the reprieve of his brother,

Claude. The cases of Ernest Melville and George Roberts are covered by Iain Adamson in his life of Reg Spooner, *The Great Detective* (Frederick Muller). There is also a file at the Public Records Office, Kew, on the Melville case, PRO/MEPO/3/3125, in which he bemoans his lack of progress, saying he believes the locals are sheltering someone. Unlike many police officers of his generation, Frederick Balmer did not publish his memoirs in book form. They appeared in the *Liverpool Echo* on his retirement in 1967.

Douglas C. Browne and T. Tullett also look at the Melville case in *Bernard Spilsbury* (Harrap), a biography of the forensic pathologist. For other views of the great man see the memoirs of pathologists Sidney Smith, *Mostly Murder* (Granada) and Keith Simpson, *Forty Years of Murder* (Panther), neither of whom were wholly enamoured with him.

INDEX